TUBE
TALK

SELECTED AND EDITED BY
Denise Ahlquist, Nancy Carr, Michael J. Elsey, Elizabeth Friedman, and Mary Klein

CONTRIBUTORS
Louise Galpine
Samantha Stankowicz

Cover and section divider design: Anne Jordan and Mitch Goldstein

Interior design: THINK Book Works

Published by the Great Books Foundation in partnership with
Harrison Middleton University.

TUBE
TALK

BIG IDEAS IN TELEVISION

THE GREAT BOOKS FOUNDATION

A nonprofit educational organization

Published and distributed by

THE GREAT BOOKS FOUNDATION

A nonprofit educational organization

233 N. Michigan Avenue, Suite 420
Chicago, IL 60601
www.greatbooks.org

Shared Inquiry™ is a trademark of the Great Books Foundation. The contents of this publication include proprietary trademarks and original materials and may be used or quoted only with permission and appropriate credit to the Foundation.

Printed in the United States of America
First printing
9 8 7 6 5 4 3 2 1

Library of Congress Cataloging-in-Publication Data has been applied for.

Notes by the author are not bracketed; notes by the Great Books Foundation, an editor, or a translator are [bracketed].

About the Great Books Foundation

The Great Books Foundation is an independent, nonprofit educational organization that creates reading and discussion opportunities for all. We believe that
literacy and critical thinking encourage reflective and well-informed citizens and
that discussion of powerful and enduring ideas promotes empathy, community,
and democratic participation.

Founded in 1947, the Great Books Foundation was established to promote
liberal education for the general public. In 1962, the Foundation extended
its mission to children with the introduction of Junior Great Books®. Since
its inception, the Foundation has helped thousands of people throughout the
United States and in other countries begin their own discussion groups in
schools, libraries, and community centers. Today, Foundation instructors conduct hundreds of workshops each year, in which educators and parents learn
to lead Shared Inquiry™ discussion.

About Harrison Middleton University

Harrison Middleton University is a great ideas, great works, great conversations,
distance learning university that offers graduate education in the humanities
with concentrations in imaginative literature, natural science, philosophy and
religion, and social science. Harrison Middleton University promotes student-
faculty scholarship through research, discussion, and the development of
collaborative publications.

Contents

Introduction

Television is a medium of simplicity. It is based on four pillars of storytelling: conflict, comedy, character, and consequences. If you think about it, almost every successful television show, from *I Love Lucy* to *Seinfeld*, from *The Twilight Zone* to *The West Wing*, from *Survivor* to *The Bachelor*, revolves around those four core principles. *I Love Lucy* is a classic example—the ongoing *conflict* between Ricky and Lucy due to her relentless desire to break into show business, the *comedy* that results from her constant struggle to seek the spotlight, the *consequences* she suffers from all her failed attempts to rise from the shadow of her husband, and the *character* she displays in her resiliency. Lucy is like all of us: she has dreams, she fails, and then she picks herself up and tries again. It is such a basic concept, so easily repeatable and relatable, yet in the hands of great writers, actors, and on-air personalities, the audience never sees the strings. That is the trick.

In all of its forms—news, sports, scripted, and reality—television has always searched for some kind of truth that lies in all of us. It is all about story, and when great stories, be they real or imagined, are brought right into your home, they somehow become more compelling, more personal, more real. The history of television is defined by the need to engage and compete, to hold a viewer's attention when the flick of a button on a remote control represents the thin line between success or failure. And it is this underlying engine of competition that has fueled the history of television.

There are various landmarks that have influenced the growth of all forms of television since its inception: Desi Arnaz popularizing the three-camera shoot with *I Love Lucy* (revolutionary at the time, and still in use to this day); the introduction of color television, promoted most successfully in 1954 by *Walt Disney's Wonderful World of Color*; and the emergence of the "live news" event (from the Nixon-Kennedy debates to the first moon landing to the Vietnam War to 9/11). But these are primarily *technological* advancements. The biggest change in television *content* has occurred in our generation. It's called reality television.

A common misconception is that reality and scripted television live in two separate worlds, equals in the overall television landscape but unaffected by each other. Nothing could be further from the truth. Today, the competition for television viewers is fierce, with an almost mind-numbing array of choices. But back in the 1990s it was like shopping at the general store, where you had four choices—NBC, ABC, CBS, and PBS—and in the majority of cases none of them were very appetizing. And where there is lack of competition, there is often lack of choice, and this lack of choice was the breeding ground for a whole new approach to television programming.

One of the primary reasons for the rise of choice in television programming over the past twenty years can be traced to the emergence of what was once the bastard stepchild of television programming, reality television. Like any invention, reality television filled a void. The rise of reality television emerged from the lack of quality scripted programming in the late 1990s. To use just one example, in 1988 Fox was a struggling young network dealing with a writers' strike—they needed material but had no way to script a new project. So they created a new kind of show, a show that required no writers and could be shot on a shoestring budget. That show was called *COPS*, and it was shot in follow-documentary style, which flipped the basic structure of making television. Instead of creating a story and then shooting from a script, cameras followed the action and then mined their story from the found footage. It felt fresh, it felt real, it had real-life consequences, and it helped launch an entire network.

In 2000 CBS took a chance on a relatively unknown television producer whose only previous experience was producing a real-life adventure race called *Eco-Challenge*. This producer, Mark Burnett, had an idea for a competition show where sixteen people would be placed on an island and only one would "survive" to become the eventual winner. Burnett shopped his idea for years, until CBS finally gave him the green light but then buried the show as a summer replacement with few expectations. *Survivor* became an instant sensation; everyone tuned in to see this outspoken guy named Richard Hatch walk around naked, and the finale of the first season attracted over 51 million viewers— more than any other show in the previous ten years of television.

The game was on. Suddenly there was programming that felt fresh, felt different. These shows relied on interesting characters living interesting lives, chock full of conflict and comedy. And the consequences somehow felt more real, since real people were doing real things in real time. And as an extra bonus, this new concept was far cheaper to produce, giving rise to a new frontier in television, cable. The idea of "pay television" had been around for years, but now instead of just licensing older content, these fledgling channels could afford to make their own original programming, shows that would not only draw eyeballs but could also brand their entire identity. Remember when MTV primarily aired music videos paid for by the record companies? *The Real World* changed all that, and soon other channels began to develop cheap reality programming. From A&E to Bravo to TLC to almost any popular cable channel you can name, the cable television world was now driven by the chase to capture younger viewers interested in watching their peers in "real" situations that felt compelling and relatable. It was a race between broadcast and cable to attract the desirable ratings numbers that in turn generated bigger ad dollars. Reality programming became a no-brainer for television executives in both worlds, who for the most part enjoy those sorts of easy, no-risk decisions.

Today, after a glut of reality TV of all types has flooded the market over the last fifteen years, scripted television has made a huge comeback. Why? Simply because it was forced to compete. Scripted television suddenly had to be more compelling than the docu-soaps and reality shows that were dominating the Nielson ratings. If you think we have now entered a second golden age for television dramas and comedies, I'm sorry to break it to you purists out there that you have reality television to thank. You like to watch sports? That's a reality show. You like to watch news? That's a reality show. The line between reality and scripted is further blurred by popular shows like *The Office* and *Modern Family*, two examples of scripted programming shot to *look like* a reality show.

And in its next, most influential and perhaps most frightening step, the reality storytelling ethic extended all the way into the Oval Office. People cringed when Reagan was elected, upset that an actor had become our commander in chief. But that pales in comparison to a president who was largely known to most as the host of a popular reality show. And how did he get elected? By selling a simple message that everyone could understand, relying on conflict, comedy, character, and consequences. The formula for reaching the American public via television has never changed.

Once Donald Trump was elected, vast audiences began tuning in to see the next "episode" of his presidency. Millions who never cared about politics were suddenly glued to cable news channels to see what was going to happen day to day. Over the years, scripted television had subtly trained audiences to experience life episodically, where everything was kept at arm's length. While oftentimes engaging, it also felt safe. Reality television is a different beast entirely, teaching audiences to view the world through a prism of instability and chaos, where tables are being flipped, violence and racism are commonplace, and raw emotions are constantly on display. For many people, especially younger viewers, this has become the normal way to view the world. So was it really a surprise to find a reality star in the White House? When you think about it, isn't the world of politics the ultimate reality show? With the highest stakes imaginable?

Television has become the most popular and influential form of media the world has ever known. It is easily accessible, affordable to almost everyone. It is sometimes the ultimate escape and sometimes profoundly moving. Driven by equal parts creativity and competition, it is constantly evolving; yet at its heart, it has never changed. Television has somehow managed to be formulaic *and* groundbreaking at the same time. It is the greatest mirror that our global society has ever held up to itself, and even though sometimes we may not like what we see, it is impossible to look away.

Especially when Lucy drinks Vitameatavegamin.

—Chris Lamson

Chris Lamson is an Emmy Award–winning television producer, with over twenty-five years of experience in the entertainment industry. His work includes docuseries, reality TV, daytime talk, film trailers, documentary, and development. He believes that compelling storytelling, in all its forms, is the most essential element of any creative endeavor.

TUBE
TALK

SITCOMS, COMEDY,
YADA, YADA, YADA

SITCOMS, COMEDY, YADA, YADA, YADA

What makes a TV show funny, and how does what we agree to laugh at on television affect our lives? The authors in this section explore the landscape of humor, including its boundaries.

In "The Great Divide: Norman Lear, Archie Bunker, and the Rise of the Bad Fan" (2014), **Emily Nussbaum** recounts what happens when audience response to a character doesn't match what the show's creator had in mind.

David Sedaris's autobiographical "Us and Them" (2004) relates the story of his family's fascination with neighbors who don't "believe in television" and what happens when Sedaris begins to spy on them to see what they substitute for viewing.

"Seven Words You Can Never Say on Television" (1972) by **George Carlin** takes up the taboos established for broadcast content and asks readers to consider how much sense they make.

In "The Amiable Madness of *Green Acres*" (2012), **Noel Murray** analyzes how this popular sitcom played on the cultural upheaval of 1960s America and explores why shows like *Green Acres* vanished in the early 1970s.

The story "Brad Carrigan, American" (2006) by **George Saunders** follows the cast of a reality show as its creators frantically remake story lines and change the characters in an effort to retain viewers.

The Great Divide

Norman Lear, Archie Bunker, and the Rise of the Bad Fan

Emily Nussbaum

"The program you are about to see is *All in the Family*. It seeks to throw a humorous spotlight on our frailties, prejudices, and concerns. By making them a source of laughter, we hope to show—in a mature fashion—just how absurd they are."

This nervous disclaimer, which was likely as powerful as a "Do not remove under penalty of law" tag on a mattress, ran over the opening credits of Norman Lear's new sitcom. It was 1971, deep into the Vietnam War and an era of political art and outrage, but television was dominated by escapist fare like *Bewitched* and *Bonanza*. *All in the Family* was designed to explode the medium's taboos, using an incendiary device named Archie Bunker. A Republican loading-dock worker living in Queens, Bunker railed from his easy chair against "coons" and "hebes," "spics" and "fags." He yelled at his wife and he screamed at his son-in-law, and even when he was quiet he was fuming about "the good old days." He was also, as played by the remarkable Carroll O'Connor, very funny, a spray of malapropisms and sly illogic.

CBS arranged for extra operators to take complaints from offended viewers, but few came in—and by season 2 *All in the Family* was TV's biggest hit. It held the No. 1 spot for five years. At the show's peak, 60 percent of the viewing public were watching the series, more than 50 million viewers nationwide, every Saturday night. Lear became the original pugnacious showrunner, long before that term existed. He produced

5

spinoff after spinoff ("cookies from my cookie cutter," he described them to *Playboy,* in 1976), including *Maude* and *The Jeffersons,* which had their own mouthy curmudgeons. At the Emmys, Johnny Carson joked that Lear had optioned his own acceptance speech. A proud liberal, Lear had clear ideological aims for his creations: he wanted his shows to be funny, and he certainly wanted them to be hits, but he also wanted to purge prejudice by exposing it. By giving bigotry a human face, Lear believed, his show could help liberate American TV viewers. He hoped that audiences would embrace Archie but reject his beliefs.

Yet, as Saul Austerlitz explains in his smart new book, *Sitcom: A History in 24 Episodes from* I Love Lucy *to* Community, Lear's most successful character managed to defy his creator, with a *Frankenstein-*like audacity. "A funny thing happened on the way to TV immortality: audiences liked Archie," Austerlitz writes. "Not in an ironic way, not in a so-racist-he's-funny way; Archie was TV royalty because fans saw him as one of their own."

This sort of audience divide, not between those who love a show and those who hate it but between those who love it in very different ways, has become a familiar schism in the past fifteen years, during the rise of—oh, God, that phrase again—golden age television. This is particularly true of the much lauded stream of cable "dark dramas," whose protagonists shimmer between the repulsive and the magnetic. As anyone who has ever read the comments on a recap can tell you, there has always been a less ambivalent way of regarding an antihero: as a hero. Some of the most passionate fans of *The Sopranos* fast-forwarded through Carmela and Dr. Melfi to freeze-frame Tony strangling a snitch with electrical wire. (David Chase satirized their bloodlust with a plot about *Cleaver,* a mob horror movie with all of the whackings, none of the Freud.) More recently a subset of viewers cheered for Walter White on *Breaking Bad,* growling threats at anyone who nagged him to stop selling meth. In a blog post about that brilliant series, I labeled these viewers "bad fans," and the responses I got made me feel as if I'd poured a bucket of oil onto a flame war from the parapets of my snobby critical castle. Truthfully, my haters had a point: who wants to hear that they're watching something *wrong*?

But television's original bad-fan crisis did not, as it happens, concern a criminal bad boy, or even take place on a drama. It involved Norman

Lear's right-wing icon, Archie Bunker, the loudmouthed buffoon who became one of TV's most resonant and beloved television characters. Archie was the first masculine powerhouse to simultaneously charm and alienate viewers, and, much like the men who came after him, he longed for an era when "guys like us, we had it made." O'Connor's noisy, tender, and sometimes frightening performance made the character unforgettable, but from the beginning he was a source of huge anxiety, triggering as many think pieces as Lena Dunham. Archie represented the danger and the potential of television itself, its ability to influence viewers rather than merely help them kill time. Ironically, for a character so desperate to return to the past, he ended up steering the medium toward the future.

All in the Family began as a British show called *Till Death Us Do Part*, a hit comedy about Alf Garnett, a Cockney xenophobe who had a sharp-tongued wife, a hip daughter, and a socialist son-in-law. The show, which first aired in 1965, was a ratings hit, spawning catchphrases ("You silly moo") and mass British identification with Garnett—a response that troubled the show's creator, Johnny Speight, even as he made the case for its pungent zingers. "To make him truthful, he's got to say those things, and they are nasty things," Speight argued.

By 1967, Norman Lear, a Second World War veteran who never finished college, had spent years cutting a path through show biz. As recounted in *Archie & Edith, Mike & Gloria*, by Donna McCrohan, he began by collecting gossip tips, ghostwrote syndicated columns, and then jumped into comedy, having scammed his way into the office of the comedy bigwig Danny Thomas by pretending to be a reporter. After a successful stretch working on 1950s showcases, including *The Martha Raye Show*, he teamed up with the producer Bud Yorkin. The two became industry *machers*, packaging TV specials and making movies, such as *Divorce American Style*. When Lear read about *Till Death* in *Variety*, he felt a stab of identification. His father, Herman Lear, a Jewish salesman from Connecticut, was a "rascal," in Norman's words, who went to prison when Norman was nine, convicted of shady dealings; like Alf Garnett, he was at once loving and bigoted. Lear bought the rights to Speight's show, without ever having seen it, and hammered out a treatment. He gave Archie one of his own father's favorite insults for him—"you meathead, dead from the neck up"—and Archie, like Herman Lear, called his wife a "dingbat" and demanded that she "stifle." It's the origin story of nearly every breakthrough sitcom, as recounted in Austerlitz's book: memoir mined for a resonant, replicable pattern—in this case, the clash between the greatest generation and the emerging baby boomers, embodied by Archie Bunker and Michael (Meathead) Stivic, his son-in-law.

ABC was interested, but the network was concerned about the show's raw language. For the next two years, the executives and Lear went through an elaborate production process, taping two pilots—the first in September 1968, titled "Justice for All" (Archie's last name was originally Justice), the second in February of the following year, called "Those Were the Days." Lear wanted to cast Mickey Rooney as the lead, but the actor thought it was too risky. (Rooney did offer to make a different show: "Listen to this—Vietnam vet. Short. Blind. Private eye. Large dog!") So Lear offered the part to O'Connor, an Irish American actor whose rare mixture of "bombast and sweetness" he described to reporters as being ideal for the role. Lear cast Jean Stapleton as Edith, who transformed the British show's battle-axe—she resembled the tart-tongued Alice of *The Honeymooners*—into a figure of genuine pathos, a quavery-voiced housewife whose tenderness cut through the show's anger, and who gradually became its voice of reason.

In those two clunky early pilots, Archie's son-in-law is Irish, not Polish. In one version, he sports a hilarious puka-shell necklace; in the other, he's a clean-cut jock. The chemistry is all wrong, a testament to how much of comedy is casting: when Archie and these lesser meat-heads spar over the insult "the laziest white man I ever seen" (another Herman Lear original), there's none of the electrical fury that the show gained once the hulking, manic Rob Reiner took the role. ABC killed the project, and Lear went back to making movies. The experiment seemed to be dead until the CBS president, Robert Wood, stepped in, in 1970. Wood, who had just taken the job, was seeking a hip property that could replace the shows that skewed to older audiences—sitcoms like *Green Acres* and tentpoles like *Lassie*—which he planned to cancel, in what would become known as "the rural purge." He pulled Lear's project from the scrap pile, and a third pilot was thrown together, with the script essentially unchanged, at Lear's insistence (although the network balked at his request to film it in black and white). O'Connor was so sure that it would be another dud that he bargained aggressively for a clause guaranteeing his family plane fare back to Europe, where they were living at the time.

There were a few more last-minute skirmishes, since Lear was determined to set a precedent for network noncooperation: in an industry that liked to sand down the pointy, he wanted to provoke viewers. He refused to eliminate what the censor called "explicit sex" (innuendo that would seem prudish these days), and he threatened to quit rather than run the milder second episode, about Richard Nixon, as the show's debut. CBS caved. In the pilot that ran, it's Archie and Edith's wedding anniversary. They return from church early, catching Michael and a miniskirted Gloria on their way to the bedroom. There's a loud belch—Lear's shows pioneered TV toilet humor—and Archie and Michael fight about atheism and Black Power. "I didn't have no million people out there marching and protesting to get me *my* job," Archie sneers. "No, his uncle got it for him," Edith replies. Some jokes stick, others fizzle, but it's Archie's volcanic charisma that lingers—at moments, it's easy to imagine him hitting Edith, though the sitcom rhythms reassure us that he won't.

Right away, critics were split. *Variety* raved that *All in the Family* was "the best TV comedy since the original *The Honeymooners*." Its sister publication, *Daily Variety*, called it "nothing less than an insult to any unbigoted televiewer." In *Life*, John Leonard wrote a virulent pan, in which he sounded a theme that became a chorus on op-ed pages: that a show like this demanded a moral response. "Why review a wretched program?" he wrote. "Well, why vacuum the living room or fix the septic tank? Every once in a while the reviewer must assume the role of a bottle of Johnson's No-Roach with the spray applicator: let's clean up this culture." The *Times* flooded the zone with pieces, from "Can Bigotry Be Laughed Away? It's Worth a Try" to "The Message Sounds Like 'Hate Thy Neighbor.'" One side felt that the show satirized bigotry; the other argued that it *was* bigotry, and that all those vaudevillian yuks and awws were merely camouflage for Archie's ugly words.

As the show's ratings rose, it began to saturate American culture, high and low. In 1971 the *Saturday Review* reported that teachers were requesting study guides, to use the show to teach their students lessons about bigotry. The literary theorist Paul de Man quoted Archie and Edith's dialogue to dramatize a point, appropriately enough, about the slipperiness of meaning: the idea that the intent of words was endlessly interpretable. A paperback called *The Wit and Wisdom of Archie Bunker* became a bestseller ("Move Over Chairman Mao—Here Comes Archie Bunker!"), with quips like "I never said a man that wears glasses is a queer. A man that wears glasses is a four-eyes. A man that's a fag is a queer!" In 1973 a poll found that Archie Bunker's was the most recognized face in America, and for a while there was a craze for bumper stickers reading "Archie Bunker for President." At the 1972 Democratic Convention in Miami, the character got a vote for vice president.

The weightiest criticism came in another *Times* essay, by Laura Z. Hobson, the elderly author of *Gentleman's Agreement*, the source for Elia Kazan's earnest Oscar-winning 1947 film about anti-Semitism. In September 1971, she published a five-thousand-word critique called "As I Listened to Archie Say 'Hebe' . . ." Hobson argued that Lear had attempted to "deodorize" bigotry, to make it safe and cute: among other things, Archie used words like "coon" and "yid," but he didn't say "nigger" or "kike." Rather than puncturing hatred, she argued, Lear had made Archie into a flattering mirror for bigots. "I don't think you can be a black-baiter and lovable, or an anti-Semite and lovable," she wrote. "And I don't think the millions who watch this show should be conned into thinking you can be."

Lear responded with his own *Times* essay, "As I Read How Laura Saw Archie," arguing that of course bigots could be lovable, as anyone with a family knew. If Archie Bunker didn't use harsher language, it was because those words were "from another decade." Besides, Michael and Gloria, the bleeding-heart liberals, always got the last word. Despite Lear's playful response, later episodes of *All in the Family* contain many echoes of this debate. The show's tone gradually softened, and the more caustic slang dropped out; Archie even stopped telling Edith to "stifle." (As with *M*A*S*H*, its creators were influenced by the rise of feminism.) In season 8, there's a trenchant sequence in which Archie, drunk and trapped in a storage room with Michael, talks about his childhood. Yes, his father said "nigger" while he was growing up, Archie says—*everybody* did—and when Michael tells him what his father said was wrong,

Archie delivers a touching, confused defense of the man who raised him, who held his hand, but who also beat him and shoved him in a closet. It was all out of love, Archie insists. "How could any man that loves you tell you anything that's wrong?" he murmurs, just before he passes out. The scene should have been grotesquely manipulative and mawkish, but, strengthened by O'Connor's affecting performance, it makes Lear's point more strongly than any op-ed, even decades later: bigotry is resilient, because rejecting it often means rejecting your own family.

Civil rights advocates, including the National Urban League and the Anti-Defamation League, tended to share Hobson's distrust of the series. (In contrast, the A.C.L.U. awarded Lear the Freedom of the Press Award in 1973.) Bill Cosby, who was a major TV star after *I Spy*, downright despised Archie Bunker. Even a decade later, on *The Phil Donahue Show*, Cosby was still expressing frustration that Bunker had never apologized for anything, making him "a hero to too many Americans for his shortsightedness, his tunnel vision." He added, "And I'm really a believer that the show never taught or tried to teach anybody anything."

To critics the show wasn't the real problem: its audience was. In 1974 the social psychologists Neil Vidmar and Milton Rokeach offered some evidence for this argument in a study published in the *Journal of Communication*, using two samples, one of teenagers, the other of adults. Subjects, whether bigoted or not, found the show funny, but most bigoted viewers didn't perceive the program as satirical. They identified with Archie's perspective, saw him as winning arguments, and, "perhaps most disturbing, saw nothing wrong with Archie's use of racial and ethnic slurs." Lear's series seemed to be even more appealing to those who shared Archie's frustrations with the culture around him, a "silent majority" who got off on hearing taboo thoughts said aloud.

This clearly wasn't true of every bigot—at least, not Richard Nixon, who eagerly recapped the series for H. R. Haldeman and John Ehrlichman. In the Watergate tapes, Nixon describes in detail an episode in which a gay friend of Michael's comes to visit, leading Archie to discover that his own football-player buddy is gay. The series "made a fool out of a good man," Nixon grumbles. He theorizes that Michael probably "goes both ways" and worries that the show will corrupt children, just as Socrates did in ancient Greece. Ehrlichman interjects, in Socrates's defense, that at least "he never had the influence that television had."

"A vast wasteland"! It's impossible to discuss TV, even today, without stumbling upon the medium's most famous libel, its own version of "meathead." The context has been lost, though. That description comes from the first official speech given by Newton Minow, shortly after President Kennedy appointed him chairman of the FCC in 1961. Minow wasn't arguing that what aired on television was bad; he was arguing that it was amoral. He quoted, with approval, the words of the industry's own Television Code and urged the networks to live up to them: "Program materials should enlarge the horizons of the viewer, provide him with wholesome entertainment, afford helpful stimulation, and remind him of the responsibilities which the citizen has toward his society."

From a modern perspective, the passage feels prissy and laughable, the residue of an era when television was considered a public utility: it was in everyone's best interest to keep it pure, and then add fluoride. No critic could support that approach, least of all those who see TV as an art form, and want to free it from anxious comparisons to novels and movies—to celebrate TV as TV. During a recent visit to a university, I bridled when an ethicist praised me for taking a moral stance. (I'd called a network show "odious torture porn.") I told her that I wanted originality, even if it was ugly, and that I'd rather watch a show that unsettled me than something that was merely "good."

That's true. And yet, like Archie himself, I have to admit to my own fascination with the good old days—in particular, that spiky, surreal moment when people found television so dangerous that they slapped warning stickers on it. Lear and his critics disagreed about how his show affected people, but they agreed that it *should* affect people. Every day marked a fresh skirmish: Should there be a "family hour"? Were Starsky and Hutch making viewers violent? Back when television was a mass phenomenon, controlled by three networks, watched live by the whole family, it was no wonder that observers wrung their hands over whether it might turn its viewers into monsters. (These days we reserve those concerns for the internet.)

Five years after *All in the Family*, Lear launched an even more radical show, *Mary Hartman, Mary Hartman*, a prophetic, neglected TV classic stuffed with anti-TV themes. A satire of soap operas, and one of the first truly serial evening shows, it was so loopy and avant-garde that its producers syndicated it independently, airing it on affiliates mostly late at night. Lear explicitly designed it to appeal to two audiences: those who enjoyed it as melodrama and those who took it as social satire. In the finale of the first season, its eponymous housewife heroine (played by Louise Lasser) has a nervous breakdown on David Susskind's talk show, as moralists hammer her with questions. "Were your orgasms better before Johnny Carson?" the ideologues shout. "Erase! Erase!" Mary Hartman begs, panicked that she has said something wrong. It was a cry of terror that seemed to symbolize the mood of that era: the world was in chaos, and viewers like Mary were tragically vulnerable to the media's influence. Yet Lasser's character's odd, raw humanity—together with the show's disorienting, deliberately ugly editing rhythms—was a form of resistance. (The next season she was institutionalized and happily became a member of the hospital's Nielsen family.)

Decades later television has a different relationship with its audience. We collect and record it; we recap it with strangers; it pours through hundreds of narrow channels. Perhaps it's not so odd that, around the time the digital revolution began, another Archie-like figure rose up, as if from TV's unconscious: the rancorous middle-aged white male antihero, nostalgic for a past when he was powerful—and often conceived by a middle-aged white male showrunner, the demographic with the greatest economic ability to shake things up. As with *All in the Family*, the best of these dramas shoved TV forward with a rough charisma, blasting through piety and formula, frightening us and turning us on—and, often, dividing the audience in two. Then this genre, too, became a pious formula.

In *Sitcom*, Austerlitz argues that, as important as *All in the Family* was, it is hard to re-watch: among other problems, its racial politics are dated, reducing racism to mere personal prejudice. There's some truth to that, and yet, these days, Lear's legacy is everywhere, often in stealthy packages. Lear set the stage for agitating comedies like *Louie* and *Girls*, acrid satires like *It's Always Sunny in Philadelphia*, and boundary-crossers less to my taste, like Seth MacFarlane's *Family Guy*. Ryan Murphy, the creator of *Glee* and *American Horror Story*, is a professed admirer of Lear, and his shows feature diva-bigots who are female variants of Archie Bunker. Lear is a hero to Judd Apatow, too. Every time a show crosses the line of good taste, from humane pulp like *Orange Is the New Black* to bleak nightmares like *Hannibal*, it enlarges Lear's territory. Some of these shows place people who look nothing like Archie at the center, helped by production models that don't require reaching every viewer.

There is no way—and maybe no reason—to unite TV's divided audience. If television creators began by trying desperately not to offend, they clearly learned that the opposite approach can work just as well: a show that speaks to multiple audiences can get ratings by offering many ways to be a fan. As for the "vast wasteland" debate, at times it feels as if the balance has shifted so far toward a reflexive cynicism (about torture as entertainment, for example) that it's difficult even to talk about the subject—at least, without getting called a Margaret Dumont. Perhaps there's another way to look at it, which is to imagine an ethical quality that is embedded in real originality. The best series rattle us and wake us up; the worst are numbing agents. Sometimes, a divided audience is a result of mixed messages, an incoherent text; sometimes, it's a sign of a bold experiment that we are still learning how to watch. But there's a lot to be said for a show that is potent without being perfect, or maybe simply perfect for its moment: storytelling that alters the audience by demanding that viewers do more than just watch.

Us and Them

David Sedaris

When my family first moved to North Carolina, we lived in a rented house three blocks from the school where I would begin the third grade. My mother made friends with one of the neighbors, but one seemed enough for her. Within a year we would move again and, as she explained, there wasn't much point in getting too close to people we would have to say goodbye to. Our next house was less than a mile away, and the short journey would hardly merit tears or even goodbyes, for that matter. It was more of a "see you later" situation, but still I adopted my mother's attitude, as it allowed me to pretend that not making friends was a conscious choice. I could if I wanted to. It just wasn't the right time.

Back in New York State, we had lived in the country, with no sidewalks or streetlights; you could leave the house and still be alone. But here, when you looked out the window, you saw other houses, and people inside those houses. I hoped that in walking around after dark I might witness a murder, but for the most part our neighbors just sat in their living rooms, watching TV. The only place that seemed truly different was owned by a man named Mr. Tomkey, who did not believe in television. This was told to us by our mother's friend, who dropped by one afternoon with a basketful of okra. The woman did not editorialize—rather, she just presented her information, leaving her listener to make of it what she might. Had my mother said, "That's the craziest thing I've ever heard in my life," I assume that the friend would have agreed, and had she said, "Three cheers for Mr. Tomkey," the friend likely would have agreed as well. It was a kind of test, as was the okra.

15

To say that you did not believe in television was different from saying that you did not care for it. Belief implied that television had a master plan and that you were against it. It also suggested that you thought too much. When my mother reported that Mr. Tomkey did not believe in television, my father said, "Well, good for him. I don't know that I believe in it, either."

"That's exactly how I feel," my mother said, and then my parents watched the news, and whatever came on after the news.

Word spread that Mr. Tomkey did not own a television, and you began hearing that while this was all very well and good, it was unfair of him to inflict his beliefs upon others, specifically his innocent wife and children. It was speculated that just as the blind man develops a keener sense of hearing, the family must somehow compensate for their loss. "Maybe they read," my mother's friend said. "Maybe they listen to the radio, but you can bet your boots they're doing *something*."

I wanted to know what this something was, and so I began peering through the Tomkeys' windows. During the day I'd stand across the street from their house, acting as though I were waiting for someone, and at night, when the view was better and I had less chance of being discovered, I would creep into their yard and hide in the bushes beside their fence.

Because they had no TV, the Tomkeys were forced to talk during dinner. They had no idea how puny their lives were, and so they were not ashamed that a camera would have found them uninteresting. They did not know what attractive was or what dinner was supposed to look like or even what time people were supposed to eat. Sometimes they wouldn't sit down until eight o'clock, long after everyone else had finished doing the dishes. During the meal, Mr. Tomkey would occasionally pound the table and point at his children with a fork, but the moment he finished, everyone would start laughing. I got the idea that he was imitating someone else, and wondered if he spied on us while we were eating.

When fall arrived and school began, I saw the Tomkey children marching up the hill with paper sacks in their hands. The son was one grade lower than me, and the daughter was one grade higher. We never spoke, but I'd pass them in the halls from time to time and attempt to view the world through their eyes. What must it be like to be so ignorant and alone? Could a normal person even imagine it? Staring at an Elmer Fudd lunch box, I tried to divorce myself from everything I already knew: Elmer's inability to pronounce the letter r, his constant pursuit of an intelligent and considerably more famous rabbit. I tried to think of him as just a drawing, but it was impossible to separate him from his celebrity.

One day in class a boy named William began to write the wrong answer on the blackboard, and our teacher flailed her arms, saying, "Warning, Will. Danger, danger." Her voice was synthetic and void of emotion, and we laughed, knowing that she was imitating the robot in a weekly show about a family who lived in outer space. The Tomkeys, though, would have thought she was having a heart attack. It occurred to me that they needed a guide, someone who could accompany them through the course of an average day and point out all the things they were unable to understand. I could have done it on weekends, but friendship would have taken away their mystery and interfered with the good feeling I got from pitying them. So I kept my distance.

In early October the Tomkeys bought a boat, and everyone seemed greatly relieved, especially my mother's friend, who noted that the motor was definitely secondhand. It was reported that Mr. Tomkey's father-in-law owned a house on the lake and had invited the family to use it whenever they liked. This explained why they were gone all weekend, but it did not make their absences any easier to bear. I felt as if my favorite show had been canceled.

Halloween fell on a Saturday that year, and by the time my mother took us to the store, all the good costumes were gone. My sisters dressed as witches and I went as a hobo. I'd looked forward to going in disguise to the Tomkeys' door, but they were off at the lake, and their house was dark. Before leaving, they had left a coffee can full of gumdrops on the front porch, alongside a sign reading DON'T BE GREEDY. In terms of Halloween candy, individual gumdrops were just about as low as you could get. This was evidenced by the large number of them floating in an adjacent dog bowl. It was disgusting to think that this was what a gumdrop might look like in your stomach, and it was insulting to be told not to take too much of something you didn't really want in the first place. "Who do these Tomkeys think they are?" my sister Lisa said.

The night after Halloween, we were sitting around watching TV when the doorbell rang. Visitors were infrequent at our house, so while my father stayed behind, my mother, sisters, and I ran downstairs in a group, opening the door to discover the entire Tomkey family on our front stoop. The parents looked as they always had, but the son and daughter were dressed in costumes—she as a ballerina and he as some kind of a rodent with terry-cloth ears and a tail made from what looked to be an extension cord. It seemed they had spent the previous evening isolated at the lake and had missed the opportunity to observe Halloween. "So, well, I guess we're trick-or-treating *now*, if that's okay," Mr. Tomkey said.

I attributed their behavior to the fact that they didn't have a TV, but television didn't teach you everything. Asking for candy on Halloween was called trick-or-treating, but asking for candy on November first was called begging, and it made people uncomfortable. This was one of the things you were supposed to learn simply by being alive, and it angered me that the Tomkeys did not understand it.

"Why of course it's not too late," my mother said. "Kids, why don't you . . . run and get . . . the candy."

"But the candy is gone," my sister Gretchen said. "You gave it away last night."

"Not *that* candy," my mother said. "The other candy. Why don't you run and go get it?"

"You mean *our* candy?" Lisa said. "The candy that we *earned*?"

This was exactly what our mother was talking about, but she didn't want to say this in front of the Tomkeys. In order to spare their feelings, she wanted them to believe that we always kept a bucket of candy lying around the house, just waiting for someone to knock on the door and ask for it. "Go on, now," she said. "Hurry up."

My room was situated right off the foyer, and if the Tomkeys had looked in that direction, they could have seen my bed and the brown paper bag marked MY CANDY. KEEP OUT. I didn't want them to know how much I had, and so I went into my room and shut the door behind me. Then I closed the curtains and emptied my bag onto the bed, searching for whatever was the crummiest. All my life chocolate has made me ill. I don't know if I'm allergic or what, but even the smallest amount leaves me with a blinding headache. Eventually, I learned to stay away from it, but as a child I refused to be left out. The brownies were eaten, and when the pounding began I would blame the grape juice or my mother's cigarette smoke or the tightness of my glasses—anything but the chocolate. My candy bars were poison but they were brand-name, and so I put them in pile no. 1, which definitely would not go to the Tomkeys.

Out in the hallway I could hear my mother straining for something to talk about. "A boat!" she said. "That sounds marvelous. Can you just drive it right into the water?"

"Actually, we have a trailer," Mr. Tomkey said. "So what we do is back it into the lake."

"Oh, a trailer. What kind is it?"

"Well, it's a *boat* trailer," Mr. Tomkey said.

"Right, but is it wooden or, you know . . . I guess what I'm asking is what *style* trailer do you have?"

Behind my mother's words were two messages. The first and most obvious was "Yes, I am talking about boat trailers, but also I am dying." The second, meant only for my sisters and me, was "If you do not immediately step forward with that candy, you will never again experience freedom, happiness, or the possibility of my warm embrace."

I knew that it was just a matter of time before she came into my room and started collecting the candy herself, grabbing indiscriminately, with no regard to my rating system. Had I been thinking straight, I would have hidden the most valuable items in my dresser drawer, but instead, panicked by the thought of her hand on my doorknob, I tore off the wrappers and began cramming the candy bars into my mouth, desperately, like someone in a contest. Most were miniature, which made them easier to accommodate, but still there was only so much room, and it was hard to chew and fit more in at the same time. The headache began immediately, and I chalked it up to tension.

My mother told the Tomkeys she needed to check on something, and then she opened the door and stuck her head inside my room. "What the *hell* are you doing?" she whispered, but my mouth was too full to answer. "I'll just be a moment," she called, and as she closed the door behind her and moved toward my bed, I began breaking the wax lips and candy necklaces pulled from pile no. 2. These were the second-best things I had received, and while it hurt to destroy them, it would have hurt even more to give them away. I had just started to mutilate a miniature box of Red Hots when my mother pried them from my hands, accidentally finishing the job for me. BB-size pellets clattered onto the floor, and as I followed them with my eyes, she snatched up a roll of Necco wafers.

"Not those," I pleaded, but rather than words, my mouth expelled chocolate, chewed chocolate, which fell onto the sleeve of her sweater. "Not those. Not those."

She shook her arm, and the mound of chocolate dropped like a horrible turd upon my bedspread. "You should look at yourself," she said. "I mean, *really* look at yourself."

Along with the Necco wafers she took several Tootsie Pops and half a dozen caramels wrapped in cellophane. I heard her apologize to the Tomkeys for her absence, and then I heard my candy hitting the bottom of their bags.

"What do you say?" Mrs. Tomkey asked.

And the children answered, "Thank you."

While I was in trouble for not bringing my candy sooner, my sisters were in more trouble for not bringing theirs at all. We spent the early part of the evening in our rooms, then one by one we eased our way back upstairs, and joined our parents in front of the TV. I was the last to arrive, and took a seat on the floor beside the sofa. The show was a Western, and even if my head had not been throbbing, I doubt I would have had the wherewithal to follow it. A posse of outlaws crested a rocky hilltop, squinting at a flurry of dust advancing from the horizon, and I thought again of the Tomkeys and of how alone and out of place they had looked in their dopey costumes. "What was up with that kid's tail?" I asked.

"Shhhh," my family said.

For months I had protected and watched over these people, but now, with one stupid act, they had turned my pity into something hard and ugly. The shift wasn't gradual, but immediate, and it provoked an uncomfortable feeling of loss. We hadn't been friends, the Tomkeys and I, but still I had given them the gift of my curiosity. Wondering about the Tomkey family had made me feel generous, but now I would have to shift gears and find pleasure in hating them. The only alternative was to do as my mother had instructed and take a good look at myself. This was an old trick, designed to turn one's hatred inward, and while I was determined not to fall for it, it was hard to shake the mental picture snapped by her suggestion: here is a boy sitting on a bed, his mouth smeared with chocolate. He's a human being, but also he's a pig, surrounded by trash and gorging himself so that others may be denied. Were this the only image in the world, you'd be forced to give it your full attention, but fortunately there were others. This stagecoach, for instance, coming round the bend with a cargo of gold. This shiny new Mustang convertible. This teenage girl, her hair a beautiful mane, sipping Pepsi through a straw, one picture after another, on and on until the news, and whatever came on after the news.

Seven Words You Can Never Say on Television

George Carlin

There are four hundred thousand words in the English language, and there are seven of them you can't say on television. What a ratio that is! Three hundred ninety-nine thousand nine hundred and ninety-three . . . to seven! They must really be bad. They'd have to be outrageous to be separated from a group that large. "All of you over here . . . You seven, you bad words."

That's what they told us, you remember? "That's a bad word." What? There are no bad words. Bad thoughts, bad intentions, but no bad words.

You know the seven, don't you, that you can't say on television? Shit, piss, fuck, cunt, cocksucker, motherfucker, and tits. Those are the Heavy Seven. Those are the ones that'll infect your soul, curve your spine, and keep the country from winning the war. Shit, piss, fuck, cunt, cocksucker, motherfucker, and tits.

Tits doesn't even belong on the list. Such a friendly sounding word. Sounds like a nickname, right? "Hey, Tits, c'mere, man!" "Hey, Tits, meet Toots. Toots, Tits, Tits, Toots." Sounds like a snack, doesn't it?

Yes I know, it IS!

But I don't mean your sexist snack. I mean new NABISCO TITS! The new cheese tits. Corn tits, and pizza tits, and sesame tits, onion tits. Tater tits. Yeah. Bet you can't eat just one, right? I usually switch off. But that word does not belong on the list.

23

Actually, none of the words belong on the list but you can understand why some of them are there. I mean, I'm not completely insensitive to people's feelings. I can dig why some of those words got on the list. Like cocksucker and motherfucker. Those are heavyweight words. There's a lot going on there, man. Besides the literal translation and the emotional feeling, they're just busy words. A lot of syllables to contend with. Those *k*'s are aggressive sounds, they jump out at you. Cocksucker, motherfucker, cocksucker, motherfucker. It's like an assault on you.

Two of the other four-letter Anglo-Saxon words are piss and cunt, which go together of course but forget that. A little accidental humor I threw in. Piss and cunt. The reason that piss and cunt are on the list is that a long time ago certain ladies said, "Those are the two I'm not going to say. I don't mind fuck and shit, but P and C are out! P and C are out!" Which led to such stupid sentences as: "Okay, you fuckers, I'm going to tinkle now."

And of course, the word fuck. I don't really—here's some more accidental humor—I don't really want to get into that now! Because it takes too long. But the word fuck is a very important word. It's the beginning of life and yet it's a word we use to hurt one another. People much wiser than I have said, "I'd rather have my son watch a film with two people making love than two people trying to kill one another." And I can agree. It's a great sentiment, I wish I knew who said it first. But I'd like to take it a step further. I'd like to substitute the word fuck for the word kill in all those movie clichés we grew up with:

"Okay, sheriff, we're going to fuck you now. But we're gonna fuck you slow."

Those are the seven you can never say on television under any circumstances, you just cannot say them ever, not even clinically, you cannot weave them in on the panel with Doc and Ed and Johnny, I mean it's just impossible. Forget those seven, they're out. There are, however, some two-way words. Like prick. It's okay to prick your finger. But don't FINGER YOUR PRICK!

The Amiable Madness of *Green Acres*

Noel Murray

W̲e had genies then. And magical Martians. We were plagued by talking horses and talking cars, and we cast sideways glances at the witches, monsters, and sexy robots who lived next door. We were comforted by thoughts of spies and private eyes, patrolling pop-art citadels to keep us safe. We enjoyed tall tales of a hillbilly family that transformed overnight into oil barons, and we heard rumors of an uncharted desert island where a movie star, a farm girl, two dopes, and two aristocrats were ruled by a benign scientist. We traveled through time with cartoon cavemen and futuristic suburbanites, and visited alternate realities where cavalrymen and Native Americans lived in harmony, and where Allied POWs toyed with neutered Nazis. The world changed from black and white to color, and then those colors grew wilder and more psychedelic, as the sets and costumes finally caught up to what was going on inside them.

And then the sitcom became self-aware.

Green Acres didn't invent postmodern TV tomfoolery, goodness knows. Ernie Kovacs was experimenting with absurdism and surrealism while the medium was still in its infancy, and television characters broke the fourth wall early and often: in variety show sketches, for example, where the host would sometimes literally wink at the audience; or in *The Many Loves of Dobie Gillis*, where the protagonist would openly plead for the audience's empathy. And reaching back even further, it could be argued that nearly everything savvy and smirky on TV had been done first on radio, where personalities like Jack Benny and

Bob & Ray refined the art of being a wiseass while simultaneously letting the audience in on the joke.

As it happens, *Green Acres* sprang *directly* from radio. In 1950, writer Jay Sommers adapted S. J. Perelman's novel *Acres and Pains* into a short-lived radio series called *Granby's Green Acres*. Sommers later became a writer for Paul Henning, the creator of *The Beverly Hillbillies* and *Petticoat Junction*. When those sitcoms became cash cows for CBS, the network gave Henning an open time slot for the fall of 1965, to fill however he pleased, with no pitch or pilot required. Sommers suggested a TV version of *Granby's Green Acres*, and Henning gave the go-ahead.

Veteran Hollywood character actor Eddie Albert stars in *Green Acres* as Oliver Wendell Douglas, a New York attorney who experiences what later generations would dub a "midlife crisis," which stirs him to buy a farm in a hick haven named Hooterville. Flamboyant Hungarian celebrity Eva Gabor plays Oliver's wife Lisa, a flighty socialite who at first protests the move, but ultimately seems more at home with the oddballs of Hooterville than Oliver ever does in any of the show's six seasons. Early in season 1, *Green Acres* is fairly closely tied to *Petticoat Junction*, and even follows something like a serialized structure, showing the Douglases' adjustment to country living. The couple buys a dilapidated farmhouse, hires gawky, childlike live-in handyman Eb Dawson (played by Tom Lester), and meets a progression of unhelpful local businessmen and bureaucrats, as Sommers and his head writer Dick Chevillat carefully build the world of Hooterville, episode by episode and kink by kink.

By the second season, though, *Green Acres'* gentle wackiness evolved into outright lunacy. Witness the opening of the episode "I Didn't Raise My Pig to Be a Soldier" (which aired early in season 2, on September 28, 1966). While Oliver works on his busted tractor—in a dress shirt, vest, and tie, as always—Lisa comes out of the house to ask him for a favor, but both of them keep getting distracted by the show's credits, which are popping up in front of their eyes. (Meanwhile, the cartoon cornpone bounce of Vic Mizzy's score keeps humming merrily in the background.)

That opening scene gives a good sense of *Green Acres'* overall sense of humor, as well as what kept the show grounded. There are outlandish gags, such as the way the wheels fall off the tractor every time Lisa points at them; and there are verbal gags, such as the way Oliver makes fun of Lisa for saying "shtuck" instead of "stuck." But there's also an appealingly flirty give-and-take between the two leads, who at the time were one of the friskiest couples on the tube—even sharing a bed before that became commonplace.

With the banter and the self-reference out of the way, Lisa gets to the point: the Douglases' elderly neighbors the Ziffels are planning to take a second honeymoon, and would like Oliver and Lisa to look after their pig, Arnold. Even people who don't know much about *Green Acres* are often aware of Arnold Ziffel, although the common reduction of *Green Acres* as "that show with the pig" undersells both the inventiveness of Sommers and Chevillat and the absurdist wonder that is Arnold. In the early '60s, Charles Schulz started drawing *Peanuts* cartoons in which Charlie Brown's dog Snoopy imagined himself having fantastical, humanlike adventures, and at the time, some of Schulz's colleagues were sure that he'd driven the strip off the rails. Instead, Schulz's recasting of Snoopy as "the WWI flying ace" or as a struggling novelist made *Peanuts* more popular than ever, and paved the way for Arnold Ziffel, who over the course of *Green Acres* would become a movie star, have love affairs, go to school, inherit millions, and generally fill the role that teen heartthrobs did on most sitcoms. (Behind the scenes, the show's producers had to keep a supply of "Arnolds" in the pipeline, since the pigs tended to outgrow the role after a couple of months. Contrary to rumor, the old Arnolds were not eaten, though the first Arnold reportedly did get slaughtered and cooked before the crew had a change of heart.)

In this episode, Lisa asks Oliver if he considers Arnold a friend, and Oliver says that he likes the pig well enough to say "hi" to him when he runs into him in town, but that he wouldn't exactly invite Arnold over to play bridge. Oliver thinks he's being funny, yet when the Ziffels drop Arnold off, they provide the Douglases with a list of the pig's quirky likes and dislikes, and make sure that Oliver and Lisa have Arnold's favorite bathtub and TV set. (Arnold's set is "easier for him to adjust," Mr. Ziffel insists.)

At about the ten-minute mark of the episode, after several scenes of Oliver being driven to distraction by Arnold's demands, the real plot of "I Didn't Raise My Pig to Be a Soldier" kicks in. Lisa picks up the Ziffels' mail and finds out that Arnold has received a draft notice. When Oliver ignores it, the county sends a couple of men by the farm to force the issue. So Oliver takes Arnold to meet with his draft board, but the officer in charge assumes this is some kind of draft-dodging prank—like that time a guy pretended to be a kangaroo—and sends the FBI to Hooterville to straighten everything out. Oliver is thus put into the position of trying to make a strange situation intelligible, explaining how he and his wife are caring for a TV-watching pig while its senior-citizen parents are on their honeymoon.

This is the flip side of what usually happens on *Green Acres*, where Oliver is frequently baffled and reduced to an inarticulate stammer by his surroundings. In Stephen Cox's *The Hooterville Handbook: A Viewer's Guide to* Green Acres, critic Mark Besten explains, "The truly inspired humor within the series springs from something far more elemental than the cultural differences between city and country. Oliver would willingly go to his grave defending his righteous belief that two plus two makes four; his Hooterville neighbors say that two plus two are five—and can often back it up with empirical evidence." Something like this occurs in "I Didn't Raise My Pig to Be a Soldier," when the FBI throws Oliver in jail for harboring a draft-dodger. When Oliver protests to Lisa that he didn't do anything wrong, she asks, "Then why are you in jail?" Her logic is airtight (sort of), and reflective in its mentality of an era where people were taught to assume that if a suspect had been arrested or a country was being bombed, then the government must have a good reason. (Then again, about all Lisa knows about the FBI is that she likes to watch their TV show, and that sometimes they have to "shoost" people.)

Like most episodes of *Green Acres*, "I Didn't Raise My Pig to Be a Soldier" was directed by Richard L. Bare, who got his big break in Hollywood in the '40s with the *Joe McDoakes* series of spoofy instructional shorts, before becoming a go-to helmer for B-movies and episodic television. In an interview in Cox's book, Bare confesses that he didn't have much to do on *Green Acres*, besides "set up the camera and let it go," and occasionally remind the actors to hold for an extra beat to make room for the laugh track. A lot of the show's comedy was constructed in the editing room. In the standard *Green Acres* flip-cut, the action jumps from one place to another, with a flip of the image and a quick burst of Mizzy. Jay Sommers was also known to trim frames out of scenes to get the pacing as tight as he wanted, and he made liberal use of insert shots to goose the gags. One of the show's regular cast members, Mary Grace Canfield, is quoted by Cox as saying that a *Green Acres* script never "read as well as it played."

Much of the humor in this episode comes from the little asides, the quick visual jokes, and the overall world that Sommers and company had built. The Douglas home itself is one big sight gag, with its crumbling fixtures serving as a backdrop to the stray bits of New York finery that Lisa had brought with her. Oliver and Lisa sleep in an elaborate bed, with a chandelier for a bedside light, and yet their closet has no back and opens up to the outside, which in "I Didn't Raise My Pig" allows Eb to let Arnold into the house when the pig won't stop whining. (Eb says that he needs his sleep, while Oliver, being the boss, doesn't "have to get up 'til 11.") Later, we see Lisa set the breakfast table by hauling all the dishes and silverware—and even a vase with a flower—in a bundled tablecloth. And there's a nice piece of deadpan acting from the draft officials, who are half-disgusted and half-pleased that they finally have their own dodger to go after. Whenever possible, the *Green Acres* writers gave a set or a costume or a piece of blocking a funky twist, to amuse themselves and the fans.

Some of the best *Green Acres* characters are missing from this episode, most notably Mr. Haney (played by Pat Buttram), the honking-voiced peddler who always seemed to roll up on the Douglases' doorstep bearing exactly the esoteric item they needed to get out of their latest predicament. But "I Didn't Raise My Pig" does feature an appearance by the Monroe "brothers," Alf and Ralph—the latter of whom is actually a woman—and a scene with Hank Kimball (Alvy Moore), the endlessly digressing county agent.

And as always, the episode has plenty of Lisa and Oliver, who were originally meant to be the straight men in this cast of oddballs, yet went a little odd themselves as the series rolled on. Gabor had such a delicate comic touch on *Green Acres*. According to Cox's book, privately the actress demanded a closed set so that no outsiders could see her without makeup (or see the elaborate system of rubber bands that kept her face taut); and while shooting, she had to deal with costumers fumbling with her bustline between takes to make sure that her cleavage didn't alarm the censors. Yet when the camera was on, Gabor had a gift for delivering the show's zippy, sometimes bone-dry jokes (such as when she boasts to her husband that she "can talk Hungarian and do imitations of Zsa Zsa Gabor") and a chipper way of saying "Oliv-ah!" several times an episode. As for Albert, there was a lightness about him that had served him well on Broadway and in the scores of movies he made during Hollywood's golden age, and which made Oliver Douglas's bluster come off as less irascible than adorable.

"I Didn't Raise My Pig to Be a Soldier" ends with Oliver finally getting Arnold a deferment, which earns Oliver a glowing mention in the local paper as "noted Hooterville pig-lawyer." But Oliver ends up back in front of the draft board again the next day with Ralph Monroe, who's just gotten *her* notice. ("Run out of pigs, huh?" the officer quips.) That's the way it goes on *Green Acres*: there's never any permanent escape from the loopiness of Hooterville.

Green Acres wasn't as big of a hit as Henning's *Beverly Hillbillies*, but it was a reliable performer for CBS until 1971, when the network killed the show as part of programming VP Fred Silverman's infamous three-year "rural purge," which also saw the demise of *The Beverly Hillbillies*, *Mayberry R.F.D.*, *Petticoat Junction*, *Hee Haw*, *Lassie*, *The Jim Nabors Hour*, and *The Glen Campbell Goodtime Hour*. (Pat Buttram dubbed it "the year CBS canceled everything with a tree.") But *Green Acres* repeats had a long run in syndication, where, removed from the pervasive freakiness of the '60s, the very specific freakiness of this show began to draw more notice. For a time, *Green Acres* became the subject of serious critical and academic study. In 1985 the prestigious cinema journal *Film Comment* even ran an appreciative essay by critic Armond White (not yet as notorious as he is today), who wrote, "Unconsciously evoking the absurdist dramatists Beckett and Ionesco, the creators of *Green Acres* questioned the stability of the world and its comprehensibility (unthinkable in a TV series), but in unpretentious terms that did not alarm the American public. Plainly put: the wonder of the series is that craziness always made sense."

In retrospect, *Green Acres* was hipper than Silverman thought, and maybe didn't deserve to be lumped in with all the other "country" shows. After all, Sommers never expressly indicated Hooterville's location—it's been variously pinpointed as the Midwest, the Ozarks,

Appalachia, and upstate New York—and the cast deployed a range of accents, from blue-collar redneck to New England innkeeper to Chicago ward boss. Sommers always said that he was inspired in part by the time he spent as a boy on a farm in Greendale, New York—not the South or the Midwest, as many might assume—which speaks to the patchwork quality of these United States, where the urban, the suburban, and the exurban are all stitched together and not confined to any one region of the country. (Also, it's apt that Sommers once lived in "Greendale," which is also the name of the location for one of the most *Green Acres*–like shows on network prime time today.)

Still, it is true that the form of *Green Acres* didn't synch up with the network soon to be known as the home of some of the most sophisticated sitcoms on television: *All in the Family, The Mary Tyler Moore Show, The Bob Newhart Show,* and *M*A*S*H* (among others). The Day-Glo pop of the '60s quickly faded into the earth tones and urban decay of the '70s, as what had once seemed like signs of a culture descending into madness—boys with long hair, rampant recreational drug use, loud music, short skirts, coarse language, war protestors, etc.—became more routine. There weren't so many genies in the '70s, or spacemen, or super-cool spies, or scientists turning coconuts into radios. For a time after the cancellation of *Green Acres* and its ilk, television instead became a home for criminals, addicts, bigots, divorcées, and genocidal profiteers. In the process, our culture diffused the crazy. Or perhaps just absorbed it into our essence.

Brad Carrigan, American

George Saunders

Morning at the Carrigans'.

Minutes ago, Chief Wayne left with the giant stick of butter. Any minute now, Brad Carrigan expects, the doorbell will ring.

Just then the doorbell rings.

Chief Wayne stands scowling in the doorway, holding the giant stick of butter.

"Gosh, what's the matter, Wayne?" says Doris, the way she always does.

"I tried to butter my toast," says Chief Wayne. "At which time I discovered that this stick of butter was actually your dog, Buddy, wearing a costume—a costume of a stick of butter!"

"Oh Buddy," says Doris. "Don't you know that, if you want someone to like you, tricking them is the last thing you should do?"

"I guess I know that now," says Buddy sadly.

"Brad? Doris?" says Chief Wayne. "I guess I also learned something today. If a dog likes you, or even a person, you should try your best to like them in return. Buddy wouldn't have to hide in this costume if I'd simply accept his friendship."

"That's a good lesson, Wayne," says Doris. "One I guess we could all stand to learn."

"What I was hoping you'd learn, Wayne?" says Buddy. "Is that just because a person spends hours at a time in front of the house, licking his or her own butt, doesn't mean he or she has no feelings."

"Although technically, Buddy, you're not really a person," says Chief Wayne.

"And technically you don't have a butt," says Doris.

"All you have is that hole where Craig puts his hand in, to make you move," says Chief Wayne.

This hurts Buddy's feelings and he runs out the dog door.

"Oh gosh," Doris says. "I hope nothing bad happens to Buddy."

"I'd feel awful if something happened to the Budster because we drove him outside with our taunts about him not having a butt," says Chief Wayne thoughtfully.

Brad, Doris, and Chief Wayne step into the yard to find Buddy hanging motionless on the clothesline, his severed genitals on the ground beneath him.

"Well, I guess we all learned something today," says Chief Wayne.

"What I learned?" says Doris. "Is you never know when someone precious to you may be snatched away."

"And therefore," says Chief Wayne, "we must show our love every day, in every way."

"That is so true," says Doris.

"Don't you think that's true, Brad?" says Chief Wayne.

"I guess so," says Brad, whose hands are shaking.

"You *guess* so?" says Chief Wayne. "Oh that's rich! You *guess* we must show our love every day, in every way?"

"As if there could be any argument about that whatsoever!" says Doris.

"Oh Brad," says Chief Wayne, with an affectionate shake of his headdress.

"Oh Brad," says Doris. "The people we know and love are all that matter in this crazy world. Someday you'll understand that."

"The people we love—and the dogs we love!" says Chief Wayne.

"If you look deep in your heart, Brad," says Doris, "I just know that's what you feel."

What Brad feels is, he's trying his best here. Trying his best to stay cheerful and positive. About a month ago, Doris passed him a note regarding possible cancellation. *It's coming*, the note said. *Our asses are grass, unless. Big changes req'd. Trust me on this. Grave crisis, no lie, love, ME.*

How did Doris know about the impending possible cancellation? When he asked, she wouldn't say. She only shook her head fiercely, as if to indicate: We're not going to discuss this any further, we're just going to fix the problem.

So whenever something's changed around here, he's tried to stay upbeat. When they got Buddy he didn't question why Buddy was a puppet-dog and not a real dog. When Chief Wayne started coming around claiming to be his oldest friend in the world, he didn't question why a Native American had red hair. When their backyard started morphing, he didn't ask how it was physically possible.

Then things started getting dumber. Plus meaner. Now it's basically all mean talk and jokes about poop and butts. He and Doris used to talk about real issues, about them, their relationship, their future hopes and plans. Once she lost her engagement ring and bought a fake so he wouldn't notice. Once he became jealous when the butcher started giving her excellent cuts of meat.

And now violence. Poor Buddy. They've never had violence before. Once a tree branch conked Brad in the head. Once he fell off a chair and landed on a knitting needle.

But a murder/castration?

No, never, this is entirely unprecedented.

"Brad, hello?" says Doris. "Have you had a stroke? Is that why you're staring off into space as if taking a dump?"

"Did you take such a difficult dump it gave you a stroke?" says Chief Wayne.

Both Doris and Chief Wayne put on their faces the expression of someone taking a difficult dump, then having a stroke. Then we see from the way they start laughing warmly, smiling affectionately at Brad, and from the happy swell of the music, that they haven't really had strokes while taking dumps, they're just trying to keep things light, and also, that it's time for a commercial.

Back at the Carrigans', Brad has placed Buddy and his genitals on a card table, along with a photo of Buddy and some of his favorite squeaky toys.

"Would anyone like to say a few words about Buddy?" Brad says.

"Poor Buddy," says Chief Wayne. "Always shooting his mouth off. I'm sure that's what happened to him. He shot his mouth off to the wrong person, who then killed and castrated him."

"Not that you're saying he deserved it," says Doris.

"I'm not saying he deserved it exactly," says Chief Wayne. "But if a person is going to have so many negative opinions, and share them with the world, eventually somebody's going to get tired of it."

"Would anyone like to say a few, other, words about Buddy?" says Brad. "Doris?"

"Hey, wait a minute," says Doris, glancing up at the TV. "Isn't this *FinalTwist*?"

"Oh, I love *FinalTwist*," says Chief Wayne.

"Guys?" says Brad. "Aren't we remembering Buddy?"

"Brad, for heaven's sake," says Doris. "Calm down and watch some *FinalTwist* with us."

"Buddy's not exactly going anywhere, Bradster," says Chief Wayne.

Also new. Previously they never watched other shows on their show. Plus they have so many TVs now, two per room, plus a backyard TV, plus one at either end of the garage, so that, wherever they go, some portion of another show is always showing.

On *FinalTwist*, five college friends take a sixth to an expensive Italian restaurant, supposedly to introduce him to a hot girl, actually to break the news that his mother is dead. This is the InitialTwist. During dessert they are told that, in fact, all of their mothers are dead. This is the SecondTwist. The ThirdTwist is, not only are all their mothers dead, the show paid to have them killed, and the fourth and FinalTwist is, the kids have just eaten their own grilled mothers.

"What a riot," says Doris.

"Doris, come on," says Brad. "These are real people, people with thoughts and hopes and dreams."

"Well, nobody got hurt," says Chief Wayne.

"Except those kids who unknowingly ate their own mothers," says Brad.

"Well, they signed the releases," says Chief Wayne.

"Releases or not, Wayne, come on," says Brad. "They killed people. They tricked people into eating their own mothers."

"I don't know that I'm all that interested in the moral ins and outs of it," says Chief Wayne. "I guess I'm just saying I enjoyed it."

"It's interesting, that's the thing," says Doris. "The expectations, the reversals, the timeless human emotions."

"Who wouldn't want to watch that?" says Chief Wayne.

"Interesting is good, Brad," says Doris. "Surprising is good."

Just then Buddy hops sheepishly off the card table, bearing his own genitals in his mouth.

"Buddy, you're alive!" says Doris.

"But I see you're still castrated?" says Chief Wayne.

"Yes, well," says Buddy, blushing.

"Maybe you could tell us who did it, Buddy," says Doris.

"Oh Doris," says Buddy, and starts to cry. "I did it myself."

"You castrated yourself?" says Doris.

"I guess you could say it was a cry for help," says Buddy.

"I'll say," says Chief Wayne.

"I just get so tired of everyone constantly making jokes about the fact that I need a certain kind of 'assistance' in order to move," Buddy says.

"You mean a hand up your keister?" says Doris.

"A fist up your poop chute?" says Chief Wayne.

"A paw up your exit ramp?" says Doris.

"You're still doing it!" barks Buddy, and runs out the dog door.

"Somebody's grumpy," says Doris.

"He'll be a lot less grumpy once we get those genitals of his sewed back on," says Chief Wayne.

Chief Wayne steps outside.

"Uh-oh, guys!" he says. "Looks like, in addition to a persnickety dog, you've got yourself *another* little problem. Your darn backyard has morphed again!"

Then we hear the familiar music that indicates the backyard has morphed again, and see that the familiar Carrigan backyard is now a vast field of charred human remains.

"Carrigan, I've about had it with this nonsense!" shouts their neighbor, Mr. Winston. "Last week my grumpy boss, Mr. Taylor, came for dinner, and right in the middle of dessert your yard morphed into ancient Egypt, and a crocodile came over and ate Mr. Taylor's toupee!"

"And when my elderly parents came to visit?" says Mrs. Winston. "Your yard morphed into some sort of nineteenth-century brothel, and a prostitute insulted my mother over the fence!"

"Oh come on, Brad," says Doris. "Let's go find Buddy."

Brad, Doris, and Chief Wayne set out across the yard.

"Jeez, where is that crazy dog?" says Chief Wayne.

"Look for the one thing not smoldering in this vast expanse of carnage," says Doris, stepping gingerly over several charred corpses in the former horseshoe pit.

From the abandoned farmhouse comes an agonized scream.

From behind a charred tree darts Buddy.

"Let's corner him by that contaminated well!" says Doris, and she and Chief Wayne rush off.

"My God," mumbles Brad. "Who were these people?"

"We're Belstonians," says one of the corpses, lying on its back, hands held out defensively, as if it died fending off a series of blows. "Our nation is comprised of three main socioethnic groups: the religious Arszani of the north, who live in small traditional agrarian communities in the mountainous northern regions; the more secular, worldly Arszani of the south, who mix freely with their Tazdit neighbors; and the Tazdit themselves, who, though superior to the southern Arszani in numbers, have always lagged behind economically. Lately this course of affairs has been exacerbated by several consecutive years of drought."

"Don't forget the complicated system of tariffs, designed to favor the southern, secular Arszani, emphasizing, as it does, the industrially driven sectors of the economy, in which the southern Arszani, along with certain more ecumenical Tazdit factions, invested heavily during the post-earthquake years," says a second corpse, whose chest cavity has been torn open, and who is missing an arm.

"Which spelled doom for us mountainous devout northern Arszani once gold was discoved in a region ostensibly under our control but legally owned by a cartel of military/industrial leaders from the south," says a third corpse, a woman, legs spread wide, mouth open in an expression of horror.

"That was our group," says the corpse missing an arm. "Northern Arszani."

"Wow," says Brad. "That's so complicated."

"Not that complicated," says the corpse who died fending off blows.

"It might seem complicated, if the person trying to understand it had lived in total plenty all his life, ignoring the rest of the world," says the corpse missing an arm, as a butterfly flits from his chest wound to his head wound.

"I agree," says the corpse who died fending off blows. "We know all about *his* country. I know who Casey Stengel was. I can quote at length from Thomas Paine."

"Who?" says Brad.

"Now, Bliorg, be fair," says the woman corpse. "Their nation occupies a larger place on the world stage. English is the lingua franca of most of the world."

"The what?" says Brad.

"I'm just saying that, occupying oneself with the genitals of a puppet, given the brutal, nightmarish things going on around the world this very instant, I find that unacceptably trivial," says the one-armed corpse.

"I miss life," says the woman corpse.

"Remember our farm?" says the corpse who died fending off blows. "Remember how delicious vorella tasted eaten directly from the traditional heated cubern?"

"How the air smelled in the Kizhdan Pass after a rain?" says the woman corpse.

"How hard we worked in the garden that final spring?" says the corpse who died fending off blows. "How suddenly it all came upon us? How unprepared we were when suddenly the militia, including some of our southern Arszani brethren, swept into our village—"

"With what violence they rended you, dear, while you were still alive," the woman corpse says, looking tenderly at the corpse who died fending off blows.

"How the men encircled you, taunting you as they . . ." The corpse who died fending off blows trails off, remembering the day the secular Arszani/southern Tazdit militia dragged his wife into the muddy yard of their shack, then held him down, forcing him to watch what followed for what might have been ten minutes and might have been three hours, after which they encircled him, bayonets fixed, and he attempted, briefly, to fend off their blows, before they eviscerated him while he was still alive, as his wife, also still alive, lifted and dropped her left arm repeatedly, for what might have been ten thousand years.

Just then Doris rushes by, bearing the re-genitaled and softly whimpering Buddy in her arms.

"Brad, honestly," she hisses. "Thanks for the help."

"Not!" says Chief Wayne.

We see from the way the corpses, devastated by memory, collapse back into the dust of the familiar Carrigan backyard, and from the sad tragic Eastern European swell of the music, that it's time for a commercial.

Back at the Carrigans', Doris and Chief Wayne come back inside to find hundreds of ears of corn growing out of the furniture, floors, and ceiling.

"What the—?" says Doris, setting Buddy down.

"I believe this is what's called a 'bumper crop,' " says Chief Wayne.

"I'll say," says Doris. "It's going to 'bump' us right out of this room if it keeps up!"

"My balls hurt so much," says Buddy.

Brad comes in, eyes moist with tears, and sits on the couch.

"What gives, Mr. Gloomy?" says Doris.

"Still moping about the corpses in the yard?" says Chief Wayne.

"Give it time, hon," says Doris. "It'll morph into something more cheerful."

"It always does," says Chief Wayne.

"Things always come out right in the end, don't they?" says Doris. "As long as you believe in your dreams?"

"And accentuate the positive," says Chief Wayne.

Just then from the TV comes the brash martial music that indicates an UrgentUpdateNewsMinute.

In California, a fad has broken out of regular people having facial surgery to look like their favorite celebrities. Sometimes they end up looking like hideous monsters. Celebrities have taken to paying surprise compassionate visits to the hideous monsters. One hideous monster, whose face looks like the face of a lion roasted in a fire, says the surprise celebrity visit made the whole ordeal worthwhile. In the Philippines, a garbage dump has exploded due to buildup of natural gas emitted by rotting garbage, killing dozens of children digging in the dump for food.

"Wait a minute," says Brad. "That gives me an idea."

"Uh-oh," says Chief Wayne. "I don't like the sound of that."

"I hope it's better than your idea about installing heat sensors in old people's underwear," says Doris.

"I also hope it's better than your idea about putting a radio transmitter on Buddy while you guys were away on vacation, which then short-circuited, causing Buddy to be continually electrocuted for two straight weeks," says Chief Wayne.

"And the Winstons thought Buddy had been taking tap lessons?" says Doris. "Oh gosh."

"So what's your idea, pal?" says Chief Wayne.

"Never mind," says Brad, blushing.

"Come on, Mr. Mopey!" says Doris. "Share it! I'm sure it's terrific."

"Well," says Brad. "My idea is, why do we need all this corn? Isn't it sort of wasteful? My idea is, let's pick this corn and send it to that village in the Philippines where the kids have to eat garbage to live. Our house gets back to normal, the kids don't have to eat trash, everybody's happy."

There is an awkward silence.

"Brad, have you finally gone totally insane?" Doris says.

"I have to say, the heat-sensor-in-the-underwear-of-the-elderly idea is starting to look pretty viable," says Chief Wayne.

"I just want to do something," says Brad, blushing again. "There's so much suffering. We have so much, and others have so little. So I was just thinking that, you know, if we took a tiny portion of what we have, which we don't really need, and sent it to the people who need it . . ."

Doris has tears in her eyes.

"Doris, what is it?" says Chief Wayne. "Tell Brad what you're feeling."

"I don't see why you always have to be such a downer, Brad," she says. "First you start weeping in our yard, then you start disparaging our indoor corn?"

"Brad, to tell the truth, there are plenty of houses with lots more indoor corn than this," says Chief Wayne. "This, relative to a lot of houses I've seen, is some very modest indoor vegetable growth."

"You probably see it as you make your rounds," says Doris. "Some people probably even have tomatoes and zucchini growing out of their furniture."

"Oh sure," says Chief Wayne. "Even watermelons."

"So this very modest amount of corn that we have, in your opinion, is nothing to feel guilty about?" says Doris.

"His 'rounds'?" says Brad. "What do you mean his 'rounds'?"

"His raids, his rounds, whatever," says Doris. "Please don't change the subject, Brad. I think we've been very fortunate, but not so fortunate that we can afford to start giving away everything we've worked so hard for. Why can't our stuff, such as corn, be *our* stuff? Why do you have to make everything so complicated? We aren't exactly made out of money, Brad!"

"Look Brad," says Chief Wayne. "Maybe you should start thinking about Doris instead of some Philippians you don't even know."

"You really get me, Wayne," says Doris.

"You're easy to get, Doris," says Chief Wayne.

Just then the doorbell rings.

On the lawn stands a delegation of deathly-pale Filipino children dressed in bloodstained white smocks.

"We've come for the corn?" says the tallest child, who has a large growth above one eyebrow.

"Brad," Doris says in a pitiful voice. "I can't believe you called these people."

"I didn't," Brad says.

And he didn't. Although he can't say he's unhappy they're here.

"Look, what's the big deal?" says Brad. "We pick the corn, give it to these kids, problem solved. If you guys would help me out, we could have all this corn picked in ten minutes."

"Brad, I've suddenly got a terrible headache," says Doris. "Would you go get me a Tylenol?"

"Brad, jeez, nice," says Chief Wayne. "Don't just stand there with your mouth hanging open when your wife is in pain."

Brad goes into the kitchen, gets Doris a Tylenol.

Buddy follows him in, hops up on a kitchen chair.

"Uh, Brad?" Buddy whispers. "I want you to know something. I've always liked you. I've consistently advocated for you. To me, you seem extremely workable, and I've said so many—"

"Buddy, no, bad dog!" Doris shouts from the living room.

"Yikes," says Buddy, and hops down from the chair, and skids out of the kitchen.

What the heck is up with Buddy? Brad wonders. He's "advocated" for Brad? He finds Brad "workable"?

Possibly the self-castration has made Buddy a little mental.

Brad returns to the living room. Doris, on the love seat, wearing the black lace bustier Brad bought her last Christmas, is straddling Chief Wayne, who, pants around his ankles, is kissing Doris's neck.

"Doris, my God!" shouts Brad.

Doris and Chief Wayne? It makes no sense. Chief Wayne is at least ten years older than they are, and is overweight and has red hair all over his back and growing out of his ears.

"Doris," Brad says. "I don't understand."

"I can explain, Bradster!" Chief Wayne says. "You've just been TotallyFukked!"

"And so have I!" says Doris. "No, just kidding! Brad, lighten up! See, look here! We kept a thin layer of protective cellophane between us at all times!"

"Come on, pal, what did you think?" says Chief Wayne. "Did you honestly think I'd let your beautiful wife straddle and pump me right here, in your living room, wearing the bustier you bought her last Christmas, without using a thin layer of protective cellophane?"

It's true. There's a thin layer of protective cellophane draped over Chief Wayne's legs, chest, and huge swollen member. A TotallyFukked cameraman steps out from behind a potted plant, with a release form, which Doris signs on Brad's behalf.

"Gosh, honey, the look on your face!" Doris says.

"He sure takes things serious," says Chief Wayne.

"Too serious," says Doris.

"Is he crying?" says Chief Wayne.

"Brad, honestly, lighten up!" says Doris. "Things are finally starting to get fun around here."

"Brad, please don't go all earnest on us," says Chief Wayne.

"Yes, don't go all earnest on us, Brad," says Doris. "Or next time we TotallyFukk you, we'll remove that thin sheet of protective cellophane."

"And wouldn't that be a relief," says Chief Wayne.

"Well yes and no," says Doris. "I love Brad."

"You love Brad but you're hot for me," says Chief Wayne.

"Well, I'm hot for Brad too," says Doris. "If only he wasn't so earnest all the time."

Brad looks at Doris. All he's ever wanted is to make her happy. But he never really has, not yet. Not when he bought her six hats, not when he covered the bedroom floor with rose petals, not when he tried to cook her favorite dish and nearly burned the house down.

What right does he have to be worrying about the problems of the world when he can't even make his own wife happy? How arrogant is that? Maybe a man's first responsibility is to make a viable home. If everybody made a viable home, the world would be a connected network of viable homes. Maybe he's been mistaken, worrying about the Belstonians and the Filipinos, when he should have been worrying about his own wife.

He thinks he knows what he has to do.

The tallest Filipino child graciously accepts Brad's apology, then leads the rest of the Filipinos away, down Eiderdown Path, across Leaping Fawn Way, Bullfrog Terrace, and Waddling Gosling Place.

Brad asks Chief Wayne to leave.

Chief Wayne leaves.

Doris stands in the middle of the corn-filled living room, looking gorgeous.

"Oh, you really do love me, don't you?" she says, and kisses Brad while sliding his hands up to her full hot breasts.

We see from the way Doris tosses her bustier over Buddy, so Buddy won't see what she and Brad are about to do, and the way Buddy winces, because the bustier has landed on his genital stitches, that Buddy is in for a very long night, as is Brad, and also, that it's time for a commercial.

Back at the Carrigans', Doris's family is over for the usual Sunday dinner of prime rib, Carolina ham, roast beef, Alaskan salmon, mashed potatoes, fresh-baked rolls, and asparagus à la Monterey.

"What a meal," says Grandpa Kirk, Doris's father.

"We are so lucky," says Grandma Sally, Doris's mother.

Brad feels incredibly lucky. Last night they did it in the living room, then in the bathroom, then twice more in the bedroom. Doris admitted she wasn't hot for Chief Wayne, exactly, just bored, plus she admired

Wayne's direct and positive way of dealing with life, so untainted by neurotic doubts and fears.

"I guess I just want some fun," she'd said. "Maybe that's how I'd put it."

"I know," Brad had said. "I get that now."

"I just want to take life as we find it and enjoy its richness," Doris had said. "I don't want to waste my life worrying worrying worrying."

"I totally agree with you," Brad had said.

Then Doris disappeared beneath the covers and took him in her mouth for the third time that night. Remembering last night, Brad starts to get what Doris calls a Twinkie, and to counteract his mild growing Twinkie, imagines the Winstons' boxer, Mr. Maggs, being hit by a car.

"This meal we just ate?" says Aunt Lydia. "In many countries, this sort of meal would only be eaten by royalty."

"There are countries where people could live one year on what we throw out in one week," says Grandpa Kirk.

"I thought it was they could live one year on what we throw out in one day," says Grandma Sally.

"I thought it was they could live ten years on what we throw out in one minute," says Uncle Gus.

"Well anyway," says Doris. "We are very lucky."

"I like what you kids have done with the place," says Aunt Lydia. "The corn and all?"

"Very autumnal," says Grandpa Kirk.

Just then from the TV comes the brash martial music that indicates an UrgentUpdateNewsMinute.

Americans are eating more quail. Special quail farms capable of producing ten thousand quail a day are being built along the Brazos River. The bad news is, Americans are eating less pig. The upside is, the excess pigs are being slaughtered for feed for the quail. The additional upside is, ground-up quail beaks make excellent filler for the new national trend of butt implants, far superior to to the traditional butt-implant filler of ground-up dog spines. Also, there has been a shocking upturn in the number of African AIDS babies. Fifteen hundred are now dying each day. Previously, only four hundred a day were dying. An emaciated baby covered with flies is shown, lying in a kind of trough.

"We are so lucky," says Aunt Lydia.

"There is no country in the history of the world as lucky as us," says Grandpa Kirk. "No country where people lived as long or as well, with as much dignity and freedom. Not the Romans. Not the Grecos."

"Not to mention infant mortality," says Uncle Gus.

"That's what I'm saying," says Grandpa Kirk. "In other countries, you go to a graveyard, you see tons of baby graves. Here, you don't see hardly any."

"Unless there was a car accident," says Uncle Gus.

"A car accident involving a daycare van," says Grandpa Kirk.

"Or if someone fell down the steps holding infant twins," suggests Grandma Sally.

Some additional babies covered with flies are shown in additional troughs, along with several grieving mothers, also covered with flies.

"That is so sad," says Aunt Lydia. "I can hardly stand to watch it."

"I can't stand to watch it," says Uncle Gus, turning away.

"So why not change it?" says Grandma Sally.

Doris changes it.

On TV six women in prison shirts move around a filthy house.

"Oh I know this one," says Grandma Sally. "This is *Kill the Ho*."

"Isn't it *Kill Which Ho*?" says Aunt Lydia.

"Isn't it *Which Ho Should We Kill*?" says Grandpa Kirk.

"All six are loose, poor, and irresponsible!" the announcer says. "But which Ho do you hate the most? Which should die? America decides, America votes, coming this fall, on *Kill the Ho*!"

"Told you," says Grandma Sally. "Told you it was *Kill the Ho*."

"They don't actually kill them though," says Grandpa Kirk. "They just do it on computers."

"They show how it would look if they killed that particular Ho," says Uncle Gus.

Then it starts to rain, and from the backyard comes a horrible scream. Brad tenses. He waits for someone to say: What the hell is that screaming?

But nobody seems to hear it. Everyone just keeps on eating.

We see from the concerned look on Brad's face, and the way he throws back his chair, and the concerned look Doris shoots him for throwing back his chair in the middle of dinner, that it's time for a commercial.

Back at the Carrigans', Brad is struggling through a downpour in the familiar Carrigan backyard.

"What is it?" Brad shouts. "Why are you screaming?"

"It's the rain," screams the corpse who died fending off blows. "We find it unbearably painful. The dead do. Especially the dead not at peace at the time of their deaths."

"I never heard that before," says Brad.

"Trust me," says the corpse who died fending off blows.

The corpses, on their backs, are doing the weirdest craziest writhing dance. They do it ceaselessly, hands opening and closing, feet bending and straightening. With all that motion, their dried hides are developing surficial cracks.

"What can I do?" says Brad.

"Get us inside," gasps the woman corpse.

Brad drags the corpses inside. Because the house is a ranch house and has no basement, he puts the corpses in the back entry, near a bag of grass seed and a sled.

"Is that better?" Brad says.

"We can't even begin to tell you," says the corpse who died fending off blows.

Brad goes back to the dining room, where Doris is serving apple pie, raspberry pie, sherbet, sorbet, coffee, and tea.

"Anything wrong, hon?" says Doris. "We're just having second dessert. Say, what's that on your shirt?"

On Brad's shirt is a black stain, which looks like charcoal but is actually corpse mud.

"Go change, silly," says Doris. "You're soaked to the bone. I can see your nipples."

Doris gives him a double-raise of her eyebrows, to indicate that the sight of his nipples has put her in mind of last night.

Brad goes into the bedroom, puts on a new button-down. Then he hears something heavy crashing to the floor and rushes out to find Doris sprawled in the back entry, staring in horror at the charred corpses.

"Bradley, how could you?" she hisses. "Is this your idea of a joke? Is this you getting revenge on me in a passive-aggressive way because I wouldn't let you waste our corn?"

"The rain hurts them," Brad says.

"Having my entry full of dead corpses hurts me, Brad," Doris says. "Did you ever think of that?"

"No, I mean it physically hurts them," says Brad.

"After all we shared last night, you pull this stunt?" Doris says. "Oh, you break my heart. Why does everything have to be so sad to you? Why do you have so many negative opinions about things you don't know about, like foreign countries and diseases and everything? Why can't you be more like Chief Wayne? He has zero opinions. He's just upbeat."

"Doris, I—" says Brad.

"I want them out," Doris says. "I want them out now, dumbass, and I want you to mop this entry, and then I want you to mop it again, shake out the rug, and also I may have you repaint that wall. Why do I have to live like this? The Elliots don't have corpses in their yard. Millie doesn't. Kate Ronston doesn't. The Winstons don't have any Filipinos trying to plunder their indoor vegetables. Only us. Only me. It's like I'm living the wrong life."

Doris storms back to the kitchen, high heels clicking sexily on the linoleum.

Dumbass? Brad thinks.

Doris has never spoken so harshly to him, not even when he accidentally threw her favorite skirt in the garbage and had to dig it out by flashlight and a raccoon came and looked at him quizzically.

Brad remembers when old Mrs. Giannelli got Lou Gehrig's disease and began losing the use of her muscles, and Doris organized over three hundred people from the community to provide round-the-clock care. He remembers when the little neighborhood retarded boy, Roger, was being excluded from ball games, and Doris herself volunteered to be captain and picked Roger first.

That was Doris.

This woman, he doesn't know who she is.

"Your wife has a temper," says the corpse who died fending off blows. "I mean, no offense."

"She is pretty, though," says the one-armed corpse.

"The way they say it here?" says the woman corpse. "They say: 'She is hot.'"

"Your wife is hot," says the one-armed corpse.

"Are you really going to put us back out there, Brad?" says the woman corpse, her voice breaking.

It seems to be raining even harder.

Once, back in Brad's childhood, Brad knows, from one of his eight Childhood Flashbacks, his grizzled grandfather, Old Rex, took him to the zoo on the Fourth of July. Near the bear cage they found a sparrow with its foot stuck in a melted marshmallow. When Old Rex stopped to pull the sparrow out, Brad felt embarrassed. Everyone was watching. Hitching up his belt, Old Rex said: *Come on, pardner, we're free, we're healthy, we've got the time—who's gonna save this little dude, if not us?*

Then Old Rex used his pocketknife to gently scrape away the residual marshmallow. Then Old Rex took the sparrow to a fountain and rinsed off its foot, and put it safely on a high branch. Then Old Rex lifted little Brad onto his shoulders and some fireworks went off and they went to watch the dolphins.

Now that was a man, Brad thinks.

Maybe the problem with their show is, it's too small-hearted. It's all just rolling up hoses and filling the birdfeeder and making smart remarks about other people's defects and having big meals while making poop jokes and sex jokes. For all its charms, it's basically a selfish show. Maybe what's needed is an enlargement of the heart of their show. What would that look like? How would one go about making that kind of show?

Well, he can think of one way right now.

He goes into the shed, finds a tarp and, using the laundry line and the tarp, makes a kind of tent. Then, using an umbrella, he carries the corpses out.

"Easy, easy," says the one-armed corpse. "Don't break my leg off by hitting it on that banister."

Just then the back door flies violently open.

"Bradley!" Doris shouts from inside. "Did I say build the ghouls a playhouse or put the ghouls in the yard?"

"The ghouls?" says the one-armed corpse.

"That isn't very nice," says the woman corpse. "We don't call her names."

Brad looks apologetically at the corpses. Apparently it's time for a little marital diplomacy, time to go inside and have a frank heart-to-heart with Doris.

Look, Doris, he'll say. What's happened to you, where has your generosity gone? Our house is huge, honey, our refrigerator is continually full. However much money we need, we automatically have that much in the bank, and neither of us even works outside of the home. There doesn't seem to be any physical limit to what we can have or get. Why not spread some of that luck around? What if that was the *point* of our show, sweetie, the radical spreading-around of our good fortune? What if we had, say, a special helicopter? And special black jumpsuits? And code names? And huge stores of food and medicine, and a team of expert consultants, and wherever there was need, there they would be, working to bring to bear on the problem whatever resources would be exactly most helpful?

Talk about positive. Talk about entertaining.

Who wouldn't want to watch that?

Brad has goose bumps. His face is suddenly hot. What an incredible idea. Will Doris get it? Of course she will. This is Doris, his Doris, the love of this life.

He can't wait to tell her.

Brad tries the door, finds it locked.

We see from the sheepish look on Brad's face, and the sudden comic wah-wah of the music, that convincing Doris may turn out to be a little harder than he thought, and also, that it's time for a commercial.

Back at the Carrigans', Grandpa Kirk, Grandma Sally, Uncle Gus, and Aunt Lydia, suddenly in formalwear, have been joined by Dr. and Mrs. Ryan, the Menendezes, the Johnsons, and Mrs. Diem, also in formalwear.

Just then the doorbell rings.

Doris, in a skimpy white Dior dress and gold spike heels, hands Grandma Sally a plate of meatballs and walks briskly toward the door.

At the door is Brad.

"Somehow I got locked out," he says.

"Hi Brad," says Doris. "Here to borrow butter?"

"Very funny," says Brad. "Hey, is that a new dress? Did you just now change dresses?"

Then Brad notices that Chief Wayne is over, and Dr. and Mrs. Ryan, the Menendezes, the Johnsons, and Mrs. Diem are over, and everyone is dressed up.

"What's all this?" he says.

"Things are kind of crazy around here at the moment, Brad," says Chief Wayne. "You could say we're in a state of transition."

"Doris, can we talk?" says Brad. "In private?"

"I'm afraid we aren't in any shape to be talking about anything in private, Bradster," says Chief Wayne. "As I said, we're in a state of transition."

"We've been so busy lately, things are so topsy-turvy lately, hardly a minute to think," Doris says. "Who knows what to think about what, you know?"

"The way I'd say it?" says Chief Wayne. "We're in a state of transition. Let's leave it at that, babe."

Brad notices that Chief Wayne is not wearing his headdress or deerskin leggings, but a pair of tight Gucci slacks and a tight Armani shirt.

Just then, from the place near the china cabinet from which their theme song and the occasional voiceover comes, comes a deep-voiced voiceover.

"Through a script error!" it says, "turns out that Chief Wayne is actually, and has actually been all along, not Chief Wayne, but *Chaz* Wayne, an epileptic pornographer with a taste for the high life and nightmarish memories of Vietnam!"

A tattooed young man Brad has never seen before steps out of the broom closet.

"I'm Whitney, Chaz Wayne's son from a disastrous previous marriage, who recently served time for killing a crooked cop with a prominent head goiter," he says.

"And I'm Buddy, their dog," says Buddy, who, Brad notices, is wearing a tiny pantless tuxedo. "I have recurring rabies and associated depression issues."

Then Chaz Wayne puts his arm around Doris.

"And this is my wife Doris, a former stripper with an imploded breast implant," says Chaz Wayne.

"I'd like to propose a toast," says Grandpa Kirk. "To the newlyweds!"

"To Doris and Chaz," says Uncle Gus.

"To Doris and Chaz!" everyone says together.

"Now wait just a minute," says Brad.

"Brad, honestly," Doris hisses. "Haven't you caused enough trouble already?"

"Here's your butter, Carrigan," says Grandma Sally, handing Brad a stick of butter. "Skedaddle on home."

Brad can't seem to breathe. It was love at first sight, he knows from their First Love Montage, when he saw Doris in a summer dress on the far side of a picket fence. On their first date, the ice cream fell off his cone. On their honeymoon, they kissed under a waterfall.

What should he do? Beg Doris's forgiveness? Punch Wayne? Start rapidly making poop jokes?

Just then the doorbell rings.

It's the Winstons.

At least Brad thinks it's the Winstons. But Mr. Winston has an arm coming out of his forehead, and impressive breasts, a vagina has been implanted in his forehead, and also he seems to have grown an additional leg. Mrs. Winston, short a leg, also with impressive breasts, has a penis growing out of her shoulder and what looks like a totally redone mouth of shining white teeth.

"May? John?" Brad says. "What happened to you?"

"Extreme Surgery," says Mrs. Winston.

"Extreme Surgery happened to us," says Mr. Winston, sweat running down his forehead-arm and into his cleavage.

"Not that we mind," says Mrs. Winston tersely. "We're just happy to be, you know, interesting."

"It's wonderful to see everyone doing their part," says Chaz Wayne.

"Nearly everyone," says Uncle Gus, frowning at Brad.

Just then from the living room comes the sound of hysterical barking.

Everyone rushes in to find Buddy staring down in terror at a naked emaciated black baby covered with open sores.

"It just magically appeared," says Buddy.

From the tribal cloth which is serving as a diaper, and the open lesions on its legs, face, and chest, Dr. Ryan concludes that the baby is an HIV-positive baby from sub-Saharan Africa.

"What should we name him?" says Buddy. "Or her?"

"Him," says Dr. Ryan, after a quick look under the tribal cloth.

"Can we name him Doug?" says Buddy.

"Don't name him anything," says Doris.

"Buddy," says Chaz Wayne. "Tell us again how this baby got in here?"

"It just magically appeared," says Buddy.

"Could you be more specific, Buddy?" says Chaz Wayne.

"It like fell in through the ceiling?" says Buddy.

"Well, that suggests an obvious solution," says Chaz Wayne. "Why not simply put it back on the roof where it came from?"

"Sounds fair to me," says Mr. Winston.

"Although that roof's got quite a pitch to it," says Grandpa Kirk. "Poor thing might roll right off."

"Maybe we could rig up a kind of mini-platform?" says Uncle Gus.

"Then duct-tape the baby in place?" suggests Mrs. Diem.

"What do you say, Brad?" says Chaz Wayne. "Would you do the honors? After all, we didn't ask for this baby, we don't know this baby, we didn't make this baby sick, we had nothing to do with the deeply unfortunate occurrence that occurred to this baby back wherever its crude regressive culture is located."

"How about it, Carrigan?" says Grandpa Kirk.

Brad looks into the baby's face. It's a beautiful face. Except for the open lesions. How did this beautiful little baby come to be here? He has no idea. But here the baby is.

"Come on, guys," says Brad. "He'll starve to death up there. Plus he'll get sunburned."

"Well, Brad," says Aunt Lydia. "He was starving to death when he got here. We didn't do it."

"Plus he's an African, Brad," says Grandma Sally. "The Africans have special pigments."

"I'm not putting any baby on any roof," Brad says.

A strange silence falls on the room.

Then we hear the familiar music that indicates the backyard has morphed again, and see that the familiar Carrigan backyard is now a bleak desert landscape full of rooting feral pigs, ferociously feeding on the corpses.

"Brad!" yells the corpse who died fending off blows. "Brad, please help us!"

"Pigs are eating us!" yells the one-armed corpse.

"A pig is eating my hip!" shouts the corpse who died fending off blows.

"Don't, Brad," says Doris. "Do not."

"Think about what you're doing, Bradster," says Chaz Wayne.

"Listen to me carefully, Brad," says Doris. "Go up onto the roof, install the roof platform, duct-tape the AIDS baby to the roof platform, then come directly down, borrow your butter, and go home."

"Or else," says Chaz Wayne.

From the yard comes the sound of sobbing.

Sobbing and grunting.

Or else? thinks Brad.

Brad remembers when Old Rex was sent to the old folks' home against his will and said: *Little pardner, sometimes a man has to take a stand, if he wants to go on being a man at all.* The next day Old Rex vanished, taking Brad's backpack, and years later they found out he'd spent the last months of his life hitchhiking around the West, involved with a series of waitresses.

What would Old Rex do in this situation? Brad wonders.

Then he knows.

Brad races outside, picks up a handful of decorative lava stones, and pelts the pigs until they flee to a bone-dry watering hole, with vultures, toward the rear of the yard.

Then he loads the corpses into the wheelbarrow, races around the side of the house, past the air-conditioning unit and the papier-mâché clown head from the episode when Doris was turning thirty and he tried to cheer her up, and loads the corpses into the back of the Suburban, after first removing the spare tire and Doris's gym bag.

Then he races back inside, grabs Doug, races out, tucks Doug between the woman corpse and the corpse who died fending off blows, and gets behind the wheel.

What he'll do is drive down Eiderdown Path, across Leaping Fawn Way, Bullfrog Terrace, and Waddling Gosling Place, and drop Doug off at the EmergiClinic, which is located in the Western Slope Mini-Mall, between PetGalaxy and House of Perms. Then he'll go live in Chief Wayne's former apartment. He'll clean out the garage for the corpses. He'll convert Chief Wayne's guest room into a nursery for Doug. He'll care for Doug and the corpses, and come over here once a day to borrow his butter, trying to catch Doris's eye, trying to persuade her to leave Chaz Wayne and join him in his important work.

Suddenly Brad's eyes are full of tears.

Oh Doris, he thinks. Did I ever really know you?

Just then a gray van screeches into the driveway and six cops jump out.

"Is this him?" says a cop.

"I'm afraid so," says Doris, from the porch.

"This is the guy who had questionable contacts with foreign Filipinos and was seen perversely loading deceased corpses into his personal vehicle for his own sick and nefarious purposes?" says another cop.

"I'm afraid so," says Chaz Wayne.

"Well, I guess we all learned something from this," says Grandma Sally.

"What I learned?" says Doris. "Is praise God we're now free to raise our future children in a hopeful atmosphere, where the predominant mode is gratitude, gratitude for all the blessings we've been given, free of neuroses and self-flagellation."

"You can say that again," says Uncle Gus.

"Actually, I'm not sure I can!" says Doris.

"Well, if you're not going to be using that hot mouth of yours, how about I use it?" says Chaz Wayne, and gives Doris an aggressive tongue kiss while sliding his hands up to Doris's full hot breasts.

This is the last thing Brad sees as the cops wrestle him into the van.

As the van doors start to close, Brad suddenly realizes that the instant the doors close completely, the van interior will become the terrifying bland gray space he's heard about all his life, the place one goes when one has been Written Out.

The van doors close completely.

The van interior becomes the bland gray space.

From the front yard TV comes the brash martial music that indicates an UrgentUpdateNewsMinute.

Animal-rights activists have expressed concern over the recent
trend of spraying live Canadian geese with a styrene coating which
instantaneously kills them while leaving them extremely malleable, so
it then becomes easy to shape them into comical positions and write
funny sayings on DryErase cartoon balloons emanating from their
beaks, which, apparently, is the new trend for outdoor summer parties. The inventor of FunGeese! has agreed to begin medicating the
geese with a knockout drug prior to the styrene-spray step. Also, the
Pentagon has confirmed the inadvertent bombing of a tribal wedding
in Taluchistan. Six bundled corpses are shown adjacent to six shallow
graves dug into some impossibly dry-looking soil near a scary gnarled-
looking dead tree.

"We've simply *got* to get some of those FunGeese!" says Doris.

"Plus a grill, and some marination trays," says Chaz Wayne. "That
way, I can have some of my slutty porn stars cook something funky for
our summer party while wearing next to nothing."

"And meanwhile I'll think of some funny things to write in those
thingies," says Doris.

"I hope I can invite some of my dog friends?" says Buddy.

"Do your dog friends have butts?" says Chaz Wayne.

"Does it matter?" says Buddy. "Can I only invite them if they have
butts?"

"I'm just wondering in terms of what I should cook," says Chaz Wayne.
"If they have no butts, I'll make something more easily digestible."

"Some of them have butts, yes," says Buddy in a hurt but
resigned tone.

Then we hear the familiar music that indicates the backyard has
morphed, and see that the familiar Carrigan backyard is the now
familiar Carrigan backyard again, only better. The lawn is lush and
green, the garden thick with roses, adjacent to the oil pit for Orgy Night
is a swimming pool with a floating wet bar, adjacent to the pool is an
attractive grouping of FunGeese! with tantalizingly blank DryErase
cartoon balloons.

We see from the joyful way Doris and Chaz Wayne lead the other
guests into the yard, and from the happy summer-party swell of the

music, that this party is just beginning, and also, that it's time for a commercial.

Back at the Carrigans', Brad floats weightlessly in the bland gray space.

Floating nearby is Wampum, Chief Wayne's former horse. Brad remembers Wampum from the episode where, while they were all inside playing cards, Wampum tried to sit in the hammock and brought it crashing down.

"He used to ride me up and down the prairie," mumbles Wampum. "Digging his bare feet into my side, praising my loyalty."

Brad knows this is too complicated. He knows that if Wampum insists on thinking in such complicated terms, he will soon devolve into a shapeless blob, and will, if he ever gets another chance, come back as someone other than Wampum. One must, Brad knows, struggle single-mindedly to retain one's memory of one's former identity throughout the long period in the gray space, if one wants to come back as oneself.

"Brad brad brad," says Brad.

"I used to eat hay, I believe," says Wampum. "Hay or corn. Or beans? Some sort of grain product, possibly? At least I think I did. Oh darn. Oh jeez."

Wampum falls silent, gradually assuming a less horselike form. Soon he is just a horse-sized blob. Then he is a pony-sized blob, then an inert dog-sized blob incapable of speech.

"Brad brad brad," says Brad.

Then his mind drifts. He can't help it. He thinks of the Belstonians, how frightened they must be, sealed in large plastic bags at the police station. He thinks of poor little Doug, probably even now starving to death sunburned on the familiar Carrigan roof.

The poor things, he thinks. The poor, poor things. I should have done more. I should have started earlier. I could have seen it all as part of me.

Brad looks down. His feet are now two mini-blobs attached to two rod-shaped blobs that seconds ago were his legs, in his khakis.

He is going, he realizes.

He is going, and will not be coming back as Brad.

He must try at least to retain this feeling of pity. If he can, whoever he becomes will inherit this feeling, and be driven to act on it, and will not, as Brad now sees he has done, waste his life on accumulation, trivia, self-protection, and vanity.

He tries to say his name, but has, apparently, forgotten his name.

"Poor things," he says, because these are now the only words he knows.

COMMERCIAL BREAK

COMMERCIAL BREAK

Streaming, binge watching, and new platforms offering original content: in "Empires of the New World" (2015), **Pamela Douglas** interviews Netflix's Ted Sarandos and explores how digital technology is changing not only our viewing habits, but also the ways in which shows are created and distributed.

Empires of the New World

(selection)

Pamela Douglas, interview with Ted Sarandos

Pamela Douglas: You are opening avenues for creativity. Other companies are already there—AMC, HBO, FX. It's not like there isn't anybody else doing good stuff, but I ran across a statistic: in prime time viewing hours, 30 percent of the viewers are watching Netflix. Shocking. Why?

Ted Sarandos: Choice. We've evolved into a culture where we want whatever we want whenever and wherever we want it. Netflix is consistent with the on-demand expectations. Now you don't ever say I wish I knew anything—you just Google it. So when you want to watch something the idea that you have to wait until Wednesday night at eight o'clock to watch the show you want is becoming ridiculous. We have so much great content to watch and we created a system to help you find it. The way people expect to find anything from Google, they expect to find anything they want to watch from us.

The moment of truth is which remote do you pick up. Once Netflix was on the TV it met the delivery demand required—that it looks beautiful and it's on your big screen. And from then it's how do I find something great to watch.

PD: Being on the big screen is recent. I heard that 30 percent of YouTube viewing, of all things, is on big screens. It's the Convergence that everyone is talking about.

TS: Your TV doesn't know where the wire came from. The fun thing about the Emmy Awards and all the debate that went into it is you're sitting there and watching a TV show on your television, so why should you distinguish what the delivery mechanism is? This is just the first time anybody stepped up.

PD: It's about the product. Netflix was the only way to see *House of Cards*.

TS: Up until *House of Cards*, television was conceived to be consumed once a week with commercial breaks. We could take the commercials out and jam the acts together. But *House of Cards* was written and created to be watched in this form with no artificial cliffhangers, and we didn't have to worry about trying to get you back next week because we knew you were going to watch the next episode in twenty seconds. Then we didn't have to worry about reminding you what happened last week because we knew you just saw it. So what you got in *House of Cards*, relative to anything else on TV, including HBO (which still has that cliff-hanger aspect), is that you have really rich, dense storytelling, more characters than a regular TV show could support, more storylines than a typical TV show could support, and more character development. You know Francis Underwood better than you know a character on almost any other show. Twenty percent of a typical episode, even on HBO, is reminding people, artificial exposition trying to tell you what happened. That's why we just have more time to do it better. Yes, you probably know more about Tony Soprano after spending eight years with him, but we're just thirteen hours in.

PD: I watched all thirteen hours in about ten days. I didn't watch it all at once.

TS: Most people don't. When they talk about binge watching, there's a mythology about that. I hope nobody watches with their eyeballs toothpicked open. It's not fun. It's great to savor and think about. But it's not rigid, like it has to be the same thing for everybody. Very few people watched all thirteen hours in the first twenty-four hours. But nobody watched just one either. They watched two or three episodes together. That's why we dropped everything at one time, because I didn't want to have to make decisions for people and then some segment of the audience wasn't going to be served. With the whole thing at once, it served the marathoners, the weekenders, and some people watched *House of Cards* at the exact same time once a week.

PD: Are you going to do that with all the shows?

TS: It works particularly well for serialized drama. I don't know that it has the same principles for procedurals or sitcoms. Right now I know that for serialized drama, having the ability to scratch the itch is important.

I have a personal background that led to my decision to drop that way. One was my old DVD behavior and even VHS tapes. I had a friend at HBO who would send me tapes of *Sopranos* a couple of years before I had HBO at home, and I always watched multiple episodes in one sitting. My kids get to watch more than one episode of their shows, that's why they're different viewers.

I personally find it frustrating to get into a show like *Breaking Bad* or *Mad Men* that I really love, and wait a week and worry if I miss a week and have to manage the DVR. To me there was too much thinking about everything but the show.

When people come up to me apologizing that they haven't watched *House of Cards* yet, I say, "Don't worry, it's going to be there for ten years. Whenever you want, just jump in."

PD: That's one element of all the options in television generally, and that's part of the reason this is such an exciting time. It's "all of the above."

TS: In the early days of pay television they took advantage of what they had over regular television in that they could curse and have nudity, and that was novel. One of the reasons stand-up comedy was so great in the early days on HBO was that there was cursing on television.

In *House of Cards*, there was very little nudity. The camera turns at the right moment. It was a sophisticated show. Yes, we killed a dog in the beginning, but we didn't show it.

PD: The scene with the dog was brilliant because it foreshadowed Underwood's character.

TS: No network would ever kill a dog on television. And in that very moment Francis does two things you don't see on television. He killed the dog, and he looked up and talked to the camera.

PD: It's not the first time a show broke the fourth wall, but this was a consistent texture of the show, that and the way you handled text on screen where you could read it.

TS: That was partly from knowing people were going to watch it on an iPhone.

PD: The size of the screen is all over the map, from phones to fifty inches for the same show. Is that a challenge for a programmer to serve both kinds of eyeballs? How do you deal with it?

TS: Right now there's user-generated shorts on YouTube—low-res, short running time, quality that doesn't matter much. For us we know the standards are much higher. The presentation of the text on screen had to be something that would work in either format. Everything counts, and you sometimes have to make a sacrifice. People who choose to watch on a small screen already know they make that sacrifice. But most Netflix viewing is on a large screen.

PD: Looking at Netflix a couple of years from now, where is it going? What are you excited about?

TS: We're going to have a lot more original programming. Most of our programming is evolving to be exclusive. Meaning the things on Netflix are not on any other services. We picked this space knowing it would be a big business, and with big businesses you have competition. So this is a way to distinguish for the viewer the reason they would have Netflix over any other. So we will continue to expand our original programming, not just in series form but also in stand-up comedy, documentary, and perhaps even some feature films. Think of us as becoming much more curated, more exclusive, and much more original over the next couple of years.

What I really want to do in the original arena is do things that would be very difficult on TV, not for the sake of being different, but to expand the audience of television.

Internet TV will change the rules of TV because the scale of it is different. You can do things for smaller audiences and they work. You scale the show to the right size of the audience. I think we can do really well with a single and a double, whereas traditional networks have to have a home run every time in prime time. For me there's no sense of prime time. There's no preciousness of the time slot, so we can let shows breathe. We can let them find their audience and discover them over time. Maybe the audience will take two or three shots at it.

Some people watched *House of Cards* and literally turned it off when he talked to the camera. We're so data-centric that we can look at the moment they stop watching. And then those same people hear about the show the next week and their friends say, just watch for a little while, and they jump back in again. You would never have the opportunity to do that on linear television.

Those are some of the things that would be deemed too difficult. I don't mean too challenging for your sensibilities. I mean they take you a little bit out of your comfort zone, like a show set in a women's prison, or a show with no good guys. Who is doing good for the sake of doing good in *House of Cards*? Everybody has a self-serving agenda. We can get there because the show is not really about politics. It's more Shakespearean than Washingtonian. So it's really about the complexity of good and evil.

PD: What is television now? What does the word mean?

TS: Television is the same as when Edward R. Morrow talked about it. It's flashing pictures in a box. It's going to remain flashing pictures in a box.

PD: How is that different from feature films?

TS: It isn't. Feature films in a theater are different because they're out of homes and shared with strangers. But other than that, it is the same, except you have to drive to the box. At its core, it's all storytelling. What it is physically is flashing pictures in a box, but in its soul it's the same as it's been since cavemen. We love to tell stories. I think we are genetically predisposed to fill in the blanks. We're not good at not knowing things, so we create stories so we can understand things better. This is why as a species we're so story-centric. The same thing that made people go west is the same thing that makes people love a good book.

PD: As a writer, I'm so glad you're saying these things. From a writer-creator's point of view, can you walk me through—imagine if somebody had a great pilot or a great idea for a show, could they possibly bring it to Netflix, and if so, how?

TS: We have a team. There is an agency system that deals with making sense of a lot of noise. We take a lot of inbound pitches. Here's where we're different:

There was something about interactivity that everybody thought the internet was all about. So then there was a whole thing about content creation where the user would influence the story. In the early days of internet entertainment I saw an interview with Steve Martin, and he said they're paying me a million dollars to write something where people can change the ending—why pay me a million dollars? That's my story, so it's funny that the roots of the internet were really disruptive to storytelling.

Now Netflix is playing a role in this where we're actually going in the opposite direction, really embracing and nurturing storytelling without interference.

I know that every great storyteller isn't published and every writer doesn't have an agent. We have to be able to peel through projects to find great ones. What emerged in the scramble to lock up great TV creators and writers: everyone had a deal. Everyone had to go through one of the programs like Warner Television. So in those cases a system started to get talent earlier and earlier who were trying to sell their stories earlier and earlier. That led to a lot of half-baked stories. They would invest a little bit to see if some of these stories played out.

So if you have a great idea, you could pitch it around, and see if you could get a development deal or something. But if it's your only great idea, you might want to hold on to it and hone it yourself. Pour your time into this project. If you come up with a great idea, I'd say thanks but I don't know what to do with that because I don't have a development system, or I'm not going to develop your script. But if you could get us a script we love, I'm going to get you a whole season of content, not just a deal where your pilot might get shot and never seen. There are thousands and thousands of projects that die in development. Your chances of getting to series on Netflix are much higher. You just have to invest a little bit of the development time yourself.

PD: Part of the reason that's such a relief is writers write. Here's a pilot. In my USC class, MFA students write the pilot, the bible, and a mid-season episode so the entire season is there on paper.

TS: That's great.

PD: Internet companies on the other side of the spectrum have told me they don't want to read anything on a piece of paper. They say if someone makes a video and gets a high YouTube number, then we might be interested. They only want to see videos. Netflix is not there, correct?

TS: Correct. Every great show starts with the writing. You could gloss up something in a video, but the flaws or the strengths of a show are in the words, absolutely. *House of Cards* is a very expensive show for a show that's just people talking. We invested in the words and the mouths that deliver them. This is not special effects driven. It's not adventure driven. There are no exotic locations. It's all words, people talking.

PD: Do you think other shows on Netflix will be like that? Would you ever do an action-adventure show?

TS: There's never been a great action-adventure tale that wasn't also great storytelling. Even with *Game of Thrones*, what people talk about are the characters.

PD: It's frustrating for writers that some companies don't seem to get it.

TS: There's a mythology about Silicon Valley versus Hollywood. It's real but it's only tribalism, that's all it is. They don't get it/we don't get it. Netflix has always done a very good job of being in Hollywood. We have a thousand people in Silicon Valley—we are a technology company—and then we have 150 people in LA for whom we are only an entertainment company. We are in the entertainment culture. We understand what makes people work creatively and the cultural aspects of the entertainment business. They're different. If you talk to a technology company about creativity, they're immediately suspicious. So we have to exist with one foot in each world. While we have more data than any entertainment company, you can't reverse engineer content. You can't reverse engineer storytelling.

PD: If you could project the future, what do you think television is going to look like, considering digital space versus cable and network?

TS: Distinctions like broadcast versus cable don't make any sense today, so I don't know how they make sense in the future. It's just a business delivery model. I hear all the time they'll never put the Super Bowl on a pay channel. For some reason it's like we have some constitutional right for the Super Bowl to be free. I think that kind of thinking will go by the wayside.

Linear television will be eventized. Everything on linear television will be super-cliffhanger stuff or competition shows and sports. If you look at the top broadcast shows, they're almost all sports of some kind. Occasionally you get a procedural in there, which is probably an effect of the aging broadcast television audience.

The reason Netflix can offer a billion hours of streaming content per month, while linear television is not really dropping that much, is that we're not substituting for watching the NBA finals. The on-demand-ness of Netflix is going to get deeper, and the event-ness of broadcast television is going to get deeper. The real business of scripted television is going to happen online.

PD: Do you see opportunities increasing for creative people coming along?

TS: Yes. More channels, more ability to aggregate efficiently, create a lot of opportunity. The internet will have the ability to channelize the audiences so they can still support the production of television because the shows have a long shelf life.

PD: Anything else you'd like to say to future generations of TV creators?

TS: Don't feel limitations because it's a TV show. On one level *House of Cards* is a thirteen-hour movie, or a thirty-nine-hour movie. I want people to write the perfect story in the perfect time. *Arrested*

Development is fifteen episodes, which is kind of an oddball number. Every episode has a different running time. The less they are connected to a linear grid for creativity, the more the show is like a novel. If every novel had to be the same number of pages, books would be pretty lousy.

So writing a twenty-two-minute sitcom you have a much harder time than you need to. Since there are no act breaks, you don't have to write up to the act break and return from the act break. This is more like a book. When it comes to great storytelling, most people discover it in their own time. People see movies at different times. They're on different pages of books. It's something funny about broadcast television. How long has it been since the majority of the country watched anything together? A long time.

EDUCATIONAL TV

(BUT YOU DON'T HAVE TO

TAKE MY WORD FOR IT)

EDUCATIONAL TV (BUT YOU DON'T HAVE TO TAKE MY WORD FOR IT)

What do children learn from watching television, whether the shows are intended to be educational or not? The authors in this section offer a range of responses to this question as they explore early viewing experiences.

In "'Time to Go': Dreaming of a Televised Future" (2008), **Dade Hayes** looks at the ways educational television has changed in the past decades and how a new generation of creators is seeking to connect with young viewers.

Jean Burnet's autobiographical "Hasta Siempre" (2016) captures how watching a long-running Spanish-language variety show with her grandmother gave the two of them a shared "strange window to somewhere new."

"From 'Lessons from Television'" (2003) by **Susan Stewart** distills how television's conventions shape both our understanding of ourselves and our reactions to that understanding.

In "Pursuit of the Public Interest in the Vast Wasteland" (2017), **Walter J. Podrazik** explores the tension between the idea of television as a "wasteland" and the aspiration for it to serve the public interest.

Nicole Chung describes in "What I Learned from Kristi Yamaguchi" (2016) why seeing a Japanese American girl celebrated on television was such a powerfully formative experience for her younger self.

"Time to Go"

Dreaming of a Televised Future

(selection)

Dade Hayes

n his classic education text *Emile*, Jean-Jacques Rousseau wrote that "reading is the scourge of childhood, for books teach us to talk about things we know nothing about." Taking it further, Neil Postman argues, "In a literate world children must become adults. But in a non-literate world there is no need to distinguish sharply between the child and the adult, for there are few secrets, and the culture does not need to provide training in how to understand itself." I kept wondering, while investigating baby/preschool entertainment, whether this booming industry was helping gradually to erode our notions of a literate society. Postman, the critic known for books such as *Amusing Ourselves to Death*, prefers the term *post-literate* in his essential polemic *The Disappearance of Childhood*. The book outlines how the concept of childhood first evolved during the Enlightenment before an "uncoordinated but powerful assault on language and literacy" occurred in the nineteenth and twentieth centuries. The result: beyond KGOY*, it is nothing less than the end of the idea of kids, with adults dressing like children and vice versa, and the pressures and seductions of adulthood setting in younger and younger. "Most people no longer understand and want the traditional, idealized model of the child because that model cannot be supported by their experience or imagination," Postman writes.

---

* Marketing shorthand for "kids getting older younger."

What new child is the media-saturated twenty-first century and its exponents, such as Little Airplane*, creating? Friends and fellow parents would often ask me to offer a bottom-line assessment that resulted from my research. "So, what did you find out? Is TV good or bad for kids?" I thought by this point I would have The Answer, a neat narrative arc describing the impact of TV on preschoolers and a corresponding code of behavior that I would introduce to my family. But the either/or proposition seems, increasingly, to be false in the face of so many choices. I found myself engrossed by Postman but not totally convinced that he was 100 percent right.

When I mentioned *The Disappearance of Childhood* to a friend, the writer Alissa Quart, whose last book examined gifted children, she dismissed it for hewing too closely to the leftist orthodoxy that considers technology a force of destruction that is sending the world toward chaos. She posits that a visually oriented society may not be such a bad thing, that kids who are more visual are typically just as smart, maybe even more so, than kids who spend more time reading. In a similar vein, Leonard Shlain, a theoretician and surgeon, has argued convincingly that screen images are reordering the contemporary brain in a way that will make print words irrelevant—a blessing, he believes, given the centuries of misogyny and repression that the alphabet has enabled.

If there are any people working in preschool TV who would likely reject those ideas outright, they are probably to be found on the fourteenth floor of an anonymous skyscraper between Manhattan's Times and Herald squares. This is where some of the main brains behind *Blue's Clues* have mobilized for a new preschool TV challenge. There, production company Out of the Blue, founded by *Blue's* creator Angela Santomero and longtime Nickelodeon executive Samantha Freeman, has been ramping up a major new series premiering on PBS at the same time as *Ni Hao, Kai-Lan*. Called *Super Why!*, it is billed as a superhero literacy show for kids ages three to six. Its 3-D animated protagonists help solve typical preschool dilemmas by traveling inside books (not unlike the way Blue once "skidooed" into a painting) to find solutions. Instead of the clues scribbled down in the "handy-dandy notebook,"

---

* [A children's TV production company.]

the puzzles embedded within each *Super Why!* episode are designed to teach spelling, reading, and comprehension. Having popularized interactive television and shown that watching it makes kids smarter, Santomero, Freeman, and *Blue's* researcher Alice Wilder have set the bar much higher with *Super Why!*

Spending a day with Out of the Blue on a research expedition and debrief helped me see why their show has the potential to add some thrust to the educational component of preschool TV. The main reason is an explicit commitment to detailed research, which comes partly from the child development backgrounds of Santomero and Wilder and partly from the rigor that results from the show's funding by a Department of Education grant. Instead of one or two adults, as in the other shows' focus groups I had observed, there were four researchers, broken into teams of two. They simultaneously tested slightly different versions of the same episode, number thirty-nine out of the series' unusually large sixty-five-episode initial order, to help ensure comprehension and interactivity scores.

The site for the research was the Acorn School, a private preschool whose students are mostly white and from higher-income families. The show has been tested all over—various socioeconomic strata in neighborhoods stretching from New Jersey to Queens, Connecticut to lower Manhattan. Even though it's intended for kids no older than six, *Super Why!* has been tested on nine-year-olds with remedial reading ability, who sparked to the superhero theme even as they struggled to follow the portions involving spelling and sentence structure. *Super Why!* also tested at a school called the IDEAL School of Manhattan (Individualized, Differentiated Education for All Learners), known for its advanced program for learning-disabled kids.

The *Super Why!* test I observed was a storybook test, but involved probably triple the number of pages of the test for *Ni Hao, Kai-Lan.* Wilder sat cross-legged in front of three different groups of four to five kids each. The session took place in a large classroom, so the noise of a typical preschool day—singing, reading aloud, and laughing—was constant. Wilder was clearly at ease in the setting. She has probably, by her own reckoning, done more than one thousand of these sessions.

Compared with other moderators I had seen in action, Wilder was far more demonstrative, pointing to the page to underscore objects, scrolling through letter choices, and generally guiding the kids' attention. Instead of just following the script dialogue, she would detour to ask, "Where's the *R*?" passing the pages around so that everyone could find it. Occasionally, she scribbled notes on the script in a red pen. She and her assistant, who took notes continuously, read from a version of the episode's script that wove in the focus-group questions.

Like *Blue's Clues*, each episode of *Super Why!* follows a set structure, with a few so-called "formal features"—that is, the Thinking Chair or Mail Time. The Super Readers, the central quartet of superheroes, meet in the Book Club after being summoned, along with the viewer, with a question-mark beam that lights up the skies over Storybrook Village as the Bat-signal does Gotham City. The Super Readers convene before the Super Computer, at the center of a meeting area tucked into packed bookcases that appear to stretch on forever. The oversize computer screen replays a video illustrating the information challenge confronting the superheroes, and they reach a decision about which book to consult for answers. The book is brought down from the shelf, the characters jump into it, and they immediately start interacting with the book's characters and scrutinizing its text. In one episode, for example, just by changing a few words, the "big bad wolf" becomes the "small good wolf," and a threat is neutralized.

After the day at Acorn, the team returned to the Out of the Blue offices, laying out stacks of sixteen-page research summaries on a conference room table. Once the data and videotape have been reviewed, a single document will summarize the day at Acorn School. The documents contain comments such as "Going up the stairs was a big moment. Research recommends that we play it up," or "Researchers noted that kids especially liked" a long list of things. "Literacy is such a hot button that we definitely expect some people not to like what we're doing," Wilder said. "So that's why we have to be committed to research because it will point us to what really gets through to kids. After *Blue's Clues*, that's just built in to our process. I didn't necessarily want to work on another show and I turned a lot of things down, but this seemed like an opportunity I couldn't pass up."

As *Super Why!* neared the starting gate, across town, *Sesame Street* was gearing up for its thirty-ninth season. Because that was the first TV show Margot and I had ever seen, I thought my mission would not be complete until I paid a visit to the people charged with keeping the longest-running preschool series current. *Sesame Street* has a reputation for quality that few of its rivals share. But that now cuts both ways, as evidenced by the *Sesame Beginnings* misadventure. New parents like me see *Sesame Street* as the gold standard and expose their kids at earlier and earlier ages, which has wreaked a bit of havoc with the curriculum.

"Parents view us as a safe alternative," said Carol-Lynn Parente, head of production at Sesame. "The alarming part about that is that a two-year-old cannot benefit from the show's design. And the curriculum is wasted on them." As a result, she continued, "we're reviewing what we do in order to constantly address the needs of our target audience. We're really trying to hit the twos and threes."

One hallmark of *Sesame Street* is its "magazine format," which involves the blending of thirty-five to forty unique segments over the course of an hour. That format "was working almost too well for younger kids and the older ones have moved on," Sesame discovered. Also, just as Selig observed, Parente conceded, "We are an hour-long show in a half-hour world."

I asked Parente how long she thought the hour-long format would last, especially given the fact that the fifteen-minute "Elmo's World" segment had grown so popular.

"The show is thought of as a playdate, never as a show," she said. "It's a playdate in an inner-city neighborhood. Within the hour, we're focusing more. It's much more continuous than it used to be as far as story. A story is broken up and told over the course of the hour, interspersed with somewhat random but themed segments. We took a look at changing to less than an hour, but we're not just a letters and numbers show."

The idea for *Sesame Street* is to return to one of its core strengths: teaching kids how to deal with emotions. "That is easier for us because we have characters getting at those story lines."

Parente cited an example from the season just passed: Rosita and Zoe are playing. The show's newest character, Abby Cadabby, comes in and bonds with Zoe, but Rosita wants to play tag. So they start to fight about it. They try to work it out themselves and then adults come in to help. The goal was to model conflict resolution.

Gary Knell, the charismatic CEO of Sesame Workshop, feels optimistic about season thirty-nine but he did not sugarcoat the challenges facing Sesame. The four "pillars" of preschool TV—license fees from broadcasters, international sales, corporate or government support, and merchandising—are all under assault, he said.

"*Dora* will die," he said, tracing a dive-bomber trajectory with his hand. "These shows usually get about five to six years where they're at their hottest point, where everyone loves them and buys their products, but not a lot of them last after that." It wasn't petty rivalry that prompted his premonition—he felt the odds were squarely against another show matching the thirty-plus-year reigns of *Sesame Street*, *Mister Rogers*, or *Captain Kangaroo*.

The environment children grow up in today has also shifted irrevocably, and not for the better, he said. "Technology dominating our culture is a bad thing," Knell said. "There is a new generation of parents who don't define things as technology. They're just *things*. They won't draw a distinction between the time they're using a device and the time when they are not. Parents are feeling overwhelmed by that shift. . . . And if you think the marketplace is crowded now, we're entering a period where everybody is a producer and distributor thanks to the internet."

Karen Hill-Scott, a veteran educational consultant who has worked on shows for Nick Jr. and the Disney Channel, is a mother and a grandmother. Watching her preschool-age grandchildren grow up in a world exponentially more media-saturated than her kids' has been eye-opening, she says. And the confluence of societal factors leaves her less than completely encouraged about the future. "This really is the era of the weak parent," she says. With the generation raising kids more apt to plan out their future and make their own fulfillment a priority, "the power these children are given is quite amazing." As an example, Hill-Scott said a family she spoke with recently had their five-year-old boy choose the make, model, and color of their new car. "The thing is, when you give them that kind of power, it gives a chance for good habit systems not to take." Indeed, the charter of many preschool shows seems to be empowerment. Chris Gifford, one of the creators of *Dora the Explorer*, says the show is addressed to "the least powerful members of society." Viewers in this age group are hungry for the message that they can do things, he explained, given their reality of needing help with almost every day-to-day task. That's commendable on its face, but when toddlers are empowered to sit in a shiny, high-tech cockpit, how will they know how to manipulate the controls and not end up in a nosedive? "When people say kids today are smarter, I disagree," Hill-Scott said. "They're just more exposed."

Anne Wood, a former schoolteacher from a northern England military town, created *Teletubbies* more than a decade ago. The show's 365 episodes proved revolutionary, by explicitly aiming at children as young as one. Its characters touched off controversy that still lingers because they had televisions in their tummies and spoke in monosyllabic gibberish that Wood contends was a realistic, relatable simulation of actual baby talk. Critics insisted the characters would harm viewers' adoption of language, and they blasted PBS for promoting the series to such young viewers.

Nearly five decades into a storied children's publishing and television career, Wood returned to British TV with *In the Night Garden*, a $30 million series that sets about to explore a heretofore untapped realm: sleep and dreams. The show stakes out an alternate world that exists between wakefulness and sleep. As with *Teletubbies*, there is less of a linear plot than a mood and an atmosphere. Set in a sunlit glen (painstakingly shot in high definition outside Stratford-upon-Avon), it brings together human-sized characters of various colors and imaginary languages, the main ones being Upsy Daisy, Makka Pakka, Igglepiggle, and the Tombliboos. With a touch of *Nutcracker* fantasy, each show brings all the characters together in one setting, which is called the night garden because Igglepiggle discovers it while sailing alone in a little boat on a starry night.

Over a live-action image of a small child's palm being caressed in a circular motion by an adult's hand, a soothing woman's voice begins to sing, as in a lullaby, "The night is black and the stars are bright and the sea is dark and deep . . ." and then the bracing diction of Shakespearean actor Derek Jacobi picks it up, continuing, ". . . but someone I know is safe and snug and they're drifting off to sleep. Round and round, a little boat no bigger than your hand, out on the ocean far away from land.

Take the sail down, light the little light. This is the way to the garden in the night."

I met Wood in the high-ceilinged dining room of London's posh Langham Hotel. Over supper and sauvignon blanc, we talked about her unorthodox path to the front ranks of preschool entertainment and her status as a cultural lightning rod. Her cardigan sweater and gentle handshake were counterbalanced by a Phyllis Diller–like hair flourish: an icing-like shock of white atop a layer of brown. Her round, button-like, deep-set eyes convey a quiet intensity. "I've been reading a lot of Kurt Vonnegut lately because I'm interested in people's last words," she said.

"It became clear to me that there was more anxiety than there used to be, more anxiety about raising children," Wood said. "Why it was, I don't know, the media, September 11, the awareness of terrorism. We live in really anxious times and the children have picked up on this. There's a lot of tension around the bedtime thing."

The show has become perhaps the purest expression of the open-ended philosophy that had long existed at Wood's company, Ragdoll, which does not test its shows in conventional ways. Instead of "research," she pointedly uses the term "observation."

"We found out by watching children that children need time to reflect," she said. "If you take them walking across the platform at a railway station, you get a lot of pigeons in London and you'll get a child hanging back to watch the pigeons. The parent wants to catch the train, but all they want to do is stand and look at the pigeons. And that's what they need to be allowed to do. That's what you can do with television. You can watch for a long time. I have been known to say to the cameraman, 'Don't take your eye off that thing!' You leave it longer, longer, longer, longer and *I'll* cut it. They always say, 'Well, we've got that shot, let's move on.' But what does it take, another thirty seconds or another minute? I want you to hold it longer."

Night Garden has been wildly popular in the United Kingdom since debuting on the BBC in March 2007. Ragdoll plans to produce one hundred episodes, fewer than the 365 it did of *Teletubbies*, but more than enough to give the show some longevity. Something is significantly different this time around, however: it is not at all clear whether an American TV network will commit to airing the show. PBS, which picked up *Teletubbies* and *Tots TV*, is in a different place than it was a decade ago.

"PBS will say it's not educational," Wood said, noting that many of its new shows (such as *Super Why!*) are funded through US Department of Education Read to Learn grants. "America is very important. It's a huge market. We get so many American shows here, it would be nice to send one back!" She laughed, but then her smile faded. The show had been a labor of love to produce, and the topic seemed both novel and important. But the American preschool landscape didn't seem to have room for it.

"They're always worried about the sixty other channels. It's such a shame," Wood said. "When you come in to *In the Night Garden*, it's very slow, with this wonderful Shakespearean actor, it's not about teaching. It's about respecting the child's right to be. And trying to understand the world from a child's perspective. . . . They have to be seen to be teaching. We are not teachers. We respect children's right to learn. That's different. *Night Garden* came from listening to the needs that were expressed, the tensions that were there."

Wood's philosophy had infuriated a lot of people over the years and her openness to the idea that one-year-olds could get something valuable from *Teletubbies* made her a target of a lot of criticism. I hadn't known what to expect when I arranged to meet her. But there was something about her approach that actually seemed quite sensible, especially as I put it in the larger context of my travels through the preschool wilderness. She puts the child at the center of things in such a way that it is hard for me to marshal significant objections. Yet debate still rages about *Teletubbies*. A 2005 study that looked in every three months on babies and toddlers aged between six and thirty months determined that those who watched *Teletubbies* knew ten fewer words at thirty months when compared with those who watched other programs. They were more prone to vocalizations than others in the study, but that didn't take the form of English words. "Children were unable to learn novel words when inserted into a *Teletubbies* clip," the authors concluded. "Multiple forms of input, including music, visual stimulation and language, were too complex to enable word learning."

Many of Wood's sternest critics will find more reason for consternation in *Night Garden*. Aside from Jacobi, few characters utter what could safely be called words. But the qualities that I have looked for in children's TV, from the time when I was a toddler to my time as a dad, all seem to be in place: high production values, an element of fantasy, and a pronounced tilt toward the child's perspective. There is no checklist of developmental concepts that have been injected into the show like vitamins into a loaf of bread.

Margot and I were recently watching Disney Channel's new show, *My Friends Tigger & Pooh*, which preschoolizes the classic Winnie-the-Pooh menagerie, inventing a new six-year-old girl, Darby, as the protagonist. Using computer animation, the show blatantly appropriates the interactive techniques of *Blue's Clues* and its progeny and seems intent on teaching lessons every couple of minutes. That busy quality drains much of the color from the Hundred Acre Wood, and I felt it had to do with the schism at the heart of the show. One of Pooh's famous lines in A. A. Milne's books is this bit of advice: "Don't underestimate the value of Doing Nothing, of just going along, listening to all the things you can't hear, and not bothering."

Author Susan Gregory Thomas latches on to Pooh in *Buy, Buy Baby*, a diatribe against the larger consumer environment preying upon parents of young children. She uses Doing Nothing as a kind of nostalgia-tinged shorthand for kids not being plugged in as they are today. I would offer a slightly different interpretation. Doing Nothing, to me, doesn't have to mean dropping out or detaching entirely. It just means meeting a work of popular imagination halfway, embracing it even if it is not machine-tooled to feed your demographic.

Anne Wood's whole career has been based on that kind of core belief that children can come to a work of art, rather than having it come to them. That notion certainly has some precedent outside of preschool entertainment. David Riesman, in his classic sociology text *The Lonely Crowd*, describes a shift in America from "inner-directed" personality types to "other-directed" ones. Inner-direction, he explains, is characterized by self-sufficiency, shaping by tradition-minded elders and movement toward "generalized but inescapable goals." Other-direction is about having one's course defined by acquaintances and the mass media, which causes one's goals to change continually. Published at the dawn of the TV age, in 1950, the book has aged creakily in some respects but magnificently in others. Its focus is generally on adults, but a fascinating passage toward the end examines the idea of "freeing the child market" with a proposal that is something of a rhetorical gimmick but also a striking comment on consumer groupthink, especially considering it is more than half a century old. To "producers and advertisers addressing themselves to the child market," Riesman suggests "the experimental creation of model consumer economies among children." In this "everyday World's Fair," luxury goods would be available for purchase. "At this 'point of sale,' there would stand market researchers able and willing to help children make their selections but having no particularly frightening charisma or overbearing charm or any interest on the employer's side in pushing one thing rather than another. The point of these 'experiment stations' would be to reveal something about what happens to childhood taste when it is given a free track away from the taste gradients and 'reasons' as well as freedom from the financial hobbles of a given peer-group."

Like Riesman, Anne Wood wants to give children the opportunity to criticize and reshape the value of objects around them, to be allowed to dawdle at the train station and watch the pigeons. As she sees it, adults are encroaching on kids' last remaining autonomous space. "The older you get, life is not simple, especially with the complexities of the shared culture children inhabit and the whole 'kidult' thing. Adults are plugging into children's culture more often."

I told Wood that everyone I had spoken with about my book had demanded a bottom-line assessment about whether exposing babies and preschoolers to TV was good or bad. She replied, "To say is television good or bad is ludicrous. You might as well say, 'Is print good or bad?' We're talking about cultural experience . . . this idea that we have in every aspect of life that it can be a quick fix. 'Tell me, is it good or bad so I can abdicate any responsibility I have for thinking about it.' It's sad, really."

Reflecting on her own roots, she added, "I come from very working-class people. Horizons were very narrow. The content on television, I firmly believe, can open windows and widen horizons for children who otherwise don't have those experiences. A lot of the comment comes from middle-class people. You have something totally innocent like *Teletubbies* and you get all these people coming out and trying to destroy its innocence. There's no room for that kind of innocence."

Wood recalled her childhood in the north of England. "You either became a nurse or a teacher," she said. "I passed up university for financial reasons. I was always interested in imaginative development, in where does imagination reside, where does consciousness reside?"

Those early years, the very stretch of time being scrutinized by pediatricians, child development experts, and TV networks, proved a grueling test for Wood. When she was three, her father went off to fight in World War II. Two brothers had died before she was born, and she was the lone child who survived. Her mother worked in the munitions factory. "I was raised by my grandmother, who had seven children, so I was well taken care of," she said. "It makes you tough. Looking back, it was good because I was never overprotected. You went out into the rough-and-tumble with the other kids. And the community looked after you. If you strayed, somebody would say, 'You shouldn't be up here, you should be over there where you belong!' Now, of course, people don't do that anymore. If you take an interest in a child who isn't your own, you are seen as some sort of sinister figure."

It isn't difficult to draw a line from Wood's own difficult childhood—a brief but unforgettable portion of our couple of hours together—straight to *In the Night Garden*. The lone, childlike figure in the boat, lowering the sail, submitting to the unknown waves. The redeeming sunshine of the garden, a secret world behind the hedge, a refuge from life's difficulties. I thought of Mister Rogers's Land of Make Believe, the empowering moshes of Milkshake.

I needed to see how Margot and I would experience this show, three years after our first voyage into the dark seas. As she watched, her breathing became heavier and deeper. It was late evening, after her bath but before bedtime. She sat in my lap, as she had done when she was much smaller, unable to talk, unable to do all the things she does now. Instead of the pop-culture heirloom of *Sesame Street*, I was introducing her to something brand-new. Halfway through the episode, Margot seemed soothed and attentive. She suddenly sat up and declared, "This show is my favorite." Of course, she says that of a lot of shows, but it indicated a connection.

Anne Wood, Josh Selig, Angela Santomero, and the people behind *Sesame Street* have a sense of idealism, even a utopian streak, and that energy allows me hope for the future. What little research exists on the effects of TV on the very young contains important clues about the importance of content, not just exposure. In other words, quality matters. It seems to me that instead of wringing hands over the steady decline of American civilization as manifested by *Little Einsteins*, parents need to recognize innovation and make quality their mantra. David Kleeman, executive director of the American Center for Children and Media, is a consultant for Prix Jeunesse, a foundation that sponsors a biannual festival billed as a "world-embracing movement for high-quality TV." Especially given how much more fixated American preschool shows are on education than other countries' programs, Kleeman says the goal should be "achieving balance. If a show is creative and engaging and also manages to teach kids something, that, to me, is a good situation." Or as the late, influential preschool TV researcher John Wright was fond of saying, "Marshall McLuhan appears to have been wrong. The medium is not the message. The *message* is the message!"

The closing minutes of *In the Night Garden* show each character settling down and going to sleep. The only one left is Igglepiggle, still wandering through the garden. Jacobi, the narrator, calls to him. "Who's not in bed? Igglepiggle's not in bed." He pauses as Igglepiggle faces the camera and waves a wave of surrender. "Don't worry, Igglepiggle. It's time to go." The last phrase has uncanny resonance, calling to mind the march upstairs at bedtime, the end of the playdate. With the magic of special effects, the garden melts into the stars and Igglepiggle is shown stretched out once again in his little boat, sleeping as it bobs in the vast sea.

Wood said that the closing sequence, meticulously designed in order to ease viewers' return to reality, is the first of any show she has produced that has elicited tears from children. "After we've lulled them into such a state of relaxation and whatever, they get terribly upset," she said. "I don't know if it's Derek Jacobi saying, 'Time to go.' I'm going to see him soon and I may ask, 'Sir Derek, could you give us another reading of that line?'" She chuckles lightly and then pauses. "It's like a much-loved toy taken away from them."

Margot has objected to many a toy being taken away, but she didn't cry at Sir Derek's farewell. When the boat finished sailing into the horizon, she rolled over and stretched. "Daddy, I want to go to sleep," she said. I wondered what kind of dreams she would have after seeing the show. Would her imagination be spurred to some kind of action as she slept, helping her tack on IQ points while her body rested? Is that the next frontier of entertaining preschoolers? More likely, *In the Night Garden* is a simple update of the bedtime story, a way of reassuring children through pure imagination and pretend play that they are safe.

I stayed on the couch, holding my daughter and two-month-old son, Finley, who had arrived as I was finishing this book. Stella and I had talked about what the effect of the book might be on him. What, if anything, would we do differently with him than we did with Margot? The *Night Garden* episode ended and the DVD menu popped up, offering a choice of two more. I could still hear the mellifluous theme song and Sir Derek's firm but soothing tone. *In the Night Garden* suddenly seemed like the only place I wanted to be.

As the show twinkled to life and the boat set sail again, Finley stirred in my lap. His head turned ever so slightly toward the screen.

Hasta Siempre

Jean Burnet

t is common in a Latin household to sit in front of the screen with one's mother, if not the entire family, and watch popular telenovelas on weeknights, and *Sábado Gigante*—the longest-running variety show in the world—every Saturday night. My family was in no way the exception to this rule.

Because we were broke, and I mean broke in the way you know life with meat and life without, life with heat and life in the Stone Age, TV was how we had fun: it was our vacations, our dinners out, our way of staying connected to what was happening out there while we lived in a world set indoors.

Back in those days we all squeezed into this one-bedroom apartment—my brother, as the man, got the bedroom—the rest of us (mom, abuela, me) shared the living room, in which we delineated bedrooms out of old refrigerator boxes. But even though we were broke as hell, somehow we still had three TVs all in varying stages of decomposition, each wearing a little foiled antenna, catching a signal despite all odds: one for my brother in his room, a tiny one for my abuela while she cooked in the kitchen, another for all-purpose family use.

My mother worked two jobs and I would only see her in the hours between them: in the morning, when she'd stop in for dinner, and then again when I'd wake up late as she was coming home for the night just long enough for her to kiss me goodnight. Our neighborhood wasn't exactly the Wonder-Bread-eating, Girl-Scout-cookie-toting kind, and between my abuela who was a hard-ass and my mother who was over-protective, I rarely saw the outside of our apartment beyond school hours. I didn't even learn how to ride a bike until I was fourteen, which puts me just a few notches above those people that show up on the news having miraculously lived in caves and shit for most of their lives. And so in the interim between these times with mom and without mom, to mark the passing of the day, there was TV. And man, did we watch.

People tell me I love television like we're in some kind of relationship, but my abuela, who never was more than a housewife and glorified babysitter—she was the OG TV-watcher. The woman could not figure out how to talk into a cell phone, but she kept a military-grade mental schedule of her telenovelas. God help you if you tried to interfere.

Of the things she watched, my favorite was Walter Mercado, our people's Liberace figure, albeit a psychic version of him. Daily we would wait for his segment on Univision until he would appear at last, wearing jewel-colored silk robes and thick eyeliner, shuffling a deck of tarot cards as he shared horoscopes for each astrological sign. For abuela, the saints may have a direct connection to God, but Mercado had a direct connection to a different and verifiable future, and whenever my sign popped up—sometimes even if it had very little to do with it—she would nod solemnly, and say something like, *"You see what I've been telling you about eating your breakfast, mija?"* On other afternoons, we watched *Jerry Springer* together, which was fascinating to us both for different reasons: hers mostly because of the white people and their strange problems, mine primarily being I did not understand what threesomes were. On Sunday mornings, she'd flip on mass, calling me into the room at the end of the hour to stand in front of the screen and receive the priest's final blessing with her.

But on Saturday nights, it was all about *Sábado Gigante*, a show she'd been watching since she lived in her own country, Ecuador. All sorts of strange segments packed the three-hour time slot—truly, a variety: sketches, games, performances, interviews. This circus was all led by Don Francisco, a handsome and congenial host who had been with the show since it started airing in 1962.

Sábado Gigante wasn't perfect. One of its best-known segments, for instance, is Miss Colita (roughly translated: Miss Ass), a pageant in which women parade around the stage in thongs while Don Francisco comments and audience members vote for their favorite buttocks.

Don Francisco is always grabbing somebody's ass—even women in the audience who just came to watch. But everyone is showing up for this willingly, enthusiastically. They are there to be a part of the spectacle of Don Francisco and his conga line of rotating models.

Everything around Don Francisco changes, except for Don Francisco, who unlike many women at the helm of a show makes a smooth transition from young and handsome host to wizened—but no less charismatic—beloved figurehead. Inevitably, the more we watched him, the more this Latin icon became enmeshed in the fabric of our family life. Many people became incorporated into our family this way.

At bedtime, the glowing light from the living room TV was the electromagnetic lullaby that soothed me to sleep, the buzz of the screen like the plainsong of grasshoppers going on and on.

When my abuela first got sick, nobody told me. As the prodigal American-born daughter, my only job was to go to school, be good at it, and not end up back where I started. Anything that would distract me from this singular journey was thus only shared with me on a need-to-know basis. I had left home by then, but I still wasn't making these decisions—*la familia* was. So when I came home from college one winter, *la familia* just said: she was in the hospital for a few days, and now she's in a nursing home. I had no idea how sick she'd been, and I felt guilty, like I should have been there all this time. I wasn't used to this kind of deception, a far cry from the days when we shared that tiny apartment: your business, everybody's business.

When you're broke you feel helpless. Like the whole country is against you—hell, maybe even the whole world. You will take it personally. I felt that for certain, and shame too, and wondered if it'd been something we'd done. That's what it was like to see her sitting there in this crummy old person home, the only one we could afford, with just one TV for everyone to share and some crazy lady yelling into her pillow all day down the hall. Watching everybody's forgotten abuelos and abuelas carted back and forth between their rooms, waiting to die.

During one of my last visits at the home, abuela told me how she was embarrassed getting her diaper changed by an orderly she described as a tall, beautiful American. Or, *gringaso*, as she called him. According to her, he was perfect for me (besides TV, finding me husbands was her second favorite activity) and during my visit she made sure that he got a good look at me. Before I left that day she pulled me down beside her, her breath hot against my ear as she whispered: "*Bueno, huvo electricidad?*" Or, in comparable English: "So was there any chemistry?" Now that was a woman who didn't know anything about shame.

She was only there for a short while before she caught a bad cold, which turned into pneumonia, and then she got moved to the hospital. My mother fussed over her room, her pillows, the temperature. She brought in a candle to St. Bernardine, which she was not allowed to light. But above all, my mother made sure abuela still had a TV to watch. Although I was rarely allowed to see her I still imagined the best of things: her falling asleep, at peace, getting better, engulfed by the pale blue light of her favorite telenovela. I continued to go on imagining like this until my mother came home from a long day away, looking more tired than she had ever looked, and said, "She tells me she's ready to be done." And that was that.

Once abuela was in hospice care, she was always asleep, breathing hard with help from the tube protruding from her mouth, a struggle in every rise and fall of her chest. Days earlier she had put us three together in a line and pointed to us one by one as if to say, it's just you three now. She brought our hands together with hers. Just us three. A gesture that said: Stick together, and don't be assholes to each other. Your life depends on it.

Even when we weren't with her, we were still with her. We started watching movies on SyFy, digestible and easy, the kind of thing that wouldn't touch the inside of our heart. There was nothing we could do then but wait for the call to come. Giant rock monsters and submarine-eating octopi flittered across our screen at home, and for many days we sat and we stared, and our three hurts, separate but equal, were absorbed inside that dim light.

When the call finally did come it was in the middle of the night. In the darkness we struggled to find an open entrance at the hospital, and my mother began to claw at every door we passed, panicked, until a security guard let us into the building. By the time we got to her room, she had already gone but was still warm, face up, jaw slack. It could have been like any other afternoon at home, her napping beside the low gurgle of some show. I waited for her to wake up.

Way back when, we could not afford the extra bed, and so I didn't have my own for a long while. Instead I'd split my time between sharing my abuela's and sharing my mother's, burrowing against their bodies like some kind of child-animal. Taking in their warmth, absorbing the strange chemistry of what makes up a woman into my own womanhood. If you've never had to do this, then you can't tell me about what it's like to share a body, get born together on that bed. And you can't tell me about what it's like to feel one-third of your body disappear right in front of your eyes.

We took turns circling the room, like clock hands. We mourned, but did not occupy the same space. If I was at her bedside, then my mother was at the doorway. If my brother was at the doorway, then I was by the window. I held her hand until eventually the only warm spot on her body was the heat from mine.

On Saturday, September 19, 2015, *Sábado Gigante* came to an end after fifty-three years on air in a huge, live television event. It is the longest-running variety show in history. As the show closes and the final lines on the script are tossed up, the camera stays on Don Francisco as he exits through the backstage. He walks between rows of fans lining the path to the luxury bus that will take him away. Every so often he stops to shake someone's hand, like some kind of TV Jesus. Every so often he looks directly into the camera and lifts two fingers in a gesture of farewell. A grown man in the crowd starts to cry.

They called the special *"Hasta Siempre."* It sounds ridiculous but I wish more than anything abuela could have seen all that. *Hasta siempre.* Until always. When he finally arrives at the bus, waving one last time before he disappears, the black screen comes up and one word fades into appearance: *Fin.* The end.

Much later, my brother would share this childhood memory of abuela with me: It starts with the two of them, still in Ecuador. I will not be born for at least another decade. For now they are together, just them. It's afternoon, and the air has a raw edge to it, heavy and wet. She is cracking a chicken's neck over an empty bucket at her feet. The blood starts to pour from the wound, slopping as it hits the bottom. While it drains she plucks feathers from the carcass in her lap absentmindedly—all the while, her eyes stay fixed on the telenovela playing in front of her on the TV. As a young boy, I can imagine that this was a somewhat horrifying scene for my brother. But now, I sometimes like to think of her like this, living through her strong hands, out in the sun, her mind churning as she watches through the eye's crystalline lens, that strange window to somewhere new.

From "Lessons from Television"

Susan Stewart

You must laugh at yourself, laugh and laugh.
Music swells the emotions;
music exists to punctuate seeing.
Emotion, therefore, is punctuation.

Formless, freedom resembles abasement.
Abasement is as infinite as desire.
You must laugh at yourself, laugh and laugh.

Those who are not demons are saints.
You are not a demon or a saint.

Women are small and want something,
so laugh at yourself, laugh and laugh.

Beds are sites of abasement.
The news is about the news.

Faces in close-up are always in anguish.
Hair and teeth are clues to class.

Clothes are changing,
changing up or down
And change itself is a laugh.

Cause can't be figured
and consequence is yet to come.

You're either awake or asleep
and that, too, is a clue to class.

Children are never with groups of children
unless they are singing in chorus.

Their mothers cannot do enough,
though there's always room for improvement.

And improvement lies in progress,
though collapsing is good for a laugh.

Saints will turn to the worse.
Demons die if they can be found.

Nature is combat, weather is sublime.
Even weather can make you laugh.

People you don't know are louder than you are,
but what is far away cannot harm you—

Books are objects, families are inspiring.
Animals protect their young;
the young come with the territory.

English is the only language.
Reading is an occasion for interruption,
and interruption is a kind of laugh.

Something is bound to get better.
And there is a pill with your name on it.

When indoors, stick with your own race—
that way you'll feel free to laugh.

Strangers are paying attention to your smell.
A camera will light like a moth on disaster.
Pity will turn to irony.

The street is a dark and frightful place.
Fires are daily.

Your car is your face.

You must laugh at yourself, laugh and laugh.

Pursuit of the Public Interest in the Vast Wasteland

Walter J. Podrazik

O n May 9, 1961, Newton Minow shook the broadcast world in his first speech to that industry's leaders following his confirmation as chairman of the Federal Communications Commission (FCC). He delivered a message that immediately made its mark, but whose ultimate impact extended far beyond that day's audience.

Minow spoke in Washington, DC, at the annual gathering of the National Association of Broadcasters (NAB), an organization that focused on advancing the business interests of its members. Over the decades, these station representatives had become accustomed to a relatively comfortable relationship with the federal agency charged with regulating them. The FCC renewed and reviewed broadcast licenses roughly every three years, but that had settled into a safely predictable business routine. Executives were not expecting a major disruption from this latest change in political administrations.

As part of a new wave of talent arriving with the 1960 election of John F. Kennedy as US president, though, the thirty-five-year-old Minow brought a fresh attitude to the task. He focused quite seriously on the FCC's mission of oversight that was meant to fashion policy designed to serve the public's "interest, convenience, and necessity."

The official title of Minow's speech for the NAB was the seemingly innocuous "Television and the Public Interest," but what followed ignited a fervent and ongoing discussion.

Minow's speech offered compliments on some of television's best recent work, citing such high-quality offerings as *CBS Reports*, *The Twilight Zone*, and *The Valiant Years* (based on the memoirs of Winston Churchill). "When television is good," he noted, "nothing—not the theater, not the magazines or newspapers—nothing is better."

Then came the rejoinder. "But when television is bad, nothing is worse." Minow directly challenged those in attendance to watch their own stations for an entire day "without a book, without a magazine, without a newspaper, without a profit and loss sheet or a rating book to distract you.

"I can assure you," he said, "that what you will observe is a vast wasteland."

Minow used the concise and potent phrase "vast wasteland" only once in his 5,400-word address, but in doing so he articulated a sense of frustration at the shortcomings of television that struck home then and remains relevant today. Minow also cemented his place in US broadcast history as virtually the *only* FCC commissioner whose name members of the general public might recognize, even more than half a century later.

Previously, no FCC official had been so blunt in criticizing the successful status quo of broadcasting. However, the assembled powerhouses of television could not simply dismiss the comments, because Minow was in a position to translate his words into action, particularly in the area of station license renewals. His agency administered the rules that defined the legal environment for every broadcast station in the country, from small independents to all the affiliates of the ABC, CBS, and NBC networks.

Yet that speech was not solely a blanket condemnation of the entire industry. Rather, Minow's harsh criticism was framed as a reminder that broadcasters were using the public's airwaves and that broadcasting was a public trust. With that trust came obligations.

When Minow revisited the speech in a 2011 article for *Atlantic* magazine, he in fact lamented that the wrong two words had been remembered. Rather than "vast wasteland," his intended message had always been to emphasize the importance of "public interest," just as the title of his speech had stated.

Nonetheless, critics of every sort have long seized on the "vast wasteland" descriptive because it captured a visceral sense that something was indeed lacking with the most powerful communication force in the country. Competing media (especially print publications) also found the phrase a convenient way to direct a dig at their biggest competitor, which had seized center stage in a remarkably short time.

The harsh criticisms of television felt particularly relevant at the time Minow spoke because, during the 1950s, broadcasters had experienced an astonishing growth spurt. In just one decade, television set ownership in the United States had gone from about 10 percent of households in 1950 to nearly 90 percent in 1961. During that same period, the total number of individual commercial broadcast stations in the country had risen from about 100 to more than 500. Between early morning sign-on and late night sign-off, programming had expanded to fill the prime time and late evening hours, mornings, afternoons, and weekends.

Along the way, the cultural axis had shifted from movie theaters, books, magazines, newspapers, and radio to the glowing tube. The medium had gone from a novelty to an assumed element of everyday life throughout the nation, from New York to Los Angeles, from Raleigh to Dubuque.

This broad influence also felt remarkably concentrated. Each individual broadcast market was home to only a handful of stations. The vast majority of those stations—some 95 percent—affiliated with one of the three commercial networks. In his 1961 speech, Minow used that pervasive presence as an important context to the broadcast leaders in that room:

> It used to be said that there were three great influences on
> a child: home, school, and church. Today, there is a fourth
> great influence, and you ladies and gentlemen in this room
> control it.

Such a specter gave an added sense of urgency to Minow's admonition to broadcasters. For while gaining influence, they had also too often created and embraced their own excesses. With living room immediacy and a reach deeper than theatrical films and radio, television seemed to exacerbate the worst tendencies of popular culture formula packaging. Minow bemoaned the procession of screwball sitcoms, police procedurals, Westerns, murderous melodramas, kids' cartoons, detective settings filled with gunfire, car chases, and physical brawls—and a constant barrage of commercial messages. Even with all that noise and movement onscreen, he observed that the overall result for viewers was "most of all, boredom."

Television was also still stinging from the scandal surrounding the rise and fall of the big-money quiz and game shows in the 1950s. Congressional hearings at the end of the decade had revealed that some of that era's top-rated programs had "fixed" the outcomes of the contests they had so heavily promoted as real. The medium had truly lost the public's trust.

Minow did not dwell on those public embarrassments—recent and familiar, there was no need. Instead, he coupled his pointed observations on television quality with a frank assessment of television's financial success while using the public's airwaves.

From the beginning of US broadcasting, the business operated exclusively under government-issued licenses to individual stations for use of a portion of the over-the-air bandwidth. There was no cash "rental" fee for each license. This vital element in the lucrative commercial communication business was a freebie. As a tradeoff for this governmental largesse, each station was expected to demonstrate regularly to the FCC that it had been a good steward of this valuable asset.

There were established benchmarks for community service and public service commitments, elements that were also to be reflected in the hours devoted to certain types of programming (including educational, informational, and local). Broadcasters, though, had quickly learned how to squirrel away those obligations into more obscure time slots, reserving most of the prime hours throughout the day for more lucrative commercial fare.

In his speech, Minow cited broadcast revenue statistics from 1959 and 1960, noting the percentage increase of profit (despite a recession at the time) of 9.7 percent (on revenues of over $1 billion, with profit before taxes of nearly $244 million). He chided broadcasters about their success: "I have confidence in your health, but not in your product."

As long as broadcasters met their minimums in the public service areas, they had rarely had their feet held to the fire about the overall television landscape. Minow, in contrast, looked at station programming over the entire broadcast day, day in and day out, and found it wanting, especially in light of what it *could be*. He took little heart looking ahead to the next season's program lineups (already announced by the networks in advance of the NAB meeting), which appeared to offer more of the same. "Is there one network president in this room who claims he can't do better?" he challenged.

Although quality-of-programming issues served as the headline-grabbing hook for Minow's speech, most of his remarks returned repeatedly to the matter of serving the public trust. Minow might not have liked many of the program types he castigated, but he stated point blank, "There will be no suppression of programming which does not meet with bureaucratic tastes." The FCC was not going to get into the business of censorship, which was outside its mission.

Instead, Minow cited areas that the commission would engage in, starting with a concerted public process for individual station license renewals, which was the cudgel that the FCC could wield to influence broadcasters. He also promised a review of the concentrated power held by the three commercial networks.

Minow also talked of potential ways to bring more creative people into the system. "I have told you that I believe in the free enterprise system," he said. "I believe that most of television's problems stem from lack of competition." To that end, he spoke of expanding the number of television options through a more viable lineup of stations in the "ultra high frequency" (UHF) portion of the bandwidth.

Even more forward-looking, Minow also expressed a willingness to consider dramatic departures from the broadcasting status quo with possible experiments in pay TV.

Concluding his NAB speech, Minow evoked the inauguration rhetoric of President Kennedy ("Ask not what your country can do for you—ask what you can do for your country"). Returning to his theme of serving the public interest, Minow challenged the industry leaders to "ask what broadcasting can do for America" and urged them to "put the people's airwaves to the service of the people."

In the immediate aftermath of the speech, the broadcast establishment was stunned, and was left in a vexing position. They had been called out and presented with the challenge to improve the state of their industry, almost as a patriotic duty, but with few specific guidelines.

More important, on a practical level, Minow's speech ignored the fact that they had limited options for quick action.

At the time, the networks took months to develop and implement plans for the following season. Key steps involved working with studios, production companies, sponsors, and individual producers to develop programs, with the need to commit talent, facilities, and budget support. The resulting schedule and program flow had to be in place by the spring in order to sell the commercial time within those programs for that fall. Even though the beginning of the 1961–62 season was four months after Minow's speech, with so many parties involved in the multilayered process, major changes would not happen instantly.

Instead, the networks touted their news departments and public affairs commitments (which were within their in-house control) and sprinkled into the fall lineup new series titles such as NBC's *David Brinkley's Journal* and *Frank McGee's Here and Now*, with the possibility of more changes to come. Later, one of these changes was increased network involvement in entertainment program execution, which stirred ire on the production side. (Producer Sherwood Schwartz expressed his displeasure at how Minow's speech affected the television process by naming the wreck of a boat on *Gilligan's Island* the SS *Minnow*. Oddly, Minow himself actually took delight at that creative critique.)

As Newton Minow had anticipated, though, the 1961–62 season that followed his speech delivered a good deal of the fare he had criticized. There were nearly two dozen returning action-adventure, crime, and Western series and more than a dozen returning situation comedies.

New fall series included violent and formulaic crime dramas such as *Cain's Hundred*, *87th Precinct*, and *Target: The Corruptors*. A particularly graphic episode of the new drama anthology *Bus Stop* drew angry criticism in the halls of Congress for the episode "A Lion Walks Among Us." Directed by Robert Altman, the story cast a popular young musical performer (Fabian) in a violent tale of robbery, seduction, murder, and suicide. Senator John Pastore observed, "I looked at it and I haven't felt clean since. I still have the stench in my nose."

At the other end of the genre spectrum, the situation comedy *The Hathaways* epitomized truly dumb television families, offering a pair of befuddled adults as surrogate "parents" acting as show business managers to a "family" of performing chimpanzees, usually dressed in human clothes.

And yet, there were new quality offerings that had been put into place even before Minow's speech, as broadcasters themselves looked for fresh faces and formulas to exploit. The fall 1961 schedule included a pair of medical dramas (*Ben Casey* and *Dr. Kildare*), Carl Reiner's autobiographical home-and-work comedy (*The Dick Van Dyke Show*), Walt Disney's longtime entertainment anthology relaunched as *The Wonderful World of Color*, a Saturday night prime time theatrical feature film showcase, and a legal drama (*The Defenders*) produced by Herb Brodkin and created by Reginald Rose, two respected names from television's 1950s "golden age" of drama.

The networks also brought back a few of the bright spots introduced in 1960, including *The Andy Griffith Show* and *The Bugs Bunny Show*, and transformed the occasional specials sponsored by DuPont into the innovative anthology *The DuPont Show of the Week*.

Together, all of these provided a respectable first response to Newton Minow's challenge to improve television content. Yet there was no guarantee that such work would consistently emerge within the structure of the three commercial networks. That's not how the business worked.

There might be an occasional happy convergence of popularity and quality, but those considerations would always be weighed in the context of ratings and profit margins. That was true before, and would continue after Minow's speech.

Nonetheless, having put broadcasters on notice regarding the twin goals of public service and content quality, Minow turned his attention to other matters in the active pursuit of those ends, focusing on expanding television options beyond the everyday business of the three commercial networks.

For example, with Congress, Minow was a strong advocate for the development of communications satellite technology. He later spoke of telling President Kennedy that communications satellites would be much more important than sending men into space, because, he observed, "they will send ideas into space. Ideas last longer than men." The first tangible product of those efforts came with the launching of the *Telstar 1* satellite in July 1962, allowing live (though limited) television transmission across the ocean.

Minow also looked to UHF, which he saw as a "sleeping giant." At the time, the television bandwidth assignments were allocated between VHF (the "very high frequency" channels 2 to 13 on the dial, the most familiar numbers to audiences) and UHF (channels 14 and above). Most television sets manufactured then did not automatically provide UHF in addition to VHF access, so UHF went largely unseen by most viewers.

Beginning in 1961, Minow successfully led an FCC effort for legislation that required new television sets to include both UHF and VHF capabilities. The All-Channel Receiver Act took effect on April 30, 1964, and subsequent models were manufactured with this required access.

That change gave UHF stations a chance to make an impression. Eventually UHF would make possible additional competing over-the-air networks to ABC, CBS, and NBC, just as Minow had predicted in his NAB speech. ("We may have a half dozen networks instead of three.")

Equally important, more widespread availability of UHF helped to support one of Minow's most cherished goals: the strengthening of educational television channels. These channels seemed to offer real hope as a source of consistent quality programming.

Many of the educational channels had been assigned to the UHF bandwidth back in the 1950s and had languished in those limited confines. For example, even in the nation's capital, lawmakers and regulators could not easily tune in hometown educational station WETA, which was located at UHF channel 26. And educational stations in the VHF bandwidth also often toiled to achieve much public awareness, as all of them were hamstrung by the budgetary limitations of being noncommercial in a hyper-commercial broadcasting world.

Greater overall visibility for both UHF and VHF educational channels helped turn that around, and educational television began to evolve into its own alternative force by the end of the 1960s. This process was boosted by the Public Broadcasting Act of 1967, which set up the Corporation for Public Broadcasting (CPB) to provide limited government funding. In 1969, the Public Broadcasting Service (PBS) replaced National Educational Television (NET), an organizing association for stations that had its roots in Ford Foundation grants in the 1950s.

Minow would become one of public television's most consistent and dedicated advocates. After his tenure at the FCC ended in June 1963, Minow returned repeatedly to the public television world. In 1969 he provided introductions to secure funding and support during the development stages of *Sesame Street*. From 1973 to 1980, he served on public television's Board of Governors (in the role of chair from 1978 to 1980), and later he was president of Carnegie Corporation, a longtime supporter of PBS.

During the 1970s, PBS solidified its image as an alternative to commercial television, building on *Sesame Street* as its flagship for children's programming, *Masterpiece Theatre* in prime time for adults, and *Monty Python's Flying Circus* for the hip and cutting edge. Through the decade, *Masterpiece Theatre* became a serious Sunday night broadcast competitor and scored consecutive multiple Emmy Award wins with such miniseries as *The First Churchills*, *Elizabeth R*, and *Upstairs, Downstairs*.

Nonetheless, one challenge that Minow could not overcome was to establish a permanent, sustained, and sufficient funding mechanism for public television. Even with the Corporation for Public Broadcasting (often buffeted by shifting political winds), there was still the need for constant fundraising and underwriting.

That pursuit of support continued as competing programming came through the doors that Minow had helped open, with the flowering of cable television, additional commercial broadcast networks, and the age of digital choice. Although public stations were generally available through local cable services (benefiting from the "must carry" rules applying to local broadcasters), they did not receive any portion of the monthly cable subscriber's fee.

Through it all, though, what made public television stand out was its noncommercial nature, an aspect few others wanted. Public television's greatest strength and selling point was successfully carving out a niche as an alternative to everything else out there, with an emphasis on such essential areas as news, documentaries, information, the performing arts, drama, and children's shows.

The public stations became just what Minow had been hoping for back in his 1961 speech—television dedicated to public service. They were available thanks in part to Minow's efforts to lower technical barriers and to open up avenues of access to as many creators as possible, making the specialized focus of public television possible.

Public television was almost the only practical response to the standards Minow had called for. Even the best efforts in commercial television were the exception, not the rule.

Attempting to better appreciate that business nature of television in the aftermath of the 1961 speech, a pair of writers later in the 1960s focused on Minow's challenge to watch an entire day of television, nonstop.

Former CBS News president Fred W. Friendly proposed such a task in his 1967 book *Due to Circumstances Beyond Our Control*, suggesting that the heads of ABC, CBS, and NBC view their respective networks from sign-on until midnight for a day and—to drive the point home— have their reactions captured on camera as they watched. However, that never happened.

In 1968, though, writer Charles Sopkin cited Friendly's suggestion and actually did subject himself to the challenge, but took the idea one step further. He watched an entire week of commercial television, jumping from channel to channel in the New York City market, and then devoted a 255-page book (*Seven Glorious Days, Seven Fun-Filled Nights*) to chronicling his experience.

The inevitable conclusion? Minow was right. Television *is* a vast wasteland.

Such a judgment was almost inescapable because American broadcasting was set up to be constantly available. The commercial programming system was designed so that there would always be *something* on the air to offer audiences—and to serve as advertising opportunities.

To fill multiple channels, day in and day out, meant that the most important aspect of any program was not the quality of the content, but simply the *existence* of content. Inevitably, there would be vast stretches of time in between higher-quality creations. What made this sometimes-chaotic enterprise work was that different people preferred different offerings. One person's wasteland was another's treasured experience. In a perfect world, commercials, consumers, and creators found each other.

With public television, Minow and like-minded viewers found their match. However, that match came with its own ongoing need: the open-ended requirement to offer sustained support financially, politically, and personally to maintain this public asset in a media world of constant choice. That support was, and continues to be, the only way to protect a welcome oasis in a vast wasteland.

What I Learned from Kristi Yamaguchi

Nicole Chung

The first time I saw her she wasn't even skating. I was flipping through the handful of channels our TV could pick up with its rabbit-ear antenna when I glimpsed her waving from the tallest podium at the 1991 World Figure Skating Championships, dazzling in rhinestone-studded hot magenta, with her high hair-sprayed bangs and million-watt smile. *She's Asian*, I thought. *There's an Asian girl on television, and everyone is cheering for her.*

I'm far from the only kid who fell hard for Kristi Yamaguchi, world and Olympic champion, in the early 1990s. But if you're an Asian American woman of a certain age, chances are Yamaguchi might also have been one of the first Asian American women you saw being publicly celebrated. What many Asian American kids felt when we watched her and, later, Michelle Kwan in the limelight was more than appreciation, more than fandom. It was recognition—all the more powerful because that feeling was often in such short supply.

Kristi Yamaguchi came along right when I needed her, filling a need I had long felt but didn't understand. I was an adopted Korean girl growing up in one of the many towns in Oregon that is not Portland, which meant that everyone who cared about me, everyone I saw around the neighborhood, everyone I met in my day-to-day life was white. In my school, where even white girls with brown hair seemed to envy the blondes, I didn't just feel invisible; I felt like a mistake.

To see a young Japanese American woman singing our national anthem with a gold medal around her neck was to feel the entire world I knew shift. I couldn't conceive of Yamaguchi's victory the way she probably did—as another crucial step on the road to the 1992 Olympics, the fulfillment of long years of training, effort, and sacrifice. To my rapt nine-year-old gaze, her triumph felt like a sudden, unexpected gift. Flanked by two white women—Tonya Harding and Nancy Kerrigan, who completed the American sweep of the medals—the person who looked most like me was the star, the golden girl. It had never occurred to me that a girl could be nationally adored without being white. It had never occurred to me that Asian American heroes might exist.

Throughout my childhood, well-meaning adults told me that my race and my heritage weren't supposed to matter. Yet claims of "colorblindness" and melting-pot platitudes did not stop people from complimenting my English or asking where my parents had gotten me, nor did they prevent my classmates from pulling back their eyes and teaching me slurs I was usually too humiliated to report to anyone. In those years there was no one I could turn to in my confusion, no one who could answer my questions: Where, exactly, did I fit in? Did my adoption mean I was supposed to try to aspire to a whiteness beyond my reach? When other people looked at me, what did they see—an Asian girl, or an American?

When I saw Kristi Yamaguchi beaming from the cover of *Newsweek*'s 1992 Olympics preview issue, I took it as an encouraging sign. Maybe I hadn't yet figured out how to be both Asian and American, but Yamaguchi, America's Olympic sweetheart, seemed to have found her place. That magazine cover occupied a place of honor on my bedroom wall for years. The article hasn't aged well. Frank Deford describes the rivalry between Yamaguchi and Midori Ito of Japan:

> The battle for the gold and all the lucre it earns sets up a duel between two young women named Yamaguchi and Ito, whose bloodlines both stretch back, pure and simple, to the same soft, cherry-blossom days on the one bold little island of Honshu. The twist is, though, that if the powerful Ito is Midori, of Nagoya, the delicate Yamaguchi is Kristi,

from the Bay Area, fourth-generation American. It's the chrysanthemum and the sword—on the ice together, worlds apart.

Comparing the two rivals' looks, body types, and styles on the ice, Deford calls it a "kicker" that Yamaguchi, while "totally of Japanese descent," exemplified "the stylish Western ideal that the stout little Midori is so envious of." He mentions the Yamaguchi siblings' "hopelessly American" interests and seems almost surprised that their parents chose not to open up about the time their families spent in World War II internment camps ("None of them want to dwell on it anymore. Or, if they do, they won't let us know"). Unsure what Yamaguchi herself thought about her potentially historic role, he concludes that her heritage might just turn out to be her secret weapon: "Certainly, deep within her, she is still Japanese—some of her must be—and if she should win it's because, while the others have the triple axel, only she has the best of both worlds."

You get the idea. I didn't know I ought to bristle at the unnecessary catalog of the skaters' physical attributes. On the contrary, I was glad the article fawned over her looks as well as her talent, because it was the first time I had ever been encouraged to think of an Asian American woman as beautiful.

The night I watched Yamaguchi win Olympic gold was one of the happiest of my young life. In the weeks following her triumph, I became increasingly aware of a wish I'd long harbored: to be seen—not as a bookish outcast or a sidekick-in-the-making, but as someone with power and potential of her own. While I knew I wasn't going to be an Olympian, I had other dreams. I was always cramming spiral notebooks with tales of sharp, spunky kids solving mysteries, outsmarting grown-ups, and saving their friends. The characters I invented usually shared some of my interests, my mannerisms, but until now they had all been blonde and blue-eyed, because that was the sort of girl I used to dream of being.

After the Albertville Games, I started a story about a new character, and for once I didn't have to stretch or struggle to figure out who she was or where she came from. Inky-haired, dark-eyed, unapologetically brilliant, she was my first Asian American protagonist. You can probably guess what I named her.

When I talked to a Malaysian Chinese American friend recently about my childhood love for Yamaguchi—who now runs her own foundation while raising two daughters—my friend reminisced with me, and then added: "It is kind of sad that we all have the same youthful touchstones." From Kristi Yamaguchi and Michelle Kwan to Claudia Kishi and the Yellow Power Ranger, our attachment to the same smattering of representatives we all treasured as children feels akin to what some Asian Americans experienced a few years ago at the height of Linsanity, the outpouring for the basketball player Jeremy Lin. Representation, when you finally get it, can be life-changing, allowing you to imagine possibilities you never entertained before. If you're seen as irrelevant, on the other hand, or rarely seen at all—if your identity is reduced time and again to a slickly packaged product or the same tired jokes and stereotypes—it can be harder to believe in your own agency and intrinsic worth.

I have two daughters now, two brown-eyed little girls who have inherited my obsessive nature and my collection of Kristi Yamaguchi memorabilia, and I often wonder who their heroes will be, who will encourage them to imagine their lives in terms of possibilities and not limitations. While they have the diverse group of friends I didn't have at their age, and I've bought them every book that I can find about Asian American kids, they have few opportunities to see girls who look like them in the media they consume. Shows centered on interracial families like ours are as rare as those featuring complex Asian American characters, and the overwhelming whiteness of the American movies we've watched once led my older daughter to ask me, in confusion, "About how many Asians *live* here?"

My childhood devotion to Kristi Yamaguchi was all the more fierce because the full burden of my pride and loyalty—which I might have split among a dozen, a hundred Asian American role models if only I'd had them—was focused on her. Today, I can't help but want more exemplars for kids like mine, whose sense of self-worth should be free to develop without the sting of such scarce representation. We should all have more heroes from whom to choose.

COMMERCIAL BREAK

COMMERCIAL BREAK

Do television characters belong to the writers who invent them, or to the audience members who love them? In "Control" (2011), **Frank Rose** recounts how
AMC and the creators of *Mad Men* were forced to reckon with a new kind of
viewer engagement when fans took to Twitter using the names of the show's
characters.

Control
(selection)

Frank Rose

One night in June 2009, Betty Draper, the frustrated suburban housewife married to sixties adman Don Draper, posted a poignant message on the three-year-old microblogging site Twitter:

> On back porch, opening jars of fireflies, releasing them into nite air. Beautiful things should be allowed to go free.

It is, of course, a small miracle that Betty Draper tweets at all. For starters, Betty is a fictional character in the television show *Mad Men*, then about to enter its third season, and fictional characters don't share their innermost thoughts online—or at least, they didn't used to. But more to the point, she's a fictional character from the early sixties, when Twitter was still decades in the future, along with the entire infrastructure that supports it—microprocessors, personal computers, the internet, the world wide web, cellular telephones, text messaging, the lot of it. As one person in the growing audience for *Mad Men* tweeters observed, that must be some powerful IBM Selectric she's using.

Yet there's something fitting about *Mad Men* on Twitter all the same. An Emmy Award–winning television program that captures Madison Avenue on the cusp of radical social change, *Mad Men* is a show that explains who we are by reminding us how far we've come. It does this in a hundred subtle and not-so-subtle ways, from the blatant homophobia and over-the-top womanizing of its main characters to its repressed-to-bursting fashion sense—white shirts and narrow-lapelled suits for the men, hip-hugging sheaths for the women (at least, the sexier ones). What little nostalgia it delivers comes with a sting. At a time when advertising, like other industries, is trying to embrace what's known as the sense-and-respond model—anticipate change, be ready to adapt—it captures the old command-and-control model at its acme. The men in this show know what you want, and they get well paid to sell you on it. Having them on Twitter only exposes the yawning chasm between then and now.

But what really reveals the depth of the chasm is this: neither the producers of the show nor the network that carries it had anything to do with putting the characters on Twitter. *Mad Men* on TV may be all about command and control, but on Twitter it became a sense-and-respond case study: What happens when viewers start seizing bits of the story and telling it themselves?

That started to happen with *Mad Men* in August 2008, shortly after the beginning of the show's second season, when Paul Isakson, a brand planner at a small ad agency in Minneapolis, took it upon himself to start tweeting as Don Draper, Betty's husband. Don was the creative director of Sterling Cooper, the fictional Madison Avenue agency in the show. Isakson began with an 11:00 a.m. aside about Don's fellow partner, Roger Sterling:

> drinking a scotch with Roger so he doesn't feel like an alcoholic.

A few days later, Carri Bugbee, who runs a marketing firm in Portland, Oregon, decided she wanted to tweet as Peggy Olson, Don's former secretary, recently promoted to the all-but-unprecedented position for a female of junior copywriter. An hour later, Bugbee phoned a friend, Michael Bissell, and told him he had to join in as well. Bissell, who runs a digital agency in Portland, decided he wanted to be Roger Sterling. Somebody else—they never found out who—started tweeting as Joan Holloway, the sexy office manager who had become Roger's playmate.

It didn't seem to matter that none of this was authorized by the show's creator, Matthew Weiner, or its network, AMC. Less than a month after the start of the second season, nine of the show's characters were on Twitter and the service was buzzing with *Mad Men* activity. Then, suddenly, it stopped. At 8:45 p.m. Pacific time on August 25, less than two weeks after Isakson started it all, Carri Bugbee logged into her Peggy Olson account and discovered it had stopped working. At first she thought Twitter had gone down—a likely enough occurrence, given the growing pains of the fast-growing site. Ten minutes later, she got an official Twitter email informing her the account had been suspended for suspicious activity. She took a deep breath and emailed her lawyer.

The next day, the Silicon Valley tech blog VentureBeat reported that "Don Draper" and "Peggy Olson" had been suspended. It soon emerged that Twitter, after being contacted by AMC, had shut down the accounts to avoid a violation of the Digital Millennium Copyright Act, the 1998 law that protects online services like Twitter and YouTube from being charged with copyright violation for anything their users post, as long as they remove any potentially infringing material at the request of the copyright holder. But no sooner were the accounts suspended than the *Mad Men* tweet stream—that is, comments about the show on Twitter—started going wild. And where "Don" and "Peggy" had been generating excitement about *Mad Men*, now the talk was all about how clueless the network was. Why would you choke off involvement from people who so clearly love the show?

Which is how Deep Focus, AMC's digital marketing agency, presented the situation to network execs. A small shop based in midtown Manhattan, Deep Focus works with clients like Samsung, Microsoft, and Electronic Arts to develop online promotional campaigns that seek to involve fans with the product. Ian Schafer, the agency's CEO, told AMC execs they shouldn't attempt to shut down something that was generating so much free publicity. "Sometimes the best thing to do in a situation like this is nothing," Schafer told me later. "But that takes a lot of self-control." Within twenty-four hours the accounts were back up, with AMC's tacit blessing but little in the way of explanation.

That's when Helen Klein Ross started tweeting as Betty. Ross had never met Carri Bugbee or the others, but she did know the ad business. She had started as a secretary in 1977 at the San Francisco office of Foote, Cone & Belding. After that she'd risen to copywriter and moved to New York, where she worked at a number of top agencies on accounts like Absolut, Dove, Nike, Revlon, and Volvo. Born around the same time as Betty's daughter Sally, she found admen in the seventies to be as casually misogynist as Peggy Olson had fifteen years earlier. Tweeting as Betty gave her a way to reconnect with that period in her life.

It was not an easy job. For starters, someone else was already tweeting as Betty Draper. Ross tried to contact that person, got no response, and decided to start tweeting anyway. To get the details right, she spent hours watching previously aired *Mad Men* episodes and poring over cookbooks and housekeeping guides from the sixties. She needed to know her way around Betty's blue Formica kitchen, because as a home-maker Betty spent much of her life there. Ross put together page after page of background notes—on Betty, on Don, on life in New York's Westchester County suburbs in the early sixties. She made a point of responding to the more interesting questions she got from people who were following Betty's remarks, because on Twitter, as she put it when we met for coffee one day in New York, "you're interacting with the audience, not just with other characters." When Betty got unexpectedly pregnant at the end of season 2 and somebody asked how she was doing, Ross replied,

> Dr. Aldrich says I'm doing fine. He wants me to smoke as much as possible so the baby will be smaller and easier to deliver.

Ross is demure in appearance but unafraid to speak her mind. She wears her hair in a boyish bob and speaks in lilting tones, a slight smile playing across her face. As Betty, she never tweets out of character. Even so, Ross can't help but expose Betty's feelings online in ways the character is never allowed to on the show. "On *Mad Men*, so much is unspoken," Ross said. "Betty can't reveal her innermost thoughts. But people now don't want subtext, they want subtitles"—clear explanations of what's going on. And that's what the characters provide on Twitter.

Unofficially, Ross and the other tweeters have been accepted by the show. The AMC blog even ran a Q&A with Carri Bugbee a few months after the shutdown. Later, at the Clio Awards, an ad industry confab in Las Vegas, Ross met Matthew Weiner, the show's famously perfection-ist creator, after he'd been honored for the program. Weiner told her he loved what she was doing as Betty. But not surprisingly, neither he nor anyone else connected with the show would reveal what was to come in season 3—like, would she keep the baby?

Well, so much for tweeting about Betty's pregnancy. To Ross, it was a missed opportunity—not just for "Betty," but for *Mad Men.* She viewed this whole Twitter thing as sort of an experiment in what entertainment could become. With this show, Weiner had created or, more correctly, re-created an entire world in incredible detail: the world of Madison Avenue in the early sixties. It was populated by humans and set on planet Earth, but as much as *Avatar* or *Star Wars* it had its own economy and technology, its own social structure and mores. And Weiner had done it brilliantly—so brilliantly that for many people, one hour a week for thirteen weeks out of the year was simply not enough. "Now you get to live in that world from 10:00 to 11:00 on Sunday night," Ross said. "But I see the potential for telling that story in a different dimension—for bringing more of that world to an audience that has expanded because the world has expanded."

Several months after she started tweeting as Betty, Ross met Michael Bissell—"Roger Sterling"—for the first time. They were at South by Southwest Interactive, the digital-culture conference in Austin, to speak at a panel discussion on *Mad Men* and Twitter. As they were preparing for the panel, she and Bissell and Carri Bugbee compared notes. Before the shutdown, she told them, she had assumed that Weiner was somehow behind the *Mad Men* Twitter campaign and that she would be engaging in some kind of online tryout. "I thought he was casting for Twitter writers," she said. "He's so brilliant—why wouldn't he do that?"

"Because he's a control freak," Bissell replied.

In a command-and-control world, we know who's telling the story; it's the author. But digital media have created an authorship crisis. Once the audience is free to step out into the fiction and start directing events, the entire edifice of twentieth-century mass media begins to crumble.

Mass media were an outgrowth of nineteenth-century technology—the development of ever more efficient presses and distribution networks, which made publishing such an expensive proposition that it made sense only on an industrial scale. Movies and television accelerated the trend. But now the internet has reversed it. An author can still speak to an audience of millions, but the communication no longer goes just one way. Newspapers and magazines don't just report events anymore, they become forums for discussing them. Movies and TV shows cease to be couch potato fodder and become catalysts for the imagination. Ad people (they're not just men anymore) begin to realize they need to stop preaching to consumers and start listening to them. That's what "sense and respond" means—a dialogue.

In the late nineties I was in London reporting a story for *Wired* on Rupert Murdoch, a man who had built a global media empire largely on the basis of an epiphany he'd had when he was much younger. In 1945, Arthur C. Clarke had published a paper in *Wireless World*, a British journal for radio buffs, positing that a spacecraft in geosynchronous orbit 22,300 miles above the equator could beam a signal to a large, stationary footprint on the Earth below. Fascinated by Clarke's vision and by his prediction that the free flow of information would challenge the authority of national governments, Murdoch had embraced the power of satellite technology. Now BSkyB, the British wing of the vast satellite fleet Murdoch had assembled, was in the process of going digital and interactive.

As Clarke had predicted, satellites were ideal for broadcasting to the masses. They gave Murdoch a gigantic fire hose in the sky—but that's all they gave him. Satellites weren't designed for pinpoint delivery of billions of web pages, nor did they make possible more than a rudimentary form of interactive TV. Murdoch wanted both. The solution seemed clear enough: partner with a phone company and run DSL lines to customers' homes. Those lines were designed to carry far more data into the home than out of it, but that didn't seem to be a problem. As Tony Ball, Sky's then CEO, offhandedly remarked, "There's not that many people sending streaming video back from their PC." It seemed almost too obvious to quote.

That was then. In June 2008, Michael Wesch, an anthropology professor at Kansas State University, pointed out in a talk at the Library of Congress that if the three leading US television networks had broadcast nonstop for the sixty years they'd been in business, that would have added up to more than 1.5 million hours of programming—which is a lot, but less than what internet users had uploaded to YouTube in the previous six months.

By that time, Murdoch had abandoned his half-romantic dream of a satellite armada circling the globe. He'd had it in his grasp when, after years of maneuvering, he won control of DIRECTV. This gave him a footprint that extended from Australia and New Zealand across China and southern Asia to India, blanketed much of Europe, and leaped across the Atlantic to cover most of North and South America. But by that time, his prize was worth more as a bargaining chip. In late 2006, after John Malone, the Denver-based cable mogul, bought up an uncomfortably large amount of stock in Murdoch's News Corporation, Murdoch gave him his satellite operations in the US and Latin America to go away.

By that time, Murdoch had made a deal that for $580 million gave him MySpace, the fast-growing social networking site, which already had 22 million members and was adding them at the rate of 2 million per month. MySpace was all about connecting people—to each other, to their favorite bands, to whatever identity they wanted to express. In early 2007, it drew 7 percent of the world's internet users every month. And when that percentage started to decline—slowly at first, then precipitously—a few years later, it was only because Facebook emerged as a more appealing way of doing the same thing.

By the standards of mass media, the rise of the web in general and social networking in particular seems to presage a revolution in human behavior—and a most unlikely one at that. "You aren't going to turn passive consumers into active trollers on the internet," a senior executive at ABC condescendingly informed Kevin Kelly, a pioneer in the Bay Area's online community and one of *Wired*'s founding editors. This was in 1989, the golden age of the couch potato. With millions of humans voluntarily reduced to a vegetative state every night in front of the TV set, it seemed a safe enough assumption at the time. But even then the audience was starting to wake up, and not because of the internet.

It started with the videocassette recorder. In 1975, when Sony introduced the notion of "time shift," as cofounder Akio Morita dubbed it, television was a staid and profitable business controlled in the United States by three national broadcast networks and in most other countries by one. *All in the Family*, America's most popular show, was watched in

30 percent of homes; cable was something you got for better reception. By 2010, thirty-five years later, the number one series in the US (Fox's *American Idol*) was being watched in less than 15 percent of households, hundreds of channels were available through cable and satellite, the broadcast networks were struggling to make a profit, and the entire apparatus of network television was beginning to break down.

The fundamental premise of broadcast television was its ability to control viewers—to deliver eyeballs to advertisers by the tens of millions. Because the networks had to attract those eyeballs and then hang on to them, programming—scheduling shows, creating effective lead-ins, countering the competition—became the network executive's highest art. The goal was to funnel eyeballs through the various day parts on the broadcasting schedule as if they were pinballs, from early evening through prime time all the way to late night—ka-ching! ka-ching! ka-ching! But the control that began eroding with the VCR has been eliminated by its successor, the digital video recorder, and blasted away entirely by the web. Americans are watching more TV than ever—but, like their counterparts around the globe, increasingly they do it on their own schedule, and at the same time they're uploading their own videos to YouTube, posting their snapshots on Flickr, sharing their thoughts on Blogger or WordPress, and connecting with one another through MySpace and Facebook. The funnel is hopelessly, irretrievably busted.

But the media industry's loss of control extends far beyond what people watch and when. Movie studios and television networks are no longer even able to control what happens in the stories they present. As Matthew Weiner discovered when the *Mad Men* characters turned up on Twitter, the people who formerly constituted the audience are now capable of running off with the show. The same tools that enable people to spontaneously coalesce online make it easy for them to start telling the story their way, if they care about it enough to do so.

What's surprising is that anyone should find this surprising. That ABC exec notwithstanding, there's nothing inherent in humans that makes them want to be passive consumers of entertainment, or of the advertising that pays for it. The couch potato era, seemingly so significant at the time, turns out to be less an era than a blip—and a blip based on faulty assumptions at that.

In 2007, the American Association of Advertising Agencies and the Advertising Research Foundation, an industry think tank, issued a report asserting that the twentieth-century approach to advertising—the approach epitomized by *Mad Men*—had it all wrong. For decades, ad people had assumed that consumers thought in a linear and essentially rational fashion. All a television spot had to do to arouse desire for the product was get the viewer's attention and make a strong case. This "input-output engineering model," as the report described it, was enshrined in ad industry thinking by Rosser Reeves, the longtime chairman of Ted Bates & Company, in his 1961 book *Reality in Advertising*: if the ad people could define the "unique selling proposition" of the product they were pitching, be it an expensive new sports car or an over-the-counter medication for headache relief, consumers would get the message and act accordingly.

Alas for Madison Avenue, it wasn't that simple. In the 1980s and '90s, the idea that creative types could input a story and get output in the form of sales began to collapse. As cognitive researchers took a closer look at the workings of the human brain, they discovered that this isn't what happens at all. People don't passively ingest a marketing message, or any type of message. They greet it with an emotional response, usually unconscious, that can vary wildly depending on their own experiences and predispositions. They don't just imbibe a story; they imbue it with meaning. Which means that perceptions of a brand aren't simply created by marketers; they're "co-created," in the words of Gerald Zaltman of Harvard Business School, by marketers and consumers together.

To anyone outside the ad business, this may seem obvious: of course the audience brings something to the table. But it's a powerful idea all the same. If individuals in the audience "co-create" a story in some sort of give-and-take with the storyteller, then the whole notion of authorial control starts to get fuzzy. The author starts the story; the audience completes it. The author creates the characters and the situation they find themselves in; the audience responds and makes it their own. Matthew Weiner produces *Mad Men*; the viewers interpret it by empathizing with its characters and imagining themselves in that scenario. Given half a chance, at least a few of them will want to start tweeting as Betty Draper or Roger Sterling—and Weiner has no choice but to accept that. People have always wanted to in some way inhabit the stories that move them. The only real variable is whether technology gives them that opportunity.

Nearly two centuries before Twitter and Wookieepedia there was the serialized novel. England in the 1830s was being transformed by technology as profoundly as the entire planet is today. Industrialization was drawing people to the cities in unimaginable numbers, crowding them together in often appalling conditions of filth and disease. Overflowing cesspools and cellars packed with "night soil"—a euphemism for human shit—were commonplace. So were cholera epidemics, which from 1831 on killed tens of thousands in an excruciating process that began with uncontrollable diarrhea and ended a day or two later with death by dehydration.

Yet the same forces of urbanization that generated such misery also led to the rise of literacy among the working and middle classes. Suddenly, there was a far bigger market for reading material than had existed even a few decades before, much less in Defoe's era. At the same time, improvements in paper manufacture, in printing, and in transportation were making it possible to print and distribute periodicals on a much greater scale. Book publishers saw a market for serial fiction—books released a few chapters at a time in flimsy paperback editions that sold for a shilling or so each (12 pence). Writers were lucky to stay one or two installments ahead of the deadline, so readers who wanted to share their thoughts could influence the plot as the books were being written—could participate, in other words.

Many authors were published in this manner, but one became identified with it above all. As a young boy, Charles Dickens had imbibed *Don Quixote* and *Tom Jones* and *Robinson Crusoe*; but when his father was sent away to a London debtor's prison, Charles, then twelve, was pulled out of school and sent to work in a rat-infested boot-blacking factory near Charing Cross. Largely deprived of a formal education, he nonetheless found success as a teenage newspaper reporter in the House of Commons, quickly rising to an enviable position at the widely read London *Morning Chronicle*. In 1836, having just turned twenty-four and published a collection of short fiction, he was commissioned by the London publishers Chapman & Hall to write a series of sketches about life in the English countryside. The picaresque adventures that made up *The Pickwick Papers* appeared in monthly installments from March of that year until October 1837. They aroused little interest at first, but when Dickens introduced Sam Weller, valet to the aristocratic Mr. Pickwick, readers clamored for more and he gave it to them. The series took off.

Dickens quickly became the most popular novelist in England, and the acknowledged master of the serial. In February 1837, while still churning out *The Pickwick Papers*, he began writing *Oliver Twist* for *Bentley's Miscellany*, a new literary journal he'd just been hired to edit. The tale of an indigent boy forced into the miasma of crime and despair that was contemporary London, *Oliver Twist* spoke directly to the new audience that cheap serials had created. In scathing tones it charged the local religious authorities with attempting to starve the poor out of existence. Yet the same technological upheaval that gave rise to the workhouses that Dickens described also created a readership for his story, and a way of reaching those readers that was cheap enough to be practicable.

Inevitably, serialization changed the structure of stories. Dickens fashioned tales with cliffhanger endings to keep readers coming back (though this technique wouldn't get its name until decades later, after Thomas Hardy literally left his hero hanging off a cliff at the end of the sixth installment of *A Pair of Blue Eyes*). More significant, however, was the way he improvised in response to his readers' reactions. Even as he was in the midst of writing *Oliver Twist*, *Nicholas Nickleby* began appearing in monthly installments. In 1841, "to shorten the intervals between himself and his readers" (as he put it in a preface), he launched a weekly periodical, *Master Humphrey's Clock*, for which he wrote *The Old Curiosity Shop* and *Barnaby Rudge*.

The weekly deadlines of *Master Humphrey's Clock* proved a bit much even for Dickens, but communication with his readers remained paramount. Not that he always heeded their wishes. As he neared the end of *The Old Curiosity Shop* in 1841, it became increasingly apparent that the saintly Nell Trent, orphaned and pursued by predators, was doomed to die. As the suspense built, readers beseeched the author to be merciful. A ship from England sailed into New York Harbor to be greeted at the pier by a crowd of people shouting, "Is Little Nell dead?" When her inevitable demise came, it was greeted with near hysteria.

Dickens knew exactly what he was doing, of course: *The Old Curiosity Shop* was his most successful novel to date. On occasions when a story was faltering, he paid much closer attention to what his readers were saying. In 1843, when monthly sales of *Martin Chuzzlewit* failed to meet expectations, he moved the action to America; and when readers latched onto Mrs. Gamp, the novel's tipsy nurse, he obligingly wrote more scenes for her.

Scholars have come to see such give-and-take as crucial to Dickens's method. "Through serial publication an author could recover something of the intimate relationship between storyteller and audience which existed in the ages of the sagas and of Chaucer," John Butt and Kathleen Tillotson observed in their 1957 study *Dickens at Work*. Princeton's E. D. H. Johnson concurred: "The drawbacks of adhering to a rigorous schedule . . . were for Dickens more than counterbalanced by the sense of immediate audience participation."

In Dickens's own time, however, serialized novels were hugely controversial. Novels themselves were only beginning to find acceptance in polite society; for upper-class commentators, serialization was entirely too much. From our perspective, Dickens is a literary master, an icon of a now threatened culture. From theirs, he represented the threat of something coming. Not for him a celebration of the old ways so romantically alluded to in John Constable's paintings of the rural English landscape. Dickens's preoccupation with the unpleasant side effects of industrialization was of a piece with the serialized novel itself—clearly the product of mass manufacture, and highly suspect as a result.

Worse, the format seemed dangerously immersive. In 1845, a critic for the patrician *North British Review* decried it as an unhealthy alternative to conversation or to games like cricket or backgammon. Anticipating Huxley and Bradbury by a century, he railed against the multiplying effects of serialization on the already hallucinatory powers of the novel:

> The form of publication of Mr. Dickens's works must be attended with bad consequences. The reading of a novel is not now the undertaking it once was, a thing to be done occasionally on holiday and almost by stealth. . . . It throws us into a state of unreal excitement, a trance,

a dream, which we should be allowed to dream out, and then be sent back to the atmosphere of reality again, cured by our brief surfeit of the desire to indulge again soon in the same delirium of feverish interest. But now our dreams are mingled with our daily business.

Toward the end of the nineteenth century, as further advances in technology continued to bring down the costs of printing and distribution, books and periodicals evolved into separate businesses and book publishers gradually moved away from serialization. The threat of immersiveness moved with them, first to motion pictures, then to television. Books, movies, TV—all were mass media, and mass media had no mechanism for audience participation. But the reader's impulse to have a voice in the story didn't vanish. It went underground and took a new form: fan fiction.

TV NEWS

AND THAT'S THE WAY IT IS

TV NEWS: AND THAT'S THE WAY IT IS

The pieces in this section grapple with the way television presents news and with how the medium encourages viewers to respond to its presentation.

In "The Age of Show Business" (1985), **Neil Postman** contends that the bias of the television medium is always toward entertaining viewers, no matter what subject matter is being broadcast.

David Margolick's "Judge in Simpson Trial Allows TV Camera in Courtroom" (1994) captures a pivotal moment in the history of television access to ongoing court cases, including the arguments for and against such broadcasting.

In his poem "To Remember History You Have to Repeat It" (2005), **Tony Hoagland** focuses on the television newscaster and her role in making the jumble of images she oversees "all right" for viewers.

In "The Moon Hours" (1969), **E. B. White** and other reporters for the *New Yorker* offer a wide range of accounts of people watching coverage of the moon landing, showing how diverse the viewing experience of the same event can be.

The Age of Show Business
(selection)

Neil Postman

A dedicated graduate student I know returned to his small apartment the night before a major examination only to discover that his solitary lamp was broken beyond repair. After a whiff of panic, he was able to restore both his equanimity and his chances for a satisfactory grade by turning on the television set, turning off the sound, and with his back to the set, using its light to read important passages on which he was to be tested. This is one use of television—as a source of illuminating the printed page.

But the television screen is more than a light source. It is also a smooth, nearly flat surface on which the printed word may be displayed. We have all stayed at hotels in which the TV set has had a special channel for describing the day's events in letters rolled endlessly across the screen. This is another use of television—as an electronic bulletin board.

Many television sets are also large and sturdy enough to bear the weight of a small library. The top of an old-fashioned RCA console can handle as many as thirty books, and I know one woman who has securely placed her entire collection of Dickens, Flaubert, and Turgenev on the top of a 21-inch Westinghouse. Here is still another use of television—as bookcase.

I bring forward these quixotic uses of television to ridicule the hope harbored by some that television can be used to support the literate tradition. Such a hope represents exactly what Marshall McLuhan used to call "rear-view mirror" thinking: the assumption that a new medium is merely an extension or amplification of an older one; that an automobile, for example, is only a fast horse, or an electric light a powerful candle. To make such a mistake in the matter at hand is to misconstrue entirely how television redefines the meaning of public discourse. Television does not extend or amplify literate culture. It attacks it. If television is a continuation of anything, it is of a tradition begun by the telegraph and photograph in the mid-nineteenth century, not by the printing press in the fifteenth.

What is television? What kinds of conversations does it permit? What are the intellectual tendencies it encourages? What sort of culture does it produce?

These are the questions to be addressed in the rest of this book, and to approach them with a minimum of confusion, I must begin by making a distinction between a technology and a medium. We might say that a technology is to a medium as the brain is to the mind. Like the brain, a technology is a physical apparatus. Like the mind, a medium is a use to which a physical apparatus is put. A technology becomes a medium as it employs a particular symbolic code, as it finds its place in a particular social setting, as it insinuates itself into economic and political contexts. A technology, in other words, is merely a machine. A medium is the social and intellectual environment a machine creates.

Of course, like the brain itself, every technology has an inherent bias. It has within its physical form a predisposition toward being used in certain ways and not others. Only those who know nothing of the history of technology believe that a technology is entirely neutral. There is an old joke that mocks that naive belief. Thomas Edison, it goes, would have revealed his discovery of the electric light much sooner than he did except for the fact that every time he turned it on, he held it to his mouth and said, "Hello? Hello?"

Not very likely. Each technology has an agenda of its own. It is, as I have suggested, a metaphor waiting to unfold. The printing press, for example, had a clear bias toward being used as a linguistic medium. It is *conceivable* to use it exclusively for the reproduction of pictures. And, one imagines, the Roman Catholic Church would not have objected to its being so used in the sixteenth century. Had that been the case, the Protestant Reformation might not have occurred, for as Luther contended, with the word of God on every family's kitchen table, Christians do not require the Papacy to interpret it for them. But in fact there never was much chance that the press would be used solely, or even very much, for the duplication of icons. From its beginning in the fifteenth century, the press was perceived as an extraordinary opportunity for the display and mass distribution of written language. Everything about its technical possibilities led in that direction. One might even say it was invented for that purpose.

The technology of television has a bias, as well. It is conceivable to use television as a lamp, a surface for texts, a bookcase, even as radio. But it has not been so used and will not be so used, at least in America. Thus, in answering the question, What is television?, we must understand as a first point that we are not talking about television as a technology but television as a medium. There are many places in the world where television, though the same technology as it is in America, is an entirely different medium from that which we know. I refer to places where the majority of people do not have television sets, and those who do have only one; where only one station is available; where television does not operate around the clock; where most programs have as their purpose the direct furtherance of government ideology and policy; where commercials are unknown, and "talking heads" are the principal image; where television is mostly used as if it were radio. For these reasons and more television will not have the same meaning or power as it does in America, which is to say, it is possible for a technology to be so used that its potentialities are prevented from developing and its social consequences kept to a minimum.

But in America, this has not been the case. Television has found in liberal democracy and a relatively free market economy a nurturing climate in which its full potentialities as a technology of images could be exploited. One result of this has been that American television programs are in demand all over the world. The total estimate of US television program exports is approximately 100,000 to 200,000 hours, equally divided among Latin America, Asia, and Europe. Over the years, programs like *Gunsmoke, Bonanza, Mission: Impossible, Star Trek, Kojak,* and more recently, *Dallas* and *Dynasty* have been as popular in England, Japan, Israel, and Norway as in Omaha, Nebraska. I have heard (but not verified) that some years ago the Lapps postponed for several days their annual and, one supposes, essential migratory journey so that they could find out who shot J.R. All of this has occurred simultaneously with the decline of America's moral and political prestige, worldwide. American television programs are in demand not because America is loved but because American television is loved.

We need not be detained too long in figuring out why. In watching American television, one is reminded of George Bernard Shaw's remark on his first seeing the glittering neon signs of Broadway and Forty-Second Street at night. It must be beautiful, he said, if you cannot read. American television is, indeed, a beautiful spectacle, a visual delight, pouring forth thousands of images on any given day. The average length of a shot on network television is only 3.5 seconds, so that the eye never rests, always has something new to see. Moreover, television offers viewers a variety of subject matter, requires minimal skills to comprehend it, and is largely aimed at emotional gratification. Even commercials, which some regard as an annoyance, are exquisitely crafted, always pleasing to the eye and accompanied by exciting music. There is no question but that the best photography in the world is presently seen on television commercials. American television, in other words, is devoted entirely to supplying its audience with entertainment.

Of course, to say that television is entertaining is merely banal. Such a fact is hardly threatening to a culture, not even worth writing a book about. It may even be a reason for rejoicing. Life, as we like to say, is not a highway strewn with flowers. The sight of a few blossoms here and there may make our journey a trifle more endurable. The Lapps undoubtedly thought so. We may surmise that the 90 million Americans who watch television every night also think so. But what I am claiming here is not that television is entertaining but that it has made entertainment itself the natural format for the representation of all experience. Our television set keeps us in constant communion with the world, but it does so with a face whose smiling countenance is unalterable. The problem is not that television presents us with entertaining subject matter but that all subject matter is presented as entertaining, which is another issue altogether.

To say it still another way: entertainment is the supra-ideology of all discourse on television. No matter what is depicted or from what point of view, the overarching presumption is that it is there for our amusement and pleasure. That is why even on news shows which provide us daily with fragments of tragedy and barbarism, we are urged by the newscasters to "join them tomorrow." What for? One would think that several minutes of murder and mayhem would suffice as material for a month of sleepless nights. We accept the newscasters' invitation because we know that the "news" is not to be taken seriously, that it is all in fun, so to say. Everything about a news show tells us this—the good looks and amiability of the cast, their pleasant banter, the exciting music that opens and closes the show, the vivid film footage, the attractive commercials—all these and more suggest that what we have just seen is no cause for weeping. A news show, to put it plainly, is a format for entertainment, not for education, reflection, or catharsis. And we must not judge too harshly those who have framed it in this way. They are not assembling the news to be read, or broadcasting it to be heard. They are televising the news to be seen. They must follow where their medium leads. There is no conspiracy here, no lack of intelligence, only a straightforward recognition that "good television" has little to do with what is "good" about exposition or other forms of verbal communication but everything to do with what the pictorial images look like.

I should like to illustrate this point by offering the case of the eighty-minute discussion provided by the ABC network on November 20, 1983, following its controversial movie *The Day After*. Though the memory of this telecast has receded for most, I choose this case because, clearly, here was television taking its most "serious" and "responsible" stance. Everything that made up this broadcast recommended it as a critical test of television's capacity to depart from an entertainment mode and rise to the level of public instruction. In the first place, the subject was the possibility of a nuclear holocaust. Second, the film itself had been attacked by several influential bodies politic, including the Reverend Jerry Falwell's Moral Majority. Thus, it was important that the network display television's value and serious intentions as a medium of information and coherent discourse. Third, on the program itself no musical theme was used as background—a significant point since almost all television programs are embedded in music, which helps to tell the audience what emotions are to be called forth. This is a standard theatrical device, and its absence on television is always ominous. Fourth, there were no commercials during the discussion, thus elevating the tone of the event to the state of reverence usually reserved for the funerals of assassinated presidents. And finally, the participants included Henry Kissinger, Robert McNamara, and Elie Wiesel, each of whom is a symbol of sorts of serious discourse. Although Kissinger, somewhat later, made an appearance on the hit show *Dynasty*, he was then and still is a paradigm of intellectual sobriety; and Wiesel, practically a walking metaphor of social conscience. Indeed, the other members of the cast—Carl Sagan, William Buckley, and General Brent Scowcroft—are, each in his way, men of intellectual bearing who are not expected to participate in trivial public matters.

The program began with Ted Koppel, master of ceremonies, so to speak, indicating that what followed was not intended to be a debate but a *discussion*. And so those who are interested in philosophies of discourse had an excellent opportunity to observe what serious television means by the word "discussion." Here is what it means: Each of six men was given approximately five minutes to say something about the subject. There was, however, no agreement on exactly what the subject was, and no one felt obliged to respond to anything anyone else said. In fact, it would have been difficult to do so, since the participants were called upon seriatim, as if they were finalists in a beauty contest, each being given his share of minutes in front of the camera. Thus, if Mr. Wiesel, who was called upon last, had a response to Mr. Buckley, who was called upon first, there would have been four commentaries in between, occupying about twenty minutes, so that the audience (if not Mr. Wiesel himself) would have had difficulty remembering the argument which prompted his response. In fact, the participants—most of whom were no strangers to television—largely avoided addressing each other's points. They used their initial minutes and then their subsequent ones to intimate their position or give an impression. Dr. Kissinger, for example, seemed intent on making viewers feel sorry that he was no longer their secretary of state by reminding everyone of books he had once written, proposals he had once made, and negotiations he had once conducted. Mr. McNamara informed the audience that he had eaten lunch in Germany that very afternoon, and went on to say that he had at least fifteen proposals to reduce nuclear arms. One would have thought that the discussion would turn on this issue, but the others seemed about as interested in it as they were in what he had for lunch in Germany. (Later, he took the initiative to mention three of his proposals but they were not discussed.) Elie Wiesel, in a series of quasi-parables and paradoxes, stressed the tragic nature of the human condition, but because he did not have the time to provide a context for his remarks, he seemed quixotic and confused, conveying an impression of an itinerant rabbi who has wandered into a coven of Gentiles.

In other words, this was no discussion as we normally use the word. Even when the "discussion" period began, there were no arguments or counterarguments, no scrutiny of assumptions, no explanations, no elaborations, no definitions. Carl Sagan made, in my opinion, the most coherent statement—a four-minute rationale for a nuclear freeze—but it contained at least two questionable assumptions and was not carefully examined. Apparently, no one wanted to take time from his own few minutes to call attention to someone else's. Mr. Koppel, for his part, felt obliged to keep the "show" moving, and though he occasionally pursued what he discerned as a line of thought, he was more concerned to give each man his fair allotment of time.

But it is not time constraints alone that produce such fragmented and discontinuous language. When a television show is in process, it is very nearly impermissible to say, "Let me think about that" or "I don't know" or "What do you mean when you say . . . ?" or "From what sources does your information come?" This type of discourse not only slows down the tempo of the show but creates the impression of uncertainty or lack of finish. It tends to reveal people in the *act of thinking*, which is as disconcerting and boring on television as it is on a Las Vegas stage. Thinking does not play well on television, a fact that television directors discovered long ago. There is not much to *see* in it. It is, in a phrase, not a performing art. But television demands a performing art, and so what the ABC network gave us was a picture of men of sophisticated verbal skills and political understanding being brought to heel by a medium that requires them to fashion performances rather than ideas. Which accounts for why the eighty minutes were very entertaining, in the way of a Samuel Beckett play: the intimations of gravity hung heavy, the meaning passeth all understanding. The performances, of course, were highly professional. Sagan abjured the turtleneck sweater in which he starred when he did *Cosmos*. He even

141

had his hair cut for the event. His part was that of the logical scientist speaking in behalf of the planet. It is to be doubted that Paul Newman could have done better in the role, although Leonard Nimoy might have. Scowcroft was suitably military in his bearing—terse and distant, the unbreakable defender of national security. Kissinger, as always, was superb in the part of the knowing world statesman, weary of the sheer responsibility of keeping disaster at bay. Koppel played to perfection the part of a moderator, pretending, as it were, that he was sorting out ideas while, in fact, he was merely directing the performances. At the end, one could only applaud those performances, which is what a good television program always aims to achieve; that is to say, applause, not reflection.

I do not say categorically that it is impossible to use television as a carrier of coherent language or thought in process. William Buckley's own program, *Firing Line*, occasionally shows people in the act of thinking but who also happen to have television cameras pointed at them. There are other programs, such as *Meet the Press* or *The Open Mind*, which clearly strive to maintain a sense of intellectual decorum and typographic tradition, but they are scheduled so that they do not compete with programs of great visual interest, since otherwise, they will not be watched. After all, it is not unheard of that a format will occasionally go against the bias of its medium. For example, the most popular radio program of the early 1940s featured a ventriloquist, and in those days, I heard more than once the feet of a tap dancer on the *Major Bowes' Amateur Hour*. (Indeed, if I am not mistaken, he even once featured a pantomimist.) But ventriloquism, dancing and mime do not play well on radio, just as sustained, complex talk does not play well on television. It can be made to play tolerably well if only one camera is used and the visual image is kept constant—as when the president gives a speech. But this is not television at its best, and it is not television that most people will choose to watch. The single most important fact about television is that people *watch* it, which is why it is called "tele*vision*." And what they watch, and like to watch, are moving pictures—millions of them, of short duration and dynamic variety. It is in the nature of the medium that it must suppress the content of ideas in order to accommodate the requirements of visual interest; that is to say, to accommodate the values of show business.

Film, records, and radio (now that it is an adjunct of the music industry) are, of course, equally devoted to entertaining the culture, and their effects in altering the style of American discourse are not insignificant. But television is different because it encompasses all forms of discourse. No one goes to a movie to find out about government policy or the latest scientific advances. No one buys a record to find out the baseball scores or the weather or the lastest murder. No one turns on radio anymore for soap operas or a presidential address (if a television set is at hand). But everyone goes to television for all these things and more, which is why television resonates so powerfully throughout the culture. Television is our culture's principal mode of knowing about itself. Therefore—and this is the critical point—how television stages the world becomes the model for how the world is properly to be staged. It is not merely that on the television screen entertainment is the metaphor for all discourse. It is that off the screen the same metaphor prevails. As typography once dictated the style of conducting politics, religion, business, education, law, and other important social matters, television now takes command. In courtrooms, classrooms, operating rooms, board rooms, churches, and even airplanes, Americans no longer talk to each other, they entertain each other. They do not exchange ideas; they exchange images. They do not argue with propositions; they argue with good looks, celebrities, and commercials. For the message of television as metaphor is not only that all the world is a stage but that the stage is located in Las Vegas, Nevada. [. . .]

Prior to the 1984 presidential elections, the two candidates confronted each other on television in what were called "debates." These events were not in the least like the Lincoln-Douglas debates or anything else that goes by the name. Each candidate was given five minutes to address such questions as, What is (or would be) your policy in Central America? His opposite number was then given one minute for a rebuttal. In such circumstances, complexity, documentation, and logic can play no role, and, indeed, on several occasions syntax itself was abandoned entirely. It is no matter. The men were less concerned with giving arguments than with "giving off" impressions, which is what television does best. Post-debate commentary largely avoided any evaluation of the candidates' ideas, since there were none to evaluate. Instead, the debates were conceived as boxing matches, the relevant question being, Who KO'd whom? The answer was determined by the "style" of the men—how they looked, fixed their gaze, smiled, and delivered one-liners. In the second debate, President Reagan got off a swell one-liner when asked a question about his age. The following day, several newspapers indicated that Ron had KO'd Fritz with his joke. Thus, the leader of the free world is chosen by the people in the Age of Television.

What all of this means is that our culture has moved toward a new way of conducting its business, especially its important business. The nature of its discourse is changing as the demarcation line between what is show business and what is not becomes harder to see with each passing day. Our priests and presidents, our surgeons and lawyers, our educators and newscasters need worry less about satisfying the demands of their discipline than the demands of good showmanship. Had Irving Berlin changed one word in the title of his celebrated song, he would have been as prophetic, albeit more terse, as Aldous Huxley. He need only have written, There's No Business But Show Business.

Judge in Simpson Trial Allows TV Camera in Courtroom

David Margolick

LOS ANGELES, Nov. 7—To the relief of millions of voyeurs, court buffs, and civic-minded students of the criminal justice system, Judge Lance A. Ito ruled today that a single television camera can remain in his courtroom for the trial of O. J. Simpson. While some pretrial hearings could still conceivably be closed, continuous coverage of the eventual trial now seems all but certain.

As Mr. Simpson sat nearby, intermittently attentive, Judge Ito spent much of the morning invoking the perils of television, including nervous witnesses, grandstanding lawyers, and salacious sound bites. He repeatedly referred to the carnival-like televised trials a generation ago of Dr. Sam Sheppard on murder charges and Billie Sol Estes on charges of fraud. At his side were twenty-one boxes filled with more than 15,000 letters, most of which, he said, had urged him to pull the plug.

But once more, the judge's threat to take such drastic action—prompted in late September by a false report on television that Nicole Brown Simpson's blood was detected on socks found in Mr. Simpson's bedroom—proved more bark than bite.

Judge Ito effectively agreed with what lawyers for both sides, along with representatives of various news groups and the American Civil Liberties Union, told him today: that whatever mistaken reporting on the case had taken place had happened outside the courtroom, not inside; that rather than encourage irresponsible reporting, cameras could both check and correct it; and that in a case crucial to public faith in courts, television was essential.

Moreover, given the public's right to attend court proceedings and the paucity of seats in the courtroom—nine to fifteen spots are set aside for the public—television represented the only alternative to holding court in the Los Angeles Coliseum. In fact 17 million people watched the second day of the preliminary hearing in the Simpson case. Mr. Simpson is charged with the murder of Ms. Simpson, his former wife, and Ronald L. Goldman, a friend of hers.

Both sides in the case urged Judge Ito to let the camera stay once testimony in the case starts, probably after the first of the year, in part because it would help legitimize whatever the verdict is.

Marcia Clark, the chief prosecutor, said cameras provided "the best way to refute unfounded rumors and wild, speculative theories" and would "enable the world to see what the jury sees."

One of Mr. Simpson's lawyers, Robert L. Shapiro, also urged that the trial be televised, but only if the price for it was not a sequestered jury.

"For Mr. Simpson to have a life after this case will require the American public to have an understanding that his acquittal was based on evidence presented in a courtroom, not on evidence that was in some way manipulated by lawyers or was excluded based on legal technicalities," he said.

But he said the defense might oppose televising some pretrial hearings in order to protect jurors from contamination, and would object to cameras at trial if the jury had to be sequestered. Judge Ito has yet to rule on that question, though he reiterated today that a six-month sequestration remained "a very real prospect" in the case.

The striking unanimity on allowing cameras showed the degree to which they have already become fixtures in most state courts.

"We are simply moving to a point where cameras are going to be accepted as a part of American justice," Floyd Abrams, a lawyer for Court TV, said afterward. Earlier, Mr. Abrams conceded that some coverage in the case had been "lurid, reckless, hysterical, beyond nonsense." But he then pointed to the camera and said it was not the problem.

"I speak for the camera, and on its behalf, I want to say the camera pleads absolutely 100 percent not guilty," said Mr. Abrams, invoking language used earlier in the case by Mr. Simpson himself.

The only skeptic around was Judge Ito himself. It quickly became apparent that the hearing was as much an exercise in devil's advocacy, professorial one-upsmanship, and an effort to create a record of conscientiousness as anything else, lest anyone accuse him of losing control of the proceedings.

Judge Ito challenged the real educational value of the Simpson case, ostensibly because it is so atypical. He noted that cameras are still not allowed in federal courts. He speculated that a snippet of testimony might be broadcast for "its excitement, its titillation value." In response to statements that cameras had enhanced public esteem for the courts, he remarked that they hadn't helped Congress.

"The public has overwhelmingly told me to pull the plug," he told Kelli L. Sager, a lawyer for several news organizations. "How do you respond to that?"

As evidence, he noted the letters he had received in response to a syndicated column by Mike Royko of the *Chicago Tribune*, urging readers to write Judge Ito to express their unhappiness with television coverage of the case.

In her response, Ms. Sager papered over her disbelief at the question and the premise underlying it with the usual deference of lawyers to judges. "My clients would be happy to organize a letter-writing campaign if that's the way the court wants to decide issues in this case," she said. He would not, she noted, determine the admissibility of DNA evidence based on a plebiscite. That comment, plus a similar observation by Douglas Mirell of the American Civil Liberties Union, prompted Judge Ito to explain himself.

"I find Mr. Royko's column thought-provoking from time to time," he said. "You should rest assured that I don't make any decision in this courtroom based on public opinion polls."

In fact, Judge Ito acknowledged he was "highly sensitive" to the Sheppard case, and not only because one of Mr. Simpson's lawyers, F. Lee Bailey, was successful in getting Dr. Sheppard's conviction overturned. He asked several lawyers what advice, if any, they would have for him in keeping things in check. Several lawyers assured him his conduct had already been exemplary, and had to be seen—on television, that is—to be fully appreciated.

"What's happened in this courtroom is the only thing that's pure in this case," Mr. Abrams said. "The public ought to see that."

To Remember History You Have to Repeat It

Tony Hoagland

The woman newscaster with the beautiful voice
is talking about the surface-to-air missiles:
What has she done to her hair? asks someone

and the flare and combustion on the screen behind her
is an orange haze against which her face is calm and clear.
She cut it back, says someone else, glancing at the menu,
raising a hand to get the waiter's attention—

The suicide bombers, they pass through her going one way,
and the funerals pass through going back the other;
The refugees are waiting at her border
like puppies waiting for adoption, the petroleum spill

gushes from her mouth, right before our eyes, but
she never cries or laughs or mispronounces.
I can imagine her going home, heating up

spaghetti from a can, telling her husband she's too tired tonight
—No wonder. She handles the hot sectors and razor wire.
She makes the failure of negotiations all right.

If I sneaked into her house tonight, if I went into her bedroom
and pressed my ear against her stomach, I believe that I could hear
troop movements and weather reports, staticky cries
of dying men, torn ligaments of this enormous body—

To remember history you have to repeat it and she does.
We stand around her like children and listen.
We stand around her like wild beasts disguised as children.

The Moon Hours

E. B. White and others

The moon, it turns out, is a great place for men. One-sixth gravity must be a lot of fun, and when Armstrong and Aldrin went into their bouncy little dance, like two happy children, it was a moment not only of triumph but of gaiety. The moon, on the other hand, is a poor place for flags. Ours looked stiff and awkward, trying to float on the breeze that does not blow. (There must be a lesson here somewhere.) It is traditional, of course, for explorers to plant the flag, but it struck us, as we watched with awe and admiration and pride, that our two fellows were universal men, not national men, and should have been equipped accordingly. Like every great river and every great sea, the moon belongs to none and belongs to all. It still holds the key to madness, still controls the tides that lap on shores everywhere, still guards the lovers who kiss in every land under no banner but the sky. What a pity that in our moment of triumph we did not forswear the familiar Iwo Jima scene and plant instead a device acceptable to all: a limp white handkerchief, perhaps, symbol of the common cold, which, like the moon, affects us all, unites us all.

By 10:00 p.m. Sunday, twelve hundred people had gathered at the intersection of Sixth Avenue and Fiftieth Street, between Radio City Music Hall and the Time-Life Plaza. Rain had been falling since 7:30 p.m., and umbrellas shifted from side to side and poked up above heads, obscuring some people's view of the thing everyone was trying to watch—a fifteen-by-fifteen-foot screen, on which NBC's coverage of the moon landing was being shown in color. A large sign read "Life and NASA Present Apollo: Man to the Moon," and huge photographs of the three Apollo astronauts stood in windows of the Time & Life Building. To the north of the television screen, a full-scale model of the lunar module was shielded from the rain by a plastic canopy, and other equipment had been given protective covers. The intersection was brightly lighted—two searchlights played on nearby buildings—and at this hour the area was extremely noisy. The noise was a constant, high-level mixture of automobile engines, horns, police whistles (twenty policemen were patrolling the area), the shouts of vendors (they moved through the crowd selling pennants, souvenir buttons, pretzels, and ice cream), the voices and beeps from the TV audio system, and the chatter of the people crowded on the sidewalks behind police barricades. But as the time for the astronauts' exit from the LM [lunar module] drew near, the crowd began to grow quiet. Anticipation was obvious in people's faces, and the talk became a sort of nervous undertone. At 10:15 p.m., a newcomer—a young man carrying a pack on his back—approached a man in a blue jacket and said, "I presume they've got to the moon."

"You don't know?" the man in blue asked. "Where have you been all day?"

"Just flown in. English," said the young man.

"Well, they're about ready to step out any second now," the man in blue said.

The young man said, "Stone me! They must be way ahead of schedule. Oh, great! This is fantastic!"

At 10:54 p.m., when the first shot of the LM—the lower part—appeared on the screen, in black and white, a cheer went up. When Neil Armstrong's foot was seen to touch the lunar surface, another cheer went up. When he stood with both feet on the moon, the people cheered and applauded a third time. Meanwhile, cars continued to roll by and the police moved incessantly in their attempt to keep the crowd behind the sidewalk barricades.

At 12:33 a.m. Monday, a No. 6 bus, without passengers, rolled silently down Seventh Avenue. A good number of people were walking west on Fiftieth Street—away from the Time-Life Plaza—and by this time only about three hundred people were left watching the big screen. The screen still showed the LM, whose legs looked bright in the sunlight. The rain, which had stopped for a while, had begun again, and people stood beneath umbrellas or improvised shelters of paper or plastic. At 12:41 a.m., a voice from Mission Control said, "This is Houston. You've got about ten minutes left now prior to commencing your EVA termination activities. Over." A young couple turned to each other and kissed. Working among the people, a man in coveralls began to sweep the plaza with a broom.

In the Eighteenth Precinct, on Fifty-Fourth Street west of Eighth Avenue, two patrolmen brought in a young man and a young woman in handcuffs. The couple were booked on suspicion of having mugged a man on West Forty-Fourth Street at about 11:00 p.m.—or at just about the time Armstrong was setting foot on the moon. Both suspects looked frightened and tired. Four police officers sat or stood in the main room. In an adjoining office, nine policemen—some in uniform and some in civilian clothes—sat relaxed in front of a television set that showed the lunar module. One man sat back with his feet on a desk, and others lounged on chairs or desks, watching the screen. They talked little, but from time to time someone spoke or laughed, and one young officer made a joke about having seen the whole thing before on *The Late Show*.

Inside the Chess & Checker Club of New York, which is upstairs at 212 West Forty-Second Street, eighteen men sat at small tables over game boards in a silence that was broken only occasionally, by desultory remarks. The Times Square Bowling Lanes, upstairs at 1482 Broadway, were similarly devoted to recreation—twenty-five people were bowling—but four people sat in the establishment's bar watching a television set, from which an announcer's voice was saying, "Heart rates of the crewmen are averaging between ninety and one hundred. The flight surgeon reports they're right on the predicted number of the B.T.U. units expended. . . . And he thinks they're in great shape."

To the customers in the Lincoln Bar, at the corner of Lenox Avenue and 135th Street, in Harlem, man's first step onto the face of the moon was greeted more with a whimper than a bang. Scarcely anyone was looking or listening when Armstrong placed his foot on the moon. A jukebox, in a dark corner, was blaring "What the World Needs Now," by the Sweet Inspirations, and a man with his back to the television set and a highball in his hand was telling a group of his friends about a girl he had just treated to a huge Chinese dinner who had declared on their way out of the restaurant that she now wanted a barbecue supper. "Man, I had to unload her," he said. "I didn't have enough left to put gas in my car." One of the customers reached out, touched him, and said, "Hey, buddy, they walking on the moon." The man with the highball put down his drink and walked out of the bar.

When Colonel Edwin Aldrin climbed down to join Armstrong, the conversations along the bar were louder than the conversation between moon and earth coming from the television set, and the jukebox in the corner had shifted to "I'm Going to Chicago, Sorry I Can't Take You." The bartender—a short, amiable white man with a bald head and a clip-on bow tie, who took care of one end of the bar while a black barmaid took care of the other—went and turned off the jukebox.

"Hey, leave that thing on, man!" a male voice yelled. "We ain't care nothin' 'bout no moon."

"I do," the bartender said. "And there's a few other people here that do, too."

"Damn!" the same voice said. "I hope those Whiteys never come back. They might just decide to stay there, too."

"Nah," a female voice said. "You can be sure the white man don't want to live up there. It's got no gold, it's got no silver, it's got no oil. And ain't that what Whitey wants? He don't want no part of all that rock up there."

At this point, the man whose girl had demanded the barbecue came back and started telling another group the story.

"Be quiet," the barmaid, a buxom, masterful-looking woman, said. "You full of nothin' but Seagram's gin. I want to see the men walking on the moon."

"Hush with your moon," he replied. "You believe any of that wild stuff?"

"You don't really believe they walking on the moon?" the barmaid said. "I can see you ain't ready for the moon yet. You still in another age, with the cotton-pickin' machine. Or maybe you just in another orbit, with your Seagram's."

"Hell!" he said. "Where *you* at?"

"I'm a moon maid, baby."

At the headquarters of the National Broadcasting Company, in Rockefeller Center, the Central Control Room, from which NBC coverage of the lunar landing was governed, was hot and stuffy, being packed with people in shirtsleeves. The controllers worked at two tiers of equipment-laden consoles, facing a wall covered with a formidable array of monitors that bore such legends as "HOUSTON," "HOUSTON POOL," "VIDEOGRAPH," "CAMERA 1," "CAMERA 2," and "CAMERA 6." The front, and lower, tier of consoles was occupied by technicians, and in the center of it sat the director—Tony Messuri, a bald man wearing a headset and a pink shirt. To the right and left of this tier were small rooms that were also packed with technicians. Executives of the NBC News Division occupied the second tier in Central Control, and the center of this tier was occupied by the executive producer of the NBC Space Unit—James Kitchell, a bushy-haired, young-looking man wearing a short-sleeved black shirt. Kitchell, too, had a headset on, and directly in front of him, within a few inches of his right hand, there was a box equipped with a row of spring-loaded switches. These switches gave Kitchell immediate access to the NBC studios—to a so-called Huntley-Brinkley Deck, which was a mezzanine arrangement a few doors away from Central Control, and in which at the moment David Brinkley and Frank McGee were occupying the anchor desk, and also to Studio 8-H, a very large area that was originally designed for broadcasting performances by Arturo Toscanini and the NBC Symphony. Just then Studio 8-H had no traces of the concert hall about it. On one wall, above a raised platform, there was a twelve-foot-wide blowup of a photographic mosaic showing at least the major craters of Apollo 11's Landing Site Two, the target area being marked off with a long elliptical line. Along the wall to the right, there was a three-dimensional model of the moon, about six feet across, set against a blue-white-and-gray backdrop presumably representing the Milky Way, and, beside this, a twenty-foot-long map of the central portion of the moon's equatorial region, showing the flight path taken by the LM and its approximate position on the lunar surface. A third section of Studio 8-H contained a twenty-two-foot-high mockup—the actual size—of the LM. It had detailed representations of the cabin and instrument facilities, of the shiny Mylar insulation covering the descent stage, and of the porch, the exit ladder, the foot pads, and the equipment-stowage area. Then, there were full-scale models of the command module and of the combined command and service modules. But Kitchell's spring-loaded switches gave him access to a great deal more than this. It was less than twenty years ago that NBC was able to boast of having accomplished the feat of showing simultaneously, in split-screen images, the East and West Coasts of the United States. Now Kitchell was able to switch in instantaneously—through commercial-satellite communication—images of NBC correspondents and people *they* had access to in London, Cologne, and Tokyo. And already during the Apollo 11 mission he had been able to relay television shots of the earth itself made from space, and of portions of the moon as the command module orbited it.

Now, a few seconds after the voice of Frank McGee said, on the air, "Neil Armstrong's on his stomach, feet first, coming out," Messuri shouted to a technician responsible for the superimposition of titles on the screen, "Set me up 'First Live Pictures from the Moon,' baby!"

"Go to Houston!" Kitchell said loudly.

"And *take it!*" Messuri cried.

"Here it comes!" Kitchell shouted.

On the monitor marked "PROGRAM" there appeared a ghostly, unclear, yet unmistakable black-and-white image of the lower portion of a heavily suited astronaut descending the LM ladder. The control room was filled with cheers and clapping.

"The foot!" Messuri cried.

Armstrong's foot descended.

"Put 'First Step on the Moon,'" Kitchell ordered, and then he said, "Wait! He's not on the moon yet. So far, he's just on the foot pad."

"That's O.K.," Messuri objected. He added, "After all, what's the foot pad connected to?"

"The shin bone," someone said, and there was some technician laughter.

Armstrong's foot could now be seen raised as he tried mounting the lowest rung of the LM ladder, and then his voice could be heard: "I'm at the foot of the ladder. . . . The surface appears to be very, very fine-grained. . . . It's one small step. . . ."

"Take it! 'First Step on the Moon.' "

Everything became very quiet in the control room as the ghostly figure, white on a white ground, against a dark sky, touched what seemed like white rigging. It all looked like an old, grained, scratchy movie showing some hooded, frost-shrouded early polar explorer standing by the bulwark of an icebound ship.

"O.K., now let's get ready for Nixon's talk with the astronauts," Kitchell said. "Better start setting up a split screen with the White House and the lunar shots." After a pause, he added, looking at the shot on the air, "It's unbelievable. Unbelievable!"

Armstrong's figure could be seen moving about the lunar surface as he tested his walk. He began walking with long, loping steps.

"Look at that!" Kitchell said, enthralled. "Look at him! Galloping across the moon!"

"The White Knight!" a technician said.

On one of the monitors, a shot of President Nixon appeared. He was not on the air, and obviously realized that he wasn't. He was gesturing toward someone out of range, holding out a hand and waggling it as though saying no. After a while, the technicians began to rearrange the image of the president so that it fitted into the upper left-hand corner of the screen; it was to be superimposed on pictures from the moon. While this was going on, Colonel Aldrin also descended from the LM, and then it became apparent, from the blurring and heaving, that Armstrong had taken the television camera from the equipment bay and was walking with it away from the LM. On one of the monitors, the image of the president, sitting at his desk, appeared in the corner of this heaving scene; he looked as though ocean waves were sweeping and swirling against him. Then the lunar camera was trained on the LM from about forty feet away, and Messuri began to complain that now the left-hand-corner picture of the president was impinging on the shot of the LM, which also stood to the left of the screen.

"I'm lousing up my moon picture," Messuri said.

Eventually, Armstrong centered the LM in his camera, and Messuri arranged the shot of the president so that the split-screen image of him did not unduly cover the image of the LM.

Then the president made his telephone call to the astronauts, the interchange went off the air, and for a few moments, before the television lights in the White House were extinguished, Mr. Nixon could be seen on the monitor, disengaging, with the help of a technician, a microphone he had had about his neck.

As the lunar broadcast proceeded, Donald Meaney, a vice-president of the NBC News Division, who was sitting immediately to Kitchell's right, left the control room for a few minutes, and then returned to remark, "One thing I think this is doing is to bring people together. The picture is going everywhere in the world by satellite. I hear they're getting a great picture in Bucharest. And in *Belgrade*. And, you know, nobody has the inside track on seeing these pictures. The scientists in Houston, the president of the United States, all of us in this room, perhaps Serbian peasants—they're all seeing the same fantastic live pictures at the same time. Nobody any better than anybody else, really. Maybe that holds something pretty good for all of us."

In the ground-floor apartment of a brownstone in the East Nineties, at around 8:30 p.m., guests began to arrive for a moon-watching party that was being given by two young men just out of law school. The male guests, most of whom were young lawyers, like their hosts, were dressed informally but expensively, some in light-colored summer suits and some in richly colored shirts. The ties in the room were wide but not flowery. The women, who seemed a few years younger than the men, were also expensively dressed, many in silky, boldly patterned bell-bottom trouser suits. The arriving guests sat down on a sofa, on chairs, or on a mattress on the floor which had been brought in from a bedroom. The political temper of the group soon established itself as liberalism-taken-for-granted. Some of the young men had spent time in the last few years working for liberal political candidates. Although so recently out of law school, many of them had already acquired the self-assured, forceful handshakes of successful lawyers, and had already adopted the lawyerish mannerisms of fixing their listeners with a frank gaze and speaking to them in carefully measured tones. On the television screen, Walter Cronkite was waiting for the astronauts to finish checking their spacecraft in preparation for their walk on the moon's surface. The people in the living room were a loosely connected collection of friends, and many of them were catching up on each other's recent past. There was a hubbub of many conversations.

"I think I met you at a skating party."

"If you have all your defense mechanisms up . . ."

"Shall we introduce them *now* or later?"

Conversation about the moon landing was restricted to jokes or brief comments. Many people seemed to want something to happen that was more exciting than what could really happen.

"It would be great if they found an animal," one man said.

"We've seen everything in simulation. They might as well do it all in simulation," a girl said.

Several people said they were not sure whether the CBS simulation of the LM landing being shown at that moment was real or not.

"Hey, those furry claws coming down the ladder!" someone said.

"No. Coming out of a crater," said a girl.

The moment when CBS expected Armstrong to emerge from the LM arrived. When the exit was delayed for ten minutes while the astronauts continued to check their equipment, a hush finally fell over the group. After several minutes, a man said, "They're having one more hand of poker." Then the voices of the astronauts began to announce Armstrong's emergence onto the porch at the top of the ladder. The hush continued. Suddenly, a telephone in the next room rang, and a young man went to answer it. When he returned, Walter Cronkite was saying, "Commander Armstrong is about to pull the ring that will give us our first live television coverage from the moon." The telephone rang again, and someone said, "Let it ring," but another man, after hesitating, went to answer it. The landscape of the moon appeared on the screen. At the top of the screen was the jet black of space. In the middle was the brilliant streak of whiteness that was the lunar landscape. At the bottom was the blackness of the LM's shadow. The ladder to the ground cut vertically across the screen. Armstrong's foot appeared. The young man returned from answering the phone and announced, "There's a girl up at the corner who can't find the party."

The group was riveted to the screen in silence during Armstrong's descent to the ground, during his first steps and his first words, and during Colonel Aldrin's descent. Then there was some more joking.

"When we find the first moon men, we'll have to decide which ones to support—the ones from the South or the ones from the North. We'll have to send military advisers." Conversations about other matters started again.

Aldrin, after taking a few steps, began to jump up and down on the moon. "Magnificent!" he said.

On the sofa, a couple began talking about a girl named Margie.

Suddenly, Armstrong emerged with amazing speed from the black shadow of the LM into the brilliant sunlight. There was a sigh from the group; then it fell silent again for a moment. As Armstrong set up the television camera to look back on the LM, conversation resumed.

"There's something interesting in a crater here!" Armstrong called out as he moved away from the LM.

A girl who was sitting on the floor began to tell about a friend of hers who had married a nun. "The nun was in the lecture course he was giving," she said. "He had her out of her robes and married in two weeks, and a year later she had twins."

On the screen, Aldrin was loping in a circle on the surface of the moon in front of the LM.

The girl looked up at the screen and cried out, "I just don't believe it!"

"I'm used to it already," a young man next to her said.

"When you get blasé about people going to the moon, you *know* you've changed," she said.

On the second floor of the living quarters of Gracie Mansion, Mayor Lindsay, in a yellow sports shirt, gray slacks, and brown loafers, was watching CBS on a color-television set. On the mayor's knees was a three-page statement on the moon walk; he had been cutting it for the past half hour and appeared still dissatisfied with it. To his left, Jay Kriegel, a young assistant, sat on a chaise longue with his shoes off, looking intently at simulations of what was to come. Other staff members—most of them in their twenties—sprawled in chairs and on the floor. The only man wearing a suit and tie was a Democratic politician from Queens who had arrived earlier in the evening to offer the mayor his support in the coming election. The room they were sitting in belonged to the mayor's daughter Anne, who was away at camp. Tacked to the door were signs: "SNOOPY LIVES HERE," "NO PED-DLERS," "ENTERING TWILIGHT ZONE." In the next room—the master bedroom—Mrs. Lindsay was also looking at a color set. Watching with her were another daughter, Kathy; a Columbia Law School student who is a friend of Kathy's; a driver for the mayor; two of the three policemen who are usually on duty outside Gracie Mansion; and a family friend. In intermittent attendance in both rooms was Detective Sergeant Pat Vecchio, a wiry, intense man who is in charge of protecting the mayor.

In Anne Lindsay's room, as the hatch of the LM was about to be opened, the Democratic politician was talking precinct strategy in Queens with Richard Aurelio, the mayor's campaign manager, while a young assistant to the mayor lying on the floor proclaimed, "Procaccino just issued a statement pledging to make the moon safe for law and order."

Two more assistants to the mayor, Sid Davidoff and Barry Gottehrer, arrived, drenched. Because of the rain, the mayor wondered aloud whether he ought to go, as he had planned, to the Moon-In, the city-sponsored celebration in the Sheep Meadow in Central Park. Mrs. Lindsay, who had appeared at the door, shook her head. "With those men walking on the moon, they won't be watching *you*," she said to her husband, and she went away, grinning.

Jay Kriegel passed a notebook to the mayor. "Here's your schedule for Wednesday."

Lindsay looked away from the television screen, studied the page, and grimaced. "That's murder," he said. "Just murder."

The first pictures of Armstrong setting foot on the moon were about to come through. Conversation in the room stopped. The mayor leaned forward, his statement slipping to the floor. "There's a foot!" he said. "There's a foot on the moon!" His eyes fixed on the screen, the mayor shook his head. "Fantastic! God, this is dramatic!"

As it became clear that Armstrong and Aldrin were having no difficulties, the moon watchers at Gracie Mansion relaxed.

Picking up his statement from the floor, the mayor read it again, and cut out another paragraph. Gottehrer and Davidoff were now convinced that he should go to the Moon-In. The mayor agreed, but he kept delaying his departure. "Look at that shot of the horizon!" he said.

Finally, at 11:45 p.m., he rose and went into the master bedroom. He returned in a beige jacket, a white shirt, and a blue-figured tie. The mayor and Mrs. Lindsay, with Davidoff, Gottehrer, Pat Vecchio, and the press secretary, Tom Morgan, squeezed into a black car in front of the mansion.

As the car moved west, Vecchio, in the front seat, announced, "No matter what's happening, I'm not going to forget about Columbus."

The mayor laughed. The car cut into Central Park, passing a hansom cab, whose driver shouted, "You're going against traffic!"

"That guy doesn't have his lamp lit," Davidoff said. "Give him a ticket."

"Come on," the mayor said. "He's right."

At the Sheep Meadow, Vecchio guided Lindsay to and from three television interviews. Just before the second one began, the mayor, who seemed blinded by the bright lights, was approached by a slender woman. She shook his hand vigorously, saying, "Congratulations, Mr. mayor!" He blinked, and blinked again. It was Mrs. Lindsay.

"Save your moon glow for November!" a woman shouted as the mayor approached his car following a swift tour of the Meadow.

"Yeah, Mayor baby!" someone else roared, to the mayor's delight.

The mayor leaned out of the car window and grabbed the hand of a policeman. "Thanks, Fred. You guys did a good job," he said. Turning to his wife as the car moved away, he remarked, "That's a great cop. King of the towaways."

Hours earlier, as the rain came down steadily and a premature darkness fell over the city, hundreds of people streamed through Central Park and converged on the center of the Sheep Meadow to join the Moon-In crowd that was already standing in a huge circle around three nine-by-twelve-foot television screens set up in a triangular formation and tuned to three different channels. The meadow was filled with puddles and mud holes, and many of the younger spectators had shucked their shoes and were negotiating the slippery terrain in bare feet. Some people carried umbrellas, others pulled coats or jackets over their heads, and a good many seemed happy simply to give themselves up to the rain and the prospect of a soaking. In front of the CBS screen, five young men in beards shared a large green-red-and-yellow-striped beach umbrella; next to them stood a couple huddled beneath a bed quilt; and nearby three girls who had contrived a makeshift tent out of an Army-surplus blanket and a pair of sanitation trash baskets were playing Scrabble. Overhead, three searchlight beams met, forming a soft halo of haze, through which the rain fell in silver sheets. Shortly before nine o'clock, Walter Cronkite announced that the hatch of the LM would be opened in half an hour, and the word was immediately carried over the meadow on hundreds of lips. "The hatch," people whispered. "The hatch is going to be opened. The hatch . . ." A few minutes later, the rain stopped and umbrellas were furled. The crowd around the television screens was so dense that movement was nearly impossible, and here and there, in a vast assemblage that filled the meadow almost as far as the eye could see, small children, their eyes blinking with sleep and wonderment, were hoisted upon their fathers' shoulders. The rain started to come down again, and hundreds of umbrellas were unfurled, only to be furled again as people in the rear protested that they couldn't see the screens.

As the scheduled moment for the hatch opening approached, the crowd grew still, and every gaze appeared to be fixed on a television screen. Then came an announcement that the moon walk would be delayed for half an hour, and there was a sustained groan of disappointment. At 9:45 p.m., Houston could be heard through a crackle of static calling to the command module, and a few minutes later the crowd, which had grown hushed again, burst into applause when the astronauts were informed by the voice of Mission Control, "You are go for cabin depressurization." The rain stopped and started several times during the next half hour, and dozens of spectators, weary from standing and long since soaked, began to sit down in the wet grass and mud. When the hatch opened, and Armstrong's booted foot could be seen groping for the rungs of the landing vehicle's ladder, and the totally unreal words "LIVE FROM THE SURFACE OF THE MOON" appeared upon the screens, there was a gasp, as if everyone had taken a quick breath. There was a smattering of applause, and then dozens of flashbulbs began popping as cameramen took pictures of a vast sea of faces held perfectly still at the same upturned angle and frozen into identical expressions of rapture and awe.

For the next twenty minutes, the crowd feasted silently upon the spectacle unfolding before it, and when Aldrin came down the ladder to join Armstrong, there was a loud burst of applause, laughter, and cheering. After a short while, there was a surge away from the screens as people started moving about and stretching their cramped legs. Some of the spectators headed for a large refreshment tent that had been set up on the east side of the meadow. Many of these people moved on to a nearby bandstand, where an orchestra had swung into a 1930s version of "Blue Moon." When, at twelve minutes before midnight, President Nixon came on the television screens to talk with the astronauts, many people turned back toward the center of the meadow to rejoin the hundreds who had stayed to watch Armstrong and Aldrin in their historic walk. After the president had finished, it was announced that Armstrong had been on the surface of the moon for fifty-nine minutes, and suddenly Aldrin could be seen floating gracefully over the lunar surface as he performed mobility exercises. The jazz band that had been blaring away in the background was replaced by a rock-and-roll ensemble, whose performance raised the decibel count in the meadow even higher, and the spectators crowded closer to the television screens in order to hear the astronauts describe the lunar landscape and to watch them walk around scooping up samples of its rock.

At one o'clock, the voice of Mission Control told Aldrin to "head on up the ladder," and announced that Armstrong had been on the surface of the moon slightly more than two hours. The rain was beating down steadily now, but only when the hatch of the landing vehicle was closed, eleven minutes later, did the last, diehard spectators turn away. Some hippies rushed by chanting "Free the moon!" Then people by the hundreds began streaming toward Fifth Avenue. Behind them, like an unblinking eye, the NBC screen still showed a picture of the LM sitting at Tranquility Base. The astronauts were safe inside and the moon walk was over, but almost everyone kept looking back over his shoulder through the downpour, as if to reassure himself that what he had seen with his eyes in the Sheep Meadow had really taken place upon the moon.

COMMERCIAL BREAK

COMMERCIAL BREAK

When is a shower not just a shower? In "Getting Dirty" (1988), **Mark Crispin Miller** takes an in-depth look at a soap commercial, anatomizing the social anxieties at work beneath its breezy surface, and answering critics who claim he's reading too much into a simple advertisement.

Getting Dirty

Mark Crispin Miller

We are outside a house, looking in the window, and this is what we see: a young man, apparently nude and half-crazed with anxiety, lunging toward the glass. "Gail!" he screams, as he throws the window open and leans outside, over a flower box full of geraniums: "The most important shower of my life, and you switch deodorant soap!" He is, we now see, only half-naked, wearing a towel around his waist; and he shakes a packaged bar of soap—"Shield"—in one accusing hand. Gail, wearing a blue man-tailored shirt, stands outside, below the window, clipping a hedge. She handles this reproach with an ease that suggests years of contempt. "Shield is better," she explains patiently, in a voice somewhat deeper than her husband's. "It's extra strength." (Close-up of the package in the husband's hand, Gail's efficient finger gliding along beneath the legend, THE EXTRA STRENGTH DEODORANT SOAP.) "Yeah," whimpers Mr. Gail, "but my first call on J. J. Siss [*sic*], the company's *toughest customer*, and now *this*!" Gail nods with broad mock-sympathy, and stands firm: "Shield fights odor better, so you'll feel *cleaner*," she assures her husband, who darts away with a jerk of panic, as Gail rolls her eyes heavenward and gently shakes her head, as if to say, "What a half-wit!"

Cut to our hero, as he takes his important shower. No longer frantic, he now grins down at himself, apparently delighted to be caked with Shield, which, in its detergent state, has the consistency of wet cement. He then goes out of focus, as if glimpsed through a shower door. "Clinical tests prove," proclaims an eager baritone, "Shield fights odor better than the *leading* deodorant soap!" A bar of Shield (green) and a bar of that other soap (yellow) zip up the screen with a festive toot, forming a sort of graph which demonstrates that Shield does, indeed, "fight odor better, so you'll feel *cleaner!*"

This particular contest having been settled, we return to the major one, which has yet to be resolved. Our hero reappears, almost transformed: calmed down, dressed up, his voice at least an octave lower. "I *do* feel cleaner!" he announces cheerily, leaning into the doorway of a room where Gail is arranging flowers. She pretends to be ecstatic at this news, and he comes toward her, setting himself up for a profound humiliation by putting on a playful air of suave command. Adjusting his tie like a real man of the world, he saunters over to his wife and her flower bowl, where he plucks a dainty purple flower and lifts it to his lapel: "And," he boasts throughout all this, trying to make his voice sound even deeper, "with old J. J.'s business and my brains—" "—you'll . . . *clean up again?*" Gail asks with suggestive irony, subverting his authoritative pose by leaning against him, draping one hand over his shoulder to dangle a big yellow daisy down his chest. Taken aback, he shoots her a distrustful look, and she titters at him.

Finally, the word SHIELD appears in extreme close-up and the camera pulls back, showing two bars of the soap, one packaged and one not, on display amidst an array of steely bubbles. "Shield fights odor better, so you'll feel *cleaner!*" the baritone reminds us, and then our hero's face appears once more, in a little square over the unpackaged bar of soap: "I feel *cleaner* than *ever before!*" he insists, sounding faintly unconvinced.

Is all this as stupid as it seems at first? Or is there, just beneath the surface of this moronic narrative, some noteworthy design, intended to appeal to (and to worsen) some of the anxieties of modern life? A serious look at this particular trifle might lead us to some strange discoveries.

We are struck, first of all, by the commercial's pseudofeminism, an advertising ploy with a long history, and one ubiquitous on television nowadays. Although the whole subject deserves more extended treatment, this commercial offers us an especially rich example of the strategy. Typically, it woos its female viewers—i.e., those who choose the soap in most households—with a fantasy of dominance; and it does so by inverting the actualities of woman's lot through a number of imperceptible details. For instance, in this marriage it is the wife, and not the husband, who gets to keep her name; and Gail's name, moreover, is a potent one, because of its brevity and its homonymic connotation. (If this housewife were more delicately named, called "Lillian" or "Cecilia," it would lessen her illusory strength.) She is also equipped in more noticeable ways: she's the one who wears the button-down shirt in this family, she's the one who's competent both outdoors and in the house, and it is she, and only she, who wields the tool.

These visual details imply that Gail is quite a powerful housewife, whereas her nameless mate is a figure of embarrassing impotence. This "man," in fact, is actually Gail's *wife*: he is utterly feminized, striking a posture and displaying attributes which men have long deplored in women. In other words, this commercial, which apparently takes the woman's side, is really the expression (and reflection) of misogyny. Gail's husband is dependent and hysterical, entirely without that self-possession which we expect from solid, manly types, like Gail. This is partly the result of his demeanor: in the opening scene, his voice sometimes cracks ludicrously, and he otherwise betrays the shrill desperation of a man who can't remember where he left his scrotum. The comic effect of this frenzy, moreover, is subtly enhanced by the mise-en-scène, which puts the man in a conventionally feminine position—in dishabille, looking down from a window. Thus we infer that he is sheltered and housebound, a modern Juliet calling for his/her Romeo; or—more appropriately—the image suggests a scene in some suburban red-light district, presenting this husband as an item on display, like the flowers just below his stomach, available for anyone's enjoyment, at a certain price. Although in one way contradictory, these implications are actually quite congruous, for they both serve to emasculate the husband, so that the wife might take his place, or play his part.

Such details, some might argue, need not have been the conscious work of this commercial's makers. The authors, that is, might have worked by instinct rather than design, and so would have been no more aware of their work's psychosocial import than we ourselves: they just wanted to make the guy look like a wimp, merely for the purposes of domestic comedy. While such an argument certainly does apply to many ads, in this case it is unlikely. Advertising agencies do plenty of research, by which we can assume that they don't select their tactics arbitrarily. They take pains to analyze the culture which they help to sicken, and then, with much wit and cynicism, use their insights in devising their small dramas. This commercial is a subtle and meticulous endorsement of castration, meant to play on certain widespread guilts and insecurities; and all we need to do to demonstrate this fact is to subject the two main scenes to the kind of visual analysis which commercials, so brief and broad, tend to resist (understandably). The ad's visual implications are too carefully achieved to have been merely accidental or unconscious.

The crucial object in the opening shot is that flower box with its bright geraniums, which is placed directly in front of the husband's groin. This clever stroke of composition has the immediate effect of equating our hero's manhood with a bunch of flowers. This is an exquisitely perverse suggestion, rather like using a cigar to represent the Eternal Feminine: flowers are frail, sweet, and largely ornamental, hardly an appropriate phallic symbol, but (of course) a venerable symbol of *maidenhood*. The geraniums stand, then, not for the husband's virility, but for its absence.

More than a clever instance of inversion, furthermore, these phallic blossoms tell us something odd about this marital relationship. As Gail, clippers in hand, turns from the hedge to calm her agitated man, she appears entirely capable of calming him quite drastically, if she hasn't done so already (which might explain his hairless chest and high-pitched voice). She has the power, that is, to take away whatever slender potency he may possess, and uses the power repeatedly, trimming her husband (we infer) as diligently as she prunes her foliage. And, as she can snip his manhood, so too can she restore it, which is what the second scene implies. Now the flower bowl has replaced the flower box as the visual crux, dominating the bottom center of the frame with a crowd of blooms. As the husband, cleaned and dressed, comes to stand beside his wife, straining to affect a new authority, the flower bowl too appears directly at his lower center; so that Gail, briskly adding flowers to the bouquet, appears to be replenishing his vacant groin with extra stalks. He has a lot to thank her for, it seems: she is his helpmate, confidante, adviser, she keeps his house and grounds in order, and she is clearly the custodian of the family jewels.

Of course, her restoration of his potency cannot be complete, or he might shatter her mastery by growing a bit too masterful himself. He could start choosing his own soap, or take her shears away, or—worst of all—walk out for good. Therefore, she punctures his momentary confidence by taunting him with that big limp daisy, countering his lordly gesture with the boutonniere by flaunting that symbol of his floral status. He can put on whatever airs he likes, but she still has his fragile vigor firmly in her hand.

Now what, precisely, motivates this sexless battle of the sexes? That is, what really underlies this tense and hateful marriage, making the man so weak, the woman so contemptuously helpful? The script, seemingly nothing more than a series of inanities, contains the answer to these questions, conveying, as it does, a concern with cleanliness that amounts to an obsession: "Shield fights odor better, so you'll feel cleaner!" "I *do* feel cleaner!" "Shield fights odor better, so you'll feel *cleaner!*" "I feel *cleaner* then *ever before!*" Indeed, the commercial emphasizes the feeling of cleanliness even more pointedly than the name of the product, implying, by its very insistence, a feeling of dirtiness, an apprehension of deep filth.

And yet there is not a trace of dirt in the vivid world of this commercial. Unlike many ads for other soaps, this one shows no sloppy children, no sweat-soaked workingmen with blackened hands, not even a bleary housewife in need of her morning shower. We never even glimpse the ground in Gail's world, nor is her husband even faintly smudged. In fact, the filth which Shield supposedly "fights" is not physical but psychological besmirchment: Gail's husband feels soiled because of what he has to do for a living, in order to keep Gail in that nice big house, happily supplied with shirts and shears.

"My first call on J. J. Siss, the company's *toughest customer,* and now *this!*" The man's anxiety is yet another feminizing trait, for it is generally women, and not men, who are consumed by doubts about the sweetness of their bodies, which must never be offensive to the guys who run the world. (This real anxiety is itself aggravated by commercials.) Gail's husband must play the female to the mighty J. J. Siss, a name whose oxymoronic character implies perversion: "J. J." is a stereotypical nickname for the potent boss, while "Sis" is a term of endearment, short for "sister" (and perhaps implying "sissy," too, in this case). Gail's husband must do his boyish best to please the voracious J. J. Siss, just as a prostitute must satisfy a demanding trick, or "tough customer." It is therefore perfectly fitting that this employee refer to the encounter, not as a "meeting" or "appointment," but as a "call"; and his demeaning posture in the window—half-dressed and bent over—conveys, we now see, a definitive implication.

Gail's job as the "understanding wife" is not to rescue her husband from these sordid obligations, but to help him meet them successfully. She may seem coolly self-sufficient, but she actually depends on her husband's attractiveness, just as a pimp relies on the charm of his whore. And, also like a pimp, she has to keep her girl in line with occasional reminders of who's boss. When her husband starts getting uppity *après la douche*, she jars him from the very self-assurance which she had helped him to discover, piercing that "shield" which was her gift.

"And, with old J. J.'s business and my brains—" "—you'll . . . *clean up again*?" He means, of course, that he'll work fiscal wonders with old J. J.'s account, but his fragmentary boast contains a deeper significance, upon which Gail plays with sadistic cleverness. "Old J. J.'s business and my brains" implies a feminine self-description, since it suggests a variation on the old commonplace of "brains vs. brawn": J. J.'s money, in the world of this commercial (as in ours), amounts to brute strength, which the flexible husband intends to complement with his mother wit. Gail's retort broadens this unconscious hint of homosexuality: "—you'll . . . *clean up again*?" Given the monetary nature of her husband's truncated remark, the retort must mean primarily, "You'll make a lot of money." If this were all it meant, however, it would not be a joke, nor would the husband find it so upsetting. Moreover, we have no evidence that Gail's husband ever "cleaned up"—i.e., made a sudden fortune—in the past. Rather, the ad's milieu and dramatis personae suggest upward mobility, gradual savings, and a yearly raise, rather than one prior killing. What Gail is referring to, in fact, with that "again," is her husband's shower: she implies that what he'll have to do, after his "call" on J. J. Siss, is, quite literally, wash himself off. Like any other tidy hooker, this man will have to clean up after taking on a tough customer, so that he might be ready to take on someone else.

These suggestions of pederasty are intended, not as a literal characterization of the husband's job but as a metaphor for what it takes to get ahead: Gail's husband, like most white-collar workers, must debase himself to make a good impression, toadying to his superiors, offering himself, body and soul, to the corporation. Maybe, therefore, it isn't really Gail who has neutered him; it may be his way of life that has wrought the ugly change. How, then, are women represented here? The commercial does deliberately appeal to women, offering them a sad fantasy of control; but it also, perhaps inadvertently, illuminates the unhappiness which makes that fantasy attractive.

The husband's status, it would seem, should make Gail happy, since it makes her physically comfortable, and yet Gail can't help loathing her husband for the degradations which she helps him undergo. For her part of the bargain is, ultimately, no less painful than his. She has to do more than put up with him; she has to prepare him for his world of affairs, and then must help him to conceal the shame. Of course, it's all quite hopeless. She clearly despises the man whom she would bolster; and the thing which she provides to help him "feel cleaner than ever before" is precisely what has helped him do the job that's always made him feel so dirty. "A little water clears us of this deed" is her promise, which is false, for she is just as soiled as her doomed husband, however fresh and well-ironed she may look.

Of course, the ad not only illuminates this mess, but helps perpetuate it, by obliquely gratifying the guilts, terrors, and resentments that underlie it and arise from it. The strategy is not meant to be noticed, but works through the apparent comedy, which must therefore be studied carefully, not passively received. Thus, thirty seconds of ingenious advertising, which we can barely stand to watch, tell us something more than we might want to know about the souls of men and women under corporate capitalism.

AFTERWORD

Advertising Age came back at this essay with an edifying two-pronged put-down. In the issue for June 7, 1982, Fred Danzig (now the magazine's editor) devoted his weekly column to the Shield analysis: "The professor prunes a television trifle," ran the headline. After a genial paraphrase of my argument, Danzig reported a few of the things I'd told him in a telephone conversation, and then finally got down to the necessary business of dismissive chuckling: "[Miller's] confession that he had watched the Shield spot more than fifteen times quickly enabled me to diagnose his problem: self-inflicted acute soap storyboard sickness. This condition inevitably leads to a mind spasm, to hallucination." The column featured the ad's crucial frames, over a caption quoting an unnamed "Lever executive": "We can hardly wait for Mr. Miller to get his hands on the Old Testament. His comments merit no comment from us; the Shield commercial speaks for itself."

Leaving aside (with difficulty) that naive crack about the Bible, I point here to the exemplary suppressiveness of his seeming "trifle" in *Advertising Age*. Indeed, "the Shield commercial speaks for itself," but the guardians of the spectacle try to talk over it, permitting it no significance beyond the superficial pitch: "—so you'll feel *cleaner!*" Through managerial scorn ("no comment") and journalistic ridicule ("mind spasm . . . hallucination"), they would shut down all discussion. (J. Walter Thompson later refused to send anyone to debate the matter with me on a radio program.) Thus was a divergent reading written off as the perversity of yet another cracked "professor"—when in fact it was the ad itself that was perverse.

Although that campaign did not appeal to its TV audience (J. Walter Thompson ultimately lost the Shield account), such belligerent "common sense" does have a most receptive public. While the ad makers—and others—insist that "people today are ad-wise," in fact most Americans still perceive the media image as transparent, a sign that simply says what it means and means what it says. They therefore tend to dismiss any intensive explication as a case of "reading too much into it"—an objection that is philosophically dubious, albeit useful to the ad makers and their allies. It is now, perhaps, one obligation of the academic humanists, empowered, as they are, by critical theory, to demonstrate at large the faultiness—and the dangers—of that objection.

A historical note on the Shield commercial's pseudofeminism. Since 1982, the contemptuous housewife has all but vanished from the antiseptic scene of advertising; Gail was among the last of an endangered species. By now, the housewife/mother is a despised figure—most despised by actual housewife/mothers, who make up 60 percent of the prime time audience. Since these viewers now prefer to see themselves represented as executives, or at least as mothers with beepers and attaché cases, the hausfrau of the past, whether beaming or sneering, has largely been obliterated by the advertisers. In 1985, Advertising to Women Inc., a New York advertising agency, found that, out of 250 current TV ads, only nine showed recognizable moms.

This is a triumph not for women's liberation, but for advertising; for, now that Mom is missing from the ads, presumably off knocking heads together in the boardroom, it is the commodity that seems to warm her home and tuck her children in at night.

In any case, the Shield strategy itself has certainly outlasted the wry and/or perky Mommy-imagoes of yesteryear. Indeed, because the sexes are now at war within the scene of advertising (and elsewhere), the nasty visual metaphors have become ubiquitous.

POLITICS AND TV

HAVE YOU NO SENSE OF DECENCY?

POLITICS AND TV: HAVE YOU NO SENSE OF DECENCY?

The writers in this section look at how television intersects with national politics and at how political questions of representation and power affect what gets televised and who controls the televised image.

In "The First Presidential Debate" (2008), **Alan Schroeder** analyzes how television coverage of candidates' debates wrought major changes in the American political landscape.

"The Revolution Will Not Be Televised" (1971) by poet and musician **Gil Scott-Heron** contrasts the television image and its comfortable consumption with a coming unmediated rebellion.

In the first-person poem "The Missing Remote" (2003), **Diane Lockward**'s speaker relates the thrill of having captured a partner's "gizmo" and exults in having exclusive use of its power.

Ariel Levy's "Dolls and Feelings: Jill Soloway's Post-Patriarchal Television" (2015) offers an in-depth look at how Soloway and her shows, including *Transparent*, have reshaped expectations of gender both onscreen and off.

In "Pop History on an Epic Scale: *Roots*" (2001), **Donald Bogle** considers how the blockbuster 1970s miniseries came to be made, how it was received at the time, and how it has affected television series since.

The First Presidential Debate

(selection)

Alan Schroeder

---

*"I should say the most important thing about the business
of government and politics is not to bore the people."*

—Richard Nixon to Jack Paar on
The Tonight Show, August 25, 1960

September 26, 1960. At exactly 7:30 p.m., a shiny Oldsmobile carrying Vice President Richard M. Nixon pulled into an interior drive at the CBS broadcast facility in downtown Chicago. As with other details surrounding the first presidential debate in history, the timing of Nixon's arrival at this skating rink turned TV station had been meticulously plotted. Like dueling divas, Nixon and his opponent, John F. Kennedy, would reach the studio a comfortable quarter hour apart.

For Richard Nixon the evening began almost as unpromisingly as it would end. Stepping out of the backseat of the car, he banged his knee sharply and painfully against the door; bystanders waiting to greet him saw the color drain from his face. Just two weeks earlier, the vice president had concluded twelve days of hospitalization for a knee infection caused by a similar mishap with a car door. Almost immediately after his release, Nixon had bounded back onto the campaign trail, hoping to make up for lost time with an intensive schedule of cross-country travel. Now heading into the most critical media event of his life, he looked exhausted, underweight, and wan—"better suited for going to a funeral, perhaps his own, than to a debate," in the view of journalist David Halberstam.[1]

At the WBBM loading dock, Nixon quickly composed himself and started through a high-power receiving line. Gathered to greet this first of the star debaters were the titans of American broadcasting: fierce competitors like William Paley of CBS, Robert Sarnoff of NBC, and Leonard Goldenson of ABC, momentarily allied in their patronage of the 1960 debates. Working the line, Nixon came to Oliver Treyz, the president of ABC News, who greeted the candidate by asking what no one else had dared: "How do you feel?"

At a dinner commemorating the debate twenty-five years later, Treyz would recall the moment: "I asked the question because he looked ill. And he said, 'Not so well. I have a temperature of a hundred and two degrees.'" When Nixon pulled from his pocket the bottle of Terramycin he was taking, Treyz asked if he wished to cancel. Nixon declined, saying he did not want to be seen as a coward.[2]

Poor physical health and a freshly injured knee were only the beginning of Richard Nixon's troubles. For weeks, a more vexing problem had been brewing: a lack of appreciation by campaign decision makers for the momentousness of the occasion. "Nixon knew the power of television very well," said Ted Rogers, Nixon's TV adviser, "but I don't think the people around him did." According to Rogers, Kennedy's staff handled their candidate as a thoroughbred, while Nixon's treated theirs like a mule, "working him to death."[3] Nixon had turned down an invitation from debate producer-director Don Hewitt for a preproduction meeting; Kennedy used his session to grill the director about staging details. As Hewitt saw it, for Nixon the debate was "just another campaign appearance."[4]

To prepare for the broadcast, Vice President Nixon studied briefing books alone, dismissing suggestions that he rehearse with aides. Senator Kennedy, by contrast, brought an entourage to Chicago two days ahead of schedule and spent much of the weekend holed up in a hotel suite practicing his responses out loud. In the hours immediately before broadcast, members of Kennedy's campaign team were still lobbing questions at him.

Fifteen minutes after Nixon's arrival at WBBM the network executives reassembled to greet the man who would emerge as the evening's undisputed champion. Unlike his Republican counterpart, John F. Kennedy arrived fit, rested, and ready. Weeks of open-air campaigning around the country had left Kennedy bronzed and glowing. Journalist Howard K. Smith, who moderated the first debate, would compare JFK to an "athlete come to receive his wreath of laurel." Said Nixon adviser Rogers, "When he came in the studio I thought he was Cochise, he was so tan."[5]

As Kennedy strode down the long corridor linking the driveway to Studio One, Nixon was already on the debate set, posing for cameramen with an air of jocularity that would quickly evaporate. "Have you ever had a picture printed yet?" Nixon teased one of the photographers, getting a laugh from the group. "You're always taking them, I never see them printed." Kennedy's entrance into the studio a few moments later immediately siphoned attention away from Nixon. "I assume you two guys know each other," Hewitt cracked, as the rivals extended their hands in greeting. The cameramen clamored for shots of the pair shaking hands; over and over they obliged, their chitchat muffled by the snap of flashbulbs.

"You get that tan the way I do?" Nixon asked Kennedy, prefiguring postdebate interest in the candidates' appearance. "Riding around in open cars? It's the wind, you know, not the sun." Though Kennedy's answer is not recorded, it is apparent from the question that the vice president was struck by how well his opponent looked. Did Nixon sense that his own post-hospital pallor was no match for Kennedy's summer glow? For weeks, TV consultant Rogers had urged Nixon to use a sunlamp. Like most of Rogers's advice, the recommendation went unheeded.

After shooing away the photographers, Don Hewitt ushered Kennedy and Nixon to their seats on the debate set for a quick orientation. Footage of this meeting shows Nixon casting his glance at a monitor offscreen, uncomfortably shifting positions in his chair, seeming to pass in and out of a daze. Kennedy, who does not deign to look at Nixon, occupies his side of the studio set with the casual presumption of a lion in his den.

To both debaters Hewitt offered the services of CBS's top makeup artist, imported from New York for the occasion. When Kennedy said no, Nixon quickly followed suit, in a show of machismo that proved to be a serious tactical blunder. "What I tried to explain to Dick," Rogers later recalled, "was he has a certain characteristic of his skin where it's almost transparent. And it was a very nice thought to say 'I don't want any makeup,' but he really needed it in order to have what we would call even an acceptable television picture."[6]

Nixon himself knew this. Two weeks before the first debate, he spoke of the cosmetic peculiarities of his skin in a TV interview with Walter Cronkite: "I can shave within thirty seconds before I go on television and still have a beard, unless we put some powder on, as we have done today."[7] Instead of a proper predebate makeup job, an aide slathered Nixon's face with an over-the-counter cosmetic called Lazy Shave, the same product the vice president had worn in his "kitchen debate" with Nikita Khrushchev a year earlier. Meanwhile, unknown to Nixon, Kennedy got a touch-up from his own people.

In the technical checks that followed, each debater took a final opportunity to sit before the lens for last-minute adjustments. Kennedy advisers examined the shade of their man's dark suit to make sure an appropriate contrast would be achieved on camera, and a staff person was dispatched back to the hotel for a blue shirt, which the senator donned for the broadcast. Another handler had brought along a pair of long socks, in case regular socks looked too short when the candidates were shown sitting on the set.

If JFK's tech check was obsessive, the other side's was fatalistic. Alarmed by Nixon's onscreen appearance, Hewitt asked Ted Rogers if he approved of the way his debater looked. Although Rogers pronounced himself "satisfied"[8]—*resigned* might have been a better word—Hewitt felt concerned enough to press the matter with his CBS boss, Frank Stanton. Stanton again asked Rogers if the shots of Nixon were acceptable, and again Rogers said yes.

Exacerbating his misfortune, Nixon had selected a light gray suit, which, according to CBS News President Sig Mickelson, "blended into the background and, if anything, exaggerated his pale appearance."[9] At the Republicans' insistence, stagehands repainted the gray backdrop several times in the hours before the debate, but each new coat dried lighter than Nixon's people had anticipated. As airtime approached, the backdrop was still moist from the latest application.

With less than half an hour to go, both candidates retired to their dressing rooms.

In Hyannis Port, Massachusetts, Jacqueline Kennedy, six months pregnant with her second child, was hosting a debate-watching party. About thirty people had gathered in the Kennedys' summer home on Nantucket Sound, where the guest list included Jackie's sister, Lee Radziwill; Professor and Mrs. Archibald Cox; Professor and Mrs. Arthur Schlesinger Jr.; Democratic committeewomen from around New England; and last but not least, about a dozen journalists.

The Kennedy "Listening Party," as the newspapers anachronistically termed it, offers further evidence of how differently the two political camps regarded the debate. While the wife of the Democratic candidate used the occasion for public relations, Pat Nixon spent a quiet evening watching at home with her two daughters in Washington, out of sight of reporters until the next day, when she would be enlisted for damage control.

The Boston press breathlessly reported every detail of Jacqueline Kennedy's party on this cool Cape Cod evening: the coffee and pastries in the dining room; the lemon-yellow couch where the hostess perched next to Professor Cox; two-and-a-half-year-old Caroline sleeping upstairs; Jackie's pearl necklace and coral-colored silk maternity dress. Sensitive to recent press reports about her expensive wardrobe, Mrs. Kennedy assured reporters that the outfit had been sewn by a local seamstress.

Jacqueline Kennedy had rented a sixteen-inch portable television set for the debate. "I own one in Washington," she told her guests, "but we don't have one here. I guess I'll have to break down and buy one." A *Boston Globe* photo showed the TV set incongruously situated atop a piece of antique furniture identified as an "early American Governor Winthrop desk."[10]

As the program drew nearer, Jacqueline confessed to being nervous. "I'm not apprehensive," she said in the debutante voice the whole country would soon recognize. "But I'm always nervous before he speaks. I must say I have no reason to be." With partygoers scattered around the room in chairs and on the floor, the moment approached. Mrs.

Kennedy herself clicked the set on, took a deep breath, and sat down to watch.

"The candidates need no introduction," began moderator Howard K. Smith. And for the next hour the country's first televised presidential debate unfolded, attracting the largest audience that had ever assembled for a political event. An estimated 70 million Americans watched on TV, while several million more listened on radio.[11]

The issues Kennedy and Nixon addressed were familiar to anyone following the news in 1960: communism and national security; labor and farm problems; the candidates' leadership experience. Though the substance of their remarks would account for most of the ink in the next day's papers, it was the debaters' personal characteristics that resonated most strongly with the viewers. "Within hours," wrote David Halberstam, "no one could recall anything that was said, only what they looked like, what they felt like."[12]

In his landmark book *The Making of the President*, campaign chronicler Theodore White famously limned the contrast between performers: Kennedy "calm and nerveless in appearance," Nixon "tense, almost frightened, at turns glowering and, occasionally, haggard-looking to the point of sickness." For Richard Nixon, White concluded, "everything that could have gone wrong that night went wrong."[13] Media historian Erik Barnouw noted that Kennedy's "air of confidence" came across not only in his statements and gestures but also, and more crucially, during the cutaway reaction shots: "A glimpse of the listening Kennedy showed him attentive, alert, with a suggestion of a smile on his lips. A Nixon glimpse showed him haggard; the lines on his face seemed like gashes and gave a fearful look."[14]

What viewers at home could not know was that these same images were igniting a parallel debate in the control room of WBBM-TV, where the issue was not public policy but visual aesthetics. Candidate cutaways had been a flashpoint in the lengthy and contentious pre-debate negotiations between the campaigns and the networks, but no firm guidelines had emerged as to how the program would be shot. By prior agreement, the candidates' television representatives sat in the control room during the program: Ted Rogers for Nixon and, for Kennedy, a former WBBM producer named Bill Wilson. With the debate under way, Wilson chided Hewitt that he "owed" Kennedy more reaction shots.

"What do you mean?" Hewitt asked. "I've cut away from Kennedy more than I've cut away from Nixon."

But the reaction shots Wilson wanted were of Nixon. The two advisers got into a heated argument with each other and with Hewitt, each side demanding more reactions of the other's candidate, each keeping a running count of the cutaways. Hewitt was hollering at them both to stop interfering with his work, which, as he saw it, was to serve as a surrogate for people watching in their living rooms. "I didn't try to catch the candidates in a grimace," Hewitt later explained. "I listened to the comments and tried to anticipate the public—to switch to a reaction shot when I thought viewers would expect one."[15] Although Nixon's close-up cutaways would loom larger in the national perception than Kennedy's, postdebate tallies showed eleven reactions of Kennedy, running a total of 118 seconds, compared to nine of Nixon, totaling 85 seconds.

The potency of these images may unintentionally have been enhanced by improvements in TV technology. The day before the debate, CBS engineers outfitted the studio cameras with new tubes that delivered a sharper than normal picture. "This was unfortunate for Nixon," CBS's Mickelson concluded. "The cameras exaggerated his paleness and heavy beard, but it was a break for Kennedy, who looked robust and healthy. As the cameras had exaggerated Nixon's apparent ill health, they likewise enhanced Kennedy's rugged vitality."[16] An additional visual factor must be considered: as black-and-white broadcasts, the debates exuded a documentary crispness that verged on the hyperreal. Especially when compared to debates from later, color TV years, the 1960 debates offer the clarity and punch of a *Life* magazine photo essay come to life.

Beyond production considerations, an eleventh-hour phone call from running mate Henry Cabot Lodge apparently helped steer Nixon onto the wrong tactical course. Lodge, who had debated Kennedy in their senatorial race in 1952, advised Nixon to take the high road and "erase the assassin image" that had dogged him throughout his political career.[17] And so it was that Richard Nixon adopted a posture of conciliation, even deference, toward his fellow debater. "The things that Senator Kennedy has said many of us can agree with," Nixon declared in his opening statement. "I can subscribe completely to the spirit that Senator Kennedy has expressed tonight."[18] At one point, the Republican nominee chose to forgo a response altogether, passing up the opportunity to rebut his opponent's remarks.

"Thank you, gentlemen. This hour has gone by all too quickly." With this coda from Howard K. Smith, the historic encounter drew to a close. In Texas, Henry Cabot Lodge, the running mate who had counseled gentility in his predebate phone call to Nixon, was heard to say, "That son of a bitch just cost us the election."[19]

Before leaving the studio, Kennedy and Nixon posed for a final round of photographs, making small talk about travel schedules and weather as the shutters clicked away. Afterward, JFK told an aide that whenever a photographer prepared to snap, Nixon "would put a stern expression on his face and start jabbing a finger into my chest, so he would look as if he was laying down the law to me about foreign policy or communism. Nice fellow."[20]

Outside the TV station, a crowd of twenty-five hundred political enthusiasts had gathered in the street. Asked by a reporter to estimate the ratio of Democrats to Republicans, a Chicago police officer quipped, "I'd say it's about twenty-five hundred to zero."[21] As Nixon slipped out the back, Kennedy triumphantly emerged at the main entrance of the building to greet his supporters. "When it was all over," Don Hewitt said, "a man walked out of this studio president of the United States. He didn't have to wait till Election Day."[22]

In what history records as the first example of postdebate spin, Jacqueline Kennedy turned to her guests at program's end and exclaimed, "I think my husband was brilliant."

For most of the hour, Mrs. Kennedy had watched the debate "almost immobile," as one observer put it, though she did get up several times to adjust the picture on the temperamental TV set. Others in the highly partisan Kennedy living room broke into laughter when Nixon misspoke and declared, "It's our responsibility that we get rid of the farmer," before correcting himself and saying, "the surpluses." The hostess concealed her reaction to this verbal slip behind a "Mona Lisa kind of smile."[23]

Fifteen minutes after the debate ended, the phone rang at the Kennedy home in Hyannis Port: the senator was on the line. Jacqueline took the call upstairs, away from the guests, and reappeared a few minutes later. Her husband had asked about the listening party, she said; otherwise their conversation remained private. One of the reporters present wrote that after the call Mrs. Kennedy was "as flushed with happiness and suppressed excitement as a schoolgirl."[24]

Richard Nixon's first indication that the debate had not gone his way came from longtime secretary Rose Mary Woods, a woman he counted among his most honest critics. Shortly after the broadcast, Woods got a call from her parents in Ohio, who asked if the vice president was feeling well. When the debate aired in California, Nixon's own mother phoned with the same question. And so the reaction went. "I recognized the basic mistake I had made," Nixon would write in *Six Crises*. "I had concentrated too much on substance and not enough on appearance. I should have remembered that 'a picture is worth a thousand words.'"[25]

Indeed. In the days that followed, the thousands of words printed about the first Kennedy-Nixon debate would be no match for the pictures that had seared themselves into the nation's consciousness. Pat Nixon, flying to her husband's side the next day, gamely told a reporter, "He looked wonderful on my TV set." Nixon himself assured interviewers that despite a weight loss, he felt fine. Press secretary Herbert G. Klein lamented that "the fault obviously was television," while other Republicans voiced public displeasure with their candidate's kid-gloves approach to his opponent.[26]

JFK, on the other hand, reaped an immediate windfall. Theodore White described the change in the crowds that turned out for Kennedy the next day in northern Ohio: "Overnight, they seethed with enthusiasm and multiplied in numbers, as if the sight of him, in their homes on the video box, had given him a 'star quality' reserved only for television and movie idols." *Time* magazine wrote that before the debate, reporters had amused themselves by counting "jumpers" in the crowds—women who hopped up and down to get a better look at Kennedy. "Now they noted 'double jumpers' (jumpers with babies in their arms). By week's end they even spotted a few 'leapers' who reached prodigious heights."[27]

Although the mythology surrounding the first Kennedy-Nixon broadcast would greatly amplify in the years to follow, the moral of the story has never varied: presidential debates are best apprehended as *television shows*, governed not by the rules of rhetoric or politics but by the demands of their host medium. The values of debates are the values of television: celebrity, visuals, conflict, and hype. On every level, Kennedy and his team perceived this, while Nixon and his did not.

After Chicago, campaigns would have no choice but to school themselves in the subtleties of the small screen, and eagerly have they taken to the task. "It didn't matter whether the televised debate had been decisive in Kennedy's victory," wrote social critic Todd Gitlin. "What mattered was that the management of television was one factor that candidates believed they could control. The time of the professional media consultant had arrived."[28]

Today, with the merger of politics and television complete, presidential debates operate as coproductions of the campaigns. Candidates and their handlers dominate every step of the process, from make-or-break issues like participation, schedule, and format, to such arcana as podium placement, camera angles, and which star gets which dressing room. Nothing is unnegotiated, nothing left to chance.

Still, when the red light blinks on to signal the start of the program, the steamroller nature of live TV supersedes the campaigns' stewardship. Spontaneity is the overriding determinant of presidential debates, and a major reason, perhaps *the* major reason, that audiences continue to watch in such staggering numbers. "Modern debates are the political version of the Indianapolis Speedway," according to political scientist Nelson Polsby. "What we're all there for—the journalist, the political pundits, the public—is to see somebody crack up in flames."[29] [. . .]

The images of John F. Kennedy and Richard M. Nixon that filled the airwaves on September 26, 1960, can be read as harbingers of change. A revolutionary programming genre burst forth that night in Chicago, one that fundamentally realigned both politics and the media in America. In the decades since Kennedy-Nixon, televised debates have lost none of their fascination for the press and the public, and none of their terror for candidates. Choreographed and unscripted, contrived and authentic, debates straddle the fault line between artifice and reality—like everything else on TV, only more so. With their clashing costars, enormous stakes, and "must-see" status, presidential debates are nothing so much as television writ large.

Notes

1. David Halberstam, "President Video," *Esquire*, June 1976, 130.
2. On September 26, 1985, the Museum of Broadcast Communications in Chicago held the Twenty-Fifth Anniversary Gala, which brought together many of the surviving principals involved in the first Kennedy-Nixon debate. The event took place in Studio One at WBBM, the site of the debate.
3. Rogers was interviewed on the *Lee Phillip Show*, WBBM, Chicago, September 22, 1985.
4. Jules Witcover, "The Bottom Line Is Style," *Washington Post*, September 19, 1976, A4.
5. Howard K. Smith, *Events Leading Up to My Death* (New York: St. Martin's, 1996), 263; *Lee Phillip Show*.
6. Rogers was interviewed on the PBS documentary *Nixon*, produced by Elizabeth Deane for the *American Experience* series, 1990.
7. Christopher Matthews, *Kennedy and Nixon: The Rivalry That Shaped Post-War America* (New York: Simon and Schuster, 1996), 145.
8. Ibid., 149.
9. Sig Mickelson, *From Whistle Stop to Sound Bite: Four Decades of Politics and Television* (New York: Praeger, 1989), 123.
10. Mary Cremmen, "Listening Party," *Boston Globe*, September 27, 1960, 1, 9.
11. Earl Mazo et al., *The Great Debates* (Santa Barbara: Center for the Study of Democratic Institutions, 1962), 4; and J. Leonard Reinsch, *Getting Elected: From Radio and Roosevelt to Television and Reagan* (New York: Hippocrene Books, 1988), 143.
12. Halberstam, "President Video," 132.
13. Theodore White, *The Making of the President 1960* (New York: Atheneum, 1961), 288–89.
14. Erik Barnouw, *The Image Empire: A History of Broadcasting in the United States from 1953* (New York: Oxford University Press, 1970), 164.
15. Terry Turner, "What 'Debate' Didn't Show," *Chicago Daily News*, September 27, 1960, 35.
16. Mickelson, *From Whistle Stop to Sound Bite*, 122.
17. White, *The Making of the President 1960*, 285.
18. Debate transcriptions used throughout this book were prepared by the Commission on Presidential Debates. They are available on the commission's website (www.debates.org).

19. Fawn M. Brodie, *Richard Nixon: The Shaping of His Character* (New York: Norton, 1981), 427.

20. Kenneth P. O'Donnell and David F. Powers, *Johnny, We Hardly Knew Ye: Memories of John Fitzgerald Kennedy* (Boston: Little, Brown, 1972), 213.

21. William Braden, "Some Tidbits for Posterity," *Chicago Sun-Times*, September 27, 1960, 18.

22. Hewitt made this remark at the Twenty-Fifth Anniversary Gala.

23. Cremmen, "Listening Party," 9.

24. Emilie Tavel, "Back at Hyannis Port . . . ," *Christian Science Monitor*, September 27, 1960, 6.

25. Richard Nixon, *Six Crises* (Garden City, NY: Doubleday, 1962), 340.

26. "Pat Sees Nixon 1st Time on TV: 'Looked Great,'" *Boston Evening Globe*, September 27, 1960, 9; Richard T. Stout, "Nixon Aides Admit Makeup Job," *Chicago Daily News*, September 30, 1960, 4.

27. White, *The Making of the President 1960*, 291; and "The Campaign: Candid Camera," *Time*, October 10, 1960, 20.

28. Todd Gitlin, "Bites and Blips: Chunk News, Savvy Talk, and the Bifurcation of American Politics," in Peter Dahlgren and Colin Sparks, eds., *Communication and Citizenship: Journalism and the Public Sphere in the New Media Age* (London: Routledge, 1991), 132.

29. George J. Church, "Debating the Debates," *Time*, October 29, 1984, 31.

The Revolution Will Not Be Televised

Gil Scott-Heron

You will not be able to stay home, brother.
You will not be able to plug in, turn on, and cop out.
You will not be able to lose yourself on skag and
skip out for beer during commercials,
because the revolution will not be televised.

The revolution will not be televised.
The revolution will not be brought to you by Xerox
in four parts without commercial interruptions.
The revolution will not show you pictures of Nixon
blowing a bugle and leading a charge by John
Mitchell, General Abrams, and Spiro Agnew to eat
hog maws confiscated from a Harlem sanctuary.
The revolution will not be televised.

The revolution will not be brought to you by the
Schaefer Award Theatre and will not star Natalie
Woods and Steve McQueen or Bullwinkle and Julia.
The revolution will not give your mouth sex appeal.
The revolution will not get rid of the nubs.
The revolution will not make you look five pounds
thinner, because the revolution will not be televised, brother.

There will be no pictures of you and Willie Mays
pushing that shopping cart down the block on the dead run,
or trying to slide that color TV into a stolen ambulance.
NBC will not be able to predict the winner at 8:32
on reports from twenty-nine districts.
The revolution will not be televised.

There will be no pictures of pigs shooting down
brothers on the instant replay.
There will be no pictures of pigs shooting down
brothers on the instant replay.
There will be no pictures of Whitney Young being
run out of Harlem on a rail with a brand new process.
There will be no slow motion or still lifes of Roy
Wilkins strolling through Watts in a red, black, and
green liberation jumpsuit that he had been saving
For just the proper occasion.

Green Acres, The Beverly Hillbillies, and Hooterville
Junction will no longer be so damned relevant, and
women will not care if Dick finally got down with
Jane on *Search for Tomorrow* because black people
will be in the street looking for a brighter day.
The revolution will not be televised.

There will be no highlights on the eleven o'clock
news and no pictures of hairy armed women
liberationists and Jackie Onassis blowing her nose.
The theme song will not be written by Jim Webb or
Francis Scott Key, nor sung by Glen Campbell, Tom
Jones, Johnny Cash, Engelbert Humperdinck, or the Rare Earth.
The revolution will not be televised.

The revolution will not be right back
after a message about a white tornado, white lightning,
or white people.
You will not have to worry about a dove in your

bedroom, the tiger in your tank, or the giant in your toilet bowl.
The revolution will not go better with Coke.
The revolution will not fight germs that may cause bad breath.
The revolution will put you in the driver's seat.

The revolution will not be televised, will not be televised,
will not be televised, will not be televised.
The revolution will be no re-run, brothers;
the revolution will be live.

The Missing Remote

Diane Lockward

Not lost or mislaid, but hidden.
While you were in Florida chasing
golf balls, I took possession
of your baton. I wanted
the thrill of clutching it,
night after night, pushing buttons
shaped like miniature nipples,
longed to mute the noise
and not listen, the way you don't
listen to me. I wanted the power
in my lap, my hand, needed
to turn on and turn off, and I did,
multiple times. I raised and lowered
the volume, returned to the previous
channel, grew dizzy with pictures
leaping, colors flashing, red, yellow,
and green. I positioned myself
in front of the screen and feasted
on sandwiches and snatches
of commercials, the tail end
of a third quarter, the opening
round of a game show. I tasted
reality. I enjoyed everything in bits
and pieces, as if nibbling
from a box of Godiva chocolates.

It wasn't *NYPD Blue* or *ER* or even
Judge Judy I craved, but the force
of that glossy little rectangle.
And now you're back, missing
your gizmo. You'll never touch
those delicate buttons again.
You'll stretch out in your favorite
recliner, night after night, unfrocked,
while I'm a swirl of primary colors
and spinning all over the globe.

Dolls and Feelings
Jill Soloway's Post-Patriarchal Television
(selection)

Ariel Levy

n a scene from *Transparent*, the television series created by Jill Soloway, a women's studies professor stands before a room of listless undergraduates, haranguing them in the accusatory tone favored by a certain strain of academic. "Because women bled without dying, men were frightened!" the professor—played by Soloway, wearing a tent of a top and a pink dreadlock in her bun—says. "The masculine insists to cut things up with exclamation points—which are in and of themselves small rapes, the way an exclamation point might end a sentence and say, 'Stop talking, *woman!*'"

At the back of the classroom, Syd, played by Carrie Brownstein, turns to her friend Ali Pfefferman (Gaby Hoffman) and asks, "Have you ever been raped by an exclamation point?"

"Actually, once I was gang-raped: question mark, exclamation point, *and* semicolon," Ali replies.

"That's brutal," Syd says stonily. "It's very underreported."

In person, Jill Soloway looks nothing like a dowdy professor. She looks more like a wide-eyed cartoon doe. Her resting facial expression is curious, attentive, intent. She has a delicate frame, brown hair that falls to her jaw, and big brown eyes. Several of her friends describe her as "a doer." Amazon, *Transparent*'s producer and distributor, has a series of governing principles; Soloway's favorite is "bias for action." She didn't want to sit around talking when I visited her, in Los

Angeles, on a warm afternoon in late October. It was a month after she won the Emmy for best director, and her star, Jeffrey Tambor, won another one, for his portrayal of Maura Pfefferman, a transgender woman who has come out at the age of sixty-eight. Soloway wanted to walk up and down the hills of Silver Lake, the hip, idyllic neighborhood where she lives, and which provides the setting for much of her show.

Sometimes, though, Soloway *sounds* not entirely unlike that women's studies professor she played. "A patriarchal society can't really handle that there's such a thing as a vagina," she said. "The untrustworthy vagina that is discerning-receiving." Soloway, who recently turned fifty, was wearing leggings and blue nail polish and a baseball cap that said "Mister." She sped past a stretch of Craftsman bungalows, whose front yards were studded with bicycles, jade plants, and toys. "So you can want sex, you can want to be entered, and then a minute later you can say, 'Stop—changed my mind,'" she continued. "That is something that our society refuses to allow for. You don't feel like it now? You're shit out of luck. You know why? Because you have a pussy! To me, that is what's underneath all this gender trouble: most of our laws are being formed by people with penises."

Most of our entertainment, of course, has also been formed by people with penises, and Soloway is trying to change that through her hiring practices, her choice of subject matter, and the way she thinks and acts at work. "We're taught that the camera is male," she said, turning to walk uphill, backward, to tone a different part of her legs. "But I'm not forcing everybody to fulfill something in my head and 'Get it right—now get it *more* right.'" Directing with "the female gaze," she asserted, is about creating the conditions for inspiration to flourish, and then "discerning-receiving."

On set, Soloway thinks of her job as akin to being a good mom: "Kids come home from school, want to put on a play in the back yard. You help them build a stage; you make sure they take breaks, have a snack." (Soloway has two sons, Isaac, nineteen, and Felix, seven.) Jeffrey Tambor told me, "I have never experienced such freedom as an actor before in my life. Often, an actor will walk on a set and do the correct take, the expected take. Then sometimes the director will say, OK, do one for yourself. That last take, that's our starting point."

The cast talks about *Transparent* as a "wonderful cult," but Soloway disputes this. "It's not a cult," she says. "It's feminism." Women, Soloway said, are naturally suited to being directors: "We all know how to do it. We fucking grew up doing it! It's *dolls.* How did men make us think we weren't good at this? It's *dolls* and *feelings.* And women are fighting to become directors? What the fuck happened?"

Soloway describes herself as "seditious." Her production company is called Topple, as in "topple the patriarchy." Ultimately, this trait has contributed to her success: while *Transparent* is, at its core, a family drama about California Jews who have a standing order at Canter's Deli and who bicker about which of the siblings should inherit the house where they grew up, it is also a radical exploration of gender and sexuality, unlike anything that preceded it on television.

But for many years Soloway's insurrectionary tendencies were a career obstacle. In 2011, after almost two decades as a television writer, Soloway was broke, with two kids, trying to recover from the recent writers' strike and the recession. Then her old friend Jane Lynch, who was starring on *Glee,* told her about a job on the show, and Soloway went to meet with the producers. "Finally, here's this moment where I'm meeting on *Glee,*" Soloway said. "Ryan Murphy wants to hire me. I've been best friends with Jane Lynch for about three decades—we're sisters. It's *happening.*" As Soloway drove home from the meeting, her agent called to say, "Pop the champagne—they loved you." A week later, he called again: Murphy had heard that Soloway was "difficult," and wasn't going to give her the job. The agent said he'd send a check to tide her over.

That night, Soloway sat in the bathtub, while her husband, Bruce Gilbert, a music supervisor for film and television, brushed his teeth. She remembers telling him, "'I don't want to use the money to pay off our debt. I want to be a director, and I want to make a film with it and get into Sundance. I want to double down on me.' And Bruce was, like, 'OK.'" Then, just as Soloway was making the leap to directing her own material, her father called one afternoon and came out as transgender. [. . .]

Transparent is a product of the female gaze: season 1 was directed exclusively by women, and four of the five primary characters are female. But it also reflects the gaze of a child—the perspective, colored by Soloway's experience, of the Pfefferman siblings, who are by turns baffled, disappointed, besotted, and enraged by the person who raised them.

Jeffrey Tambor's Maura is a retired professor who has, after decades of dreaming about it, finally grown her sparse gray hair past her shoulders. She wears flowing pants and long skirts and has a broad frame and a poignant ungainliness. She is wary, but also prone to radiant bursts of daring and disarming maternal love. She doesn't want to live in the big, expensive, modern house in Pacific Palisades where she spent decades being a distant father and husband and "dressing up like a man." She wants her children to live there while she finds out where she belongs. At nearly seventy, Maura has been reborn.

One consequence of rebirth is a second coming of age, and both Maura and her children act out with the heedless egocentrism of adolescents. The eldest sibling, Sarah, leaves her husband to pursue an affair with her college girlfriend, after they reunite at the school that their children attend. In the second season, their relationship moves from illicit to domestic, and Sarah finds herself trapped in her own escape plan, as restless and unmoored as ever. Her brother, Josh, keeps accidentally getting women pregnant and pitching fits: he throws a chair at his boss, and shrieks at other drivers from behind the wheel. Ali, the youngest, drifts between interests and lovers, experimenting with drugs, lesbianism, yellow eye shadow, and academia. ("You can not *do* anything!" Maura explodes at her.)

The upside of immaturity is guileless delight, and *Transparent* has a child's sense of amazement about the world—especially secret places where different rules apply. Maura seems free for the first time at a sylvan cross-dressing camp, where she bikes along the dirt road wearing a purple dress. The Michigan Womyn's Music Festival—which ended this summer, after forty years, largely because of conflicts over whether trans women ought to be included—is re-created in the second season as a muddy, magical oasis where women receive visions by staring into bonfires. "I'm always trying to bring the concept of play into the female gaze," Soloway told me.

There is even an innocence to the sex scenes, which are radical and plentiful. Sarah gets a spanking—but in the forest, with a grin on her face. In season 2, Maura has sex for the first time since her transition, with an earth mother played by Anjelica Huston. She says aloud what so many virgins have said in their minds: "I don't know what to do."

I walked into the den of Soloway's rambling house one morning as she was watching that scene on her computer. Originally, the Huston character felt Maura's erection pressing against her and said, seductively, "What do we have here?" To which Maura replied, "We have a penis." One of Soloway's writers—a transgender woman—had suggested that Maura might not think of her genitals that way anymore, and that she ought to say, "We have a big clit."

Soloway looked at me intently, discerning-receiving, and said, "What do you think? Too much?" (In the end, both lines were cut.)

Like Maura, the transgender movement in this country is just coming out, even though it has a long secret history. *Transparent* both reflects and advances its agenda, and the people who make the show feel an acute responsibility. "It's an extremely tough line to walk," Bridget Bedard, the head writer, told me. "We're making a comedy—or a 'trauma-dy,' we've started saying—and comedy comes from people being fallible." But they want to make the characters believably flawed without reinforcing stereotypes: "Like, a trans woman looking in the mirror and crying—don't do that."

Every decision on the show is vetted by Rhys Ernst and Zackary Drucker, trans activists and artists whose work about their relationship appeared in the most recent Whitney Biennial. "We monitor the politics of representation—if we catch things in the writing stage, it's kind of optimal because then there's time to shape it," Drucker told me. "We're kind of starting over with *Transparent*, and with the trans tipping point in general."

Despite the uniformity of experience suggested by the label LGBT, the gay community has been accepted into American life and politics in a way that trans people have not. The city of Houston elected its first lesbian mayor in 2009, but when she passed a broad anti-discrimination ordinance—which addressed race, age, and sexual orientation as well as gender identity—opponents launched a campaign with the slogan "No Men in Women's Bathrooms," and voters easily repealed the measure.

But, if trans people are scapegoats for the right, they are also requiring the left to undertake a momentous shift in thinking. "We're asking the whole world to transition with us to a less binary way of being,"

Drucker said. "It's the next step in the fight for gender equality: removing the habit of always qualifying a person as a man or a woman. If we start thinking of each other as just people, it allows us to identify with each other in a way that has never really been possible before."

If the point of this kind of identity transition is to reconcile the way the world sees you with the way you see yourself, the details of perception and representation become crucial. "A really interesting thought exercise is to say 'they' and 'them' for all genders," Soloway instructed me. I was confused, so she explained. "If you said, 'I have to go pick up my friend at the airport,' I could very easily say, 'What time do they get here?' So there is a structure for talking about your friend and not knowing their gender—and it's perfect English."

I pointed out that strict grammar forbids using a plural pronoun for a single person; it would sound crazy, for instance, to describe Soloway by saying, "They are my favorite director."

Soloway shook her head vigorously. "All of the magazines and newspapers need to begin to do this," she said. "The language is evolving daily—even gender reassignment, people are now calling it gender confirmation!" She was getting excited. "The promise of this revolution is not having to say, 'Men do this, women do this.'"

In the utopia that Soloway envisions, I suggested, there would be no need to transition, because there would be no gender in the first place. Soloway parsed it differently: "In a few years, we're going to look back and say, 'When we were little, we used to think that all women had vaginas and all men had penises, but now, of course, we know that's not true.'"

Pop History on an Epic Scale: *Roots*

Donald Bogle

E pic, sweeping, and larger than life, the twelve-hour, six-million-dollar miniseries *Roots* told American history from an African American perspective. Based on Alex Haley's famous 1976 book, the drama traced the struggles of the author's family from its life in Africa to its enslavement and ultimate "freedom" in America. At first, *Roots* looked downright hokey. The initial episode opened in 1750 with the birth of the Haley forefather, the young Kunta Kinte (LeVar Burton), the son of two loving parents, Binta (Cicely Tyson) and Omoro (Thalmus Rasulala). Often the idealized portrait of life in Gambia seemed more Hollywood than West African, with a sequence in which young Kunta underwent tribal manhood rites that looked much like the activities of college pledges during a fraternity initiation.

But *Roots* grew forceful and urgent once Kunta Kinte was captured by white slave traders and sent across the sea on a slave ship. Proud and confident, he rebels once put into slavery in America, attempting to escape (and losing part of a foot because of it) and refusing to let the slaveholders give him the name Toby. It is the older slave Fiddler (Louis Gossett Jr.), known on the plantation for his mastery of the fiddle, who teaches the boy the techniques of survival in America—and also the game of masks that any slave must learn to play. Around whites, Fiddler plays his fiddle, grins, and cavorts; the real man hides behind the self-imposed mask of a contented, happy darky who delights his slave owners. But away from the white master, Fiddler is his own man, dignified and assured. Kunta learns to respond to the name Toby. But from Fiddler, he understands that in his heart and his head he will always be

Kunta Kinte. He learns to preserve the customs and traditions of the culture from whence he has come.

Roots followed Kunta into adulthood (the role then played by John Amos) through his marriage to Bell (Madge Sinclair) and the loss of his only child, Kizzy, who is sold by a "good" master to a brutal slaveholder on another plantation. From there, the drama traced Kizzy's experiences—her rape by her new master, the birth of her son, and the hope always of freedom. The last episode of *Roots* followed the life of Kizzy's son Chicken George and her grandson Tom, who finally, following the Civil War, see the freedom their ancestors always dreamed of.

During the eight consecutive nights the series aired, *Roots* became one of the most watched television programs in the history of the medium. It was also the topic of conversation throughout the nation: in classrooms, dormitories, offices, elevators—and on the streets. It was a great shared national experience; its concluding episode was seen by approximately 130 million viewers, nearly half the nation's population. Later *Newsweek* reported that the drama had inspired hundreds of colleges to start *Roots* courses and that the National Archives in Washington, DC, was flooded with requests by citizens seeking information on how to trace their family genealogies.

Though *Roots* became the type of cultural phenomenon that might never be duplicated, it almost wasn't produced. Network executives had not expected such an extraordinary response and even initially feared that white viewers might not watch it. As early as 1974, producer David Wolper had approached ABC about a series to be based on the book that Alex Haley had not yet completed. ABC, however, was lukewarm to the idea because *Roots* "violated two long-standing truisms of network television," reported television journalist Sally Bedell Smith. First, historical dramas were thought to put viewers to sleep. Second, of course, was the belief that "dramatic protrayals of nonwhites held little appeal for most viewers." But then came the remarkable success of *The Autobiography of Miss Jane Pittman*. ABC fed Wolper $50,000 for the development of a miniseries that might run three to four hours. Once Wolper submitted some scripts to ABC, he was given a budget of $6 million to do the entire miniseries.

Still, all types of safeguards were taken by the network to ensure that *Roots* would not be a TV debacle. Foremost, ABC had approval of the cast. At first, one executive, said Sally Bedell Smith, balked at using drama student LeVar Burton for the young Kunta "because his lips were too thick." Others at ABC argued, however, that Burton had a sensitive look that would make him sympathetic. To help draw a large white viewership, ABC insisted that white actors be prominently cast in the drama. Such recognizable white television performers as Ed Asner, Sandy Duncan, Robert Reed, Chuck Connors, Lorne Greene, and Lynda Day George were hired for the production.

David Wolper's team of writers also made changes from the Haley book that gave the series more of an emphasis on sex and violence. The sexy character Fanta, whom the young Kunta Kinte beds, was nowhere to be found in the book. The creation of a guilt-ridden slave ship captain (Ed Asner) seemed to be a plot device to comfort mainstream viewers, assuring them that indeed there were sensitive whites trapped in the inhumanity of the slave system as much as the African captives. Haley had not written of such a character. In the African segment, women were seen bare-breasted but were shot from a distance without any close-ups.

The writers for the eight episodes of *Roots* were all white. Many of the episodes were directed as rather routine television melodrama, the result being that the actors looked as if they were heroically and triumphantly directing themselves. The directors, however, had sense enough not to pull back from the actors' emotions. Only one of the series's directors was African American, Gilbert Moses, who directed the sixth and seventh episodes. Originally, the network would approve only Black directors Gordon Parks Sr. and Michael Schultz, neither of whom was available. Producer Stan Marguiles felt that at first Moses (originally a stage director) was not familiar with film. But Moses learned quickly and, said Margulies, "made a difference to the actors."

Roots was promoted as an elaborate piece of entertainment; twelve hours of glorious, high-flung soap opera. ABC did not want the miniseries to be perceived as *only* a recounting of Black history. "Our concern," said network executive Larry Sullivan, "was to put a lot of white people in the promos. Otherwise we felt the program would be a turnoff." "I think we fooled the audience," ABC executive Lou Rudolph said later. "Because the white stories in most cases were irrelevant, it was a matter of having some white faces particularly in the opening episodes."

Originally, the network planned to air the program over eight weeks in eight installments, as it had done with the miniseries *Rich Man, Poor Man*. But Fred Silverman, then a top ABC executive, took the episodes home to view with his wife, Cathy, over eight consecutive nights. Both were overwhelmed and moved. Silverman realized, "To spread it out would have dissipated the impact." He decided it should air nightly. ABC executives didn't argue. They decided by airing it in one week they'd dispose of it quickly. Should it bomb, the ABC brass felt, "they would only lose a single week of the ratings competition instead of dragging down their average over two months." Fred Silverman decided to air *Roots* in January rather than during the important February sweeps because, he admitted, "I did not have enough faith in it."

But, concessions, compromises, and campaign strategies aside, *Roots* was a powerful viewing experience. It told the flip side of the story of *Gone with the Wind*, revealing the horrors and tragedy of slavery, taking viewers away from the mist and magnolia to the slave quarters, the family separations, the beatings, the wholesale trading of Black lives. The miniseries form permitted the writers to develop stronger characters than generally seen on television.

Roots was also distinguished by first-rate performances from a gallery of talented African American actors and actresses: Madge Sinclair, Ben Vereen, Olivia Cole, LeVar Burton, Leslie Uggams, Georg Stanford Brown, Moses Gunn, Hari Rhodes, Beverly Todd, Ren Woods, Scatman Crothers, Lawrence-Hilton Jacobs, Richard Roundtree, Hilly Hicks, and Lynne Moody. After all his troubles on *Good Times*, John Amos looked as if he finally had a part he could identify with: a strong, rebellious, unyielding older Kunta Kinte. His performance was complemented by that of Madge Sinclair as his wife Bell. Sinclair delineated a complicated woman, who has foolishly taken her master at his word and tragically made the mistake of actually believing in his goodness. When her daughter is sold, Sinclair's Bell falls on her knees, pleading with him in a sequence that was both shocking and moving. Later she turns her blind anger toward her husband, Kunta. Every movement of her body, every twitch or blink of her eyes, every sound of ache and desperation in her voice were all perfectly modulated and coordinated to create a wholly believable human being: a woman who knows she is dying at the very moment she is begging for her child's life—and in essence, her own.

Louis Gossett Jr. (billed as such for the first time), who won an Emmy for his portrayal of Fiddler, gave perhaps the most dazzling performance; perfectly illustrating a slave's awareness of his fate as well as his crafty maneuvers to make the system work to his advantage. Yet ultimately even Fiddler ends a heartbroken man, betrayed by the master he has so shrewdly served.

Perhaps most moving was the graveyard sequence with Leslie Uggams as Kizzy. Returning as an adult woman to the plantation where she had grown up, Uggams's Kizzy kneels before her father's tombstone, which is marked Toby. Having suffered and endured, she fully understands how her father's pride has sustained and strengthened her. She speaks in front of the gravesite, letting her dead father know of her new life, of her son George, and of her vow never to forget what her father taught her. She ends by scratching out the name Toby, replacing it with the name Kunta Kinte.

Watching Uggams in the sequence was one of those moments when a viewer responds as much to the person onscreen as to the character being portrayed. *Roots* helped Leslie Uggams find herself as a performer. Having been in show business since her childhood, she had appeared on *Beulah* and served a young apprenticeship, singing on a host of variety programs: *The Ed Sullivan Show*, *The Jack Paar Show*, *The Arthur Godfrey Show*, and *The Garry Moore Show*. Finally, she arrived at early stardom as a singer on Mitch Miller's weekly program *Sing Along with Mitch*. Afterward she won a Tony for her performance in the Broadway show *Hallelujah, Baby!*, and then had her own short-lived variety program, *The Leslie Uggams Show*, in 1969.

Every time a viewer saw her in this earlier phase of her career, Leslie Uggams looked like a well-mannered girl—really a windup doll—doing everything exactly as she had been taught: smiling, pleasing, singing on cue. She seemed bland without a single idiosyncrasy that might have made her distinct or interesting. One wondered what was underneath the plastic smile; if, indeed, there was a person inside this show business creation. But in her key scenes in *Roots*, she attained a newfound maturity, washing away any signs of the eager-to-please child star, going all the way emotionally to indicate she fully understood Kizzy's torment.

Knowing something about Leslie Uggams's past made her performance all the more moving. Here was a real woman suddenly come to life.

Most of the performers in *Roots* had spent years playing trivial or trashy roles. Some would return to such parts afterward, but in *Roots* they seemed invigorated by doing something of worth and meaning. They proved that the theory about television acting—the idea that performers had to play "tiny" rather than grand; that the little tube still wasn't comfortable with big, searing emotions—simply wasn't true. Even though the medium still was best at showcasing ordinary lives, *Roots* proved that larger-than-life experiences could engross an audience.

Roots altered television history. Not only did its success elevate the miniseries's stature (indicating that audiences would stay home night after night to follow a drama) but it also proved the popularity of a family saga that spanned many generations. Many *white-cast* imitations followed. Nominated for thirty-seven Emmy awards, *Roots* won nine. (Some of the actors canceled each other out for awards. In the category of Outstanding Actor for a Single Performance in a Drama or Comedy Series, all the nominees—LeVar Burton, John Amos, Ben Vereen, and Louis Gossett Jr., who won—were in *Roots*.) Olivia Cole won the Emmy for Outstanding Single Performance by a Supporting Actress in a Comedy or Drama Series. Ed Asner won the same award in the actor category. Quincy Jones was awarded the Emmy for Outstanding Music Composition for a series. *Roots* also won the Emmy for Outstanding Limited Series.

Most important, both *The Autobiography of Miss Jane Pittman* and *Roots* indicated that the race question—indeed the race drama—was still, despite the beliefs of network executives, very much on the minds of the American public. Intelligent African American dramatic presentations could be mainstream hits. Yet, sadly, neither program had a lasting effect on Black television programming. One might have assumed a flock of similar serious Black dramas would have paraded across the airwaves. But no such thing happened. Nonetheless some unusual Black specials did appear.

Two years after *The Autobiography of Miss Jane Pittman*, ABC broadcast a two-hour adaptation of African American playwright Lonne

Elder III's *Ceremonies in Dark Old Men*. Under the direction of Black director Michael Schultz, this drama—set in Harlem in 1958—depicted a Black family in conflict with itself and a new set of values in an increasingly violent culture. Though tied more to theater than film, the production nonetheless had some fine moments and exciting performances by Douglas Turner Ward, Godfrey Cambridge, Robert Hooks (as the cool, sinister gangster Blue Haven), and Rosalind Cash. It also marked the television debut of the Negro Ensemble theater company. In 1974, the theme of interracial love was explored in fairly serious terms in *The Wedding Band* with Ruby Dee and James Broderick.

The two-hour TV movie *Green Eyes* starred Paul Winfield as an embittered war veteran who returns to Vietnam in search of the son he fathered with a Vietnamese prostitute. The story of Olympic runner Wilma Rudolph was dramatized in *Wilma*, which starred newcomer Shirley Jo Finney as Rudolph and Cicely Tyson as her mother. Maya Angelou's moving memoir *I Know Why the Caged Bird Sings* was also adapted—unfortunately, disappointingly so—as a two-hour TV movie with Diahann Carroll, Esther Rolle, and Roger Mosley. LeVar Burton also starred in such TV movies as *Dummy* and *Billy: Portrait of a Street Kid*.

An unusual telecast was *The Minstrel Man*, a somber glimpse into the world of the African American minstrel show that told the story of two brothers struggling to maintain their dignity while pursuing careers as blackface entertainers—even though they themselves are Black. The all-star presentation *Freedom Road* featured Muhammad Ali as a former slave who becomes a United States senator.

The lavishly mounted six-hour miniseries *King* dramatized the life of Dr. Martin Luther King Jr. Directed and written by Abby Mann, it featured Cicely Tyson (as Coretta Scott King) and Paul Winfield in the title role. Giving a stirring performance, Winfield managed to do the impossible: he vividly re-created King's legendary speeches without sounding like a parody. Yet King's lieutenant, Dr. Ralph Abernathy, complained that the role of a white adviser to King was overstated—and a distortion of history that made it appear that even the most successful African Americans relied on guidance and help from whites.

The Killing Affair dramatized the interracial affair of a white female police officer (Elizabeth Montgomery) and her African American partner (O. J. Simpson), who are drawn together as they pursue a psychopathic killer. Though *The Killing Affair* was—for 1977—strong television material (willing to acknowledge sexism and racism on a big-city police force), it was often predictably clichéd. Montgomery, however, gave a convincing performance while Simpson glided along on his charm surprisingly well. Perhaps the most interesting character was the Black cop's wife, played by Rosalind Cash. When she realizes her husband is involved with a white woman, Cash's intensity makes the drama searingly *real*. One almost wishes *The Killing Affair* was about her. As for Simpson, the part led the way to starring roles in such other TV dramas as *Goldie and the Boxer* and the sequel *Goldie and the Boxer Go to Hollywood* (in which he played the good-hearted protector of a sweet little white girl). Then came the famous Hertz rent-a-car commercials and, finally, his starring role in the most riveting TV of the 1990s, his trial for the murder of his former wife, Nicole Brown Simpson.

The Depression-era Black family drama *Roll of Thunder, Hear My Cry* also appeared in 1978. An unusual—and uneven—drama was *The Hollow Image*, the tale of a young African American woman (Saundra Sharp) struggling with conflicts over her career and her life in Harlem.

But the best of the post-*Roots* TV dramas were *Backstairs at the White House* (1979) and the sequel *Roots: The Next Generations*. The beautifully made nine-hour *Backstairs at the White House* seemed a mix of *Roots* and the PBS British import *Upstairs, Downstairs*. Based on a 1961 book and broadcast over four consecutive Monday nights, *Backstairs at the White House* chronicled the experiences of a real-life African American mother and daughter—Maggie (Olivia Cole) and Lillian (Leslie Uggams) Rogers, who worked as domestics in the White House from the Taft administration on through the presidencies of Wilson, Harding, Coolidge, Hoover, Roosevelt, Truman, and Eisenhower. Here again American history was seen from another perspective. *Backstairs at the White House* also dramatized the conflict between a stern mother and a sensitive, insecure daughter. The production was strengthened by a powerful performance by Olivia Cole, who looked as if she might follow in the heels of Cicely Tyson. Also cast were Louis Gossett Jr., Robert Hooks, Eileen Heckart, Claire Bloom, George Kennedy, and Cloris Leachman.

Roots: The Next Generations was a real surprise: a sequel almost as good (in a very different way) as the original. This fourteen-hour, seven-part production traced the lives of four generations of Alex Haley's ancestors: opening with Tom Harvey (Georg Stanford Brown), the great-grandson of Kunta Kinte, and ending with Alex Haley himself on his trip to Africa to trace his family's roots. Throughout, the family members witness important times in American history: the Reconstruction era, the rise of Jim Crow laws and the Ku Klux Klan, segregation in the modern South and de facto segregation in the modern North, World Wars I and II, race riots, and the civil rights era.

Though the characters in the sequel had none of the pop tragic grandeur of the earlier characters—and though it was more soap-opera-ish—*Roots: The Next Generations* still engaged viewers. Perhaps the most unexpectedly moving sequence occurred when Beah Richards as Cynthia Harvey Palmer took her grandson, the young Alex (Christoff St. John), aside and explained the family history. Richards performed so simply yet with such a felt and credible intensity—not an actorish performance, just a *supremely* real one—that a viewer could be saddened by a dawning awareness of who Beah Richards herself was: yet another immensely talented African American performer who rarely got the parts she deserved. Yet she couldn't utter a line of dialogue without making it a thing of truth and beauty. Equally impressive was Al Freeman Jr., who played Malcolm X.

Also in the cast of this $16 million production (nearly three times the cost of the original) were: Dorian Harewood, Irene Cara, Stan Shaw, Bernie Casey, Debbie Allen, Brock Peters, Ossie Davis, Diahann Carroll, James Earl Jones (giving one of the few *un*convincing performances as Alex Haley), Fay Hauser, Lynne Moody, Debbi Morgan, Bever-Leigh Banfield, Henry Fonda, Ruby Dee, Olivia de Havilland, Avon Long, Roger Mosley, Rosey Grier, and Lynn Hamilton. Making his television debut was Marlon Brando as the American Nazi leader George Lincoln Rockwell. This time around David Wolper's production company also employed African American directors like Lloyd Richards and Georg Stanford Brown and Black writer Thad Mumford.

And so the 1970s ended with the very look of the prime time schedule having been radically altered. Not only had more Black-oriented programs appeared than ever before in the medium's history but some—*Sanford and Son, The Jeffersons, The Autobiography of Miss Jane Pittman, Roots,* and *Roots: The Next Generations*—had been among the era's most successful broadcasts. African American performers—Cicely Tyson, Redd Foxx, Flip Wilson, Sherman Hemsley—were now also among the medium's great stars.

But still African American viewers often felt conflicted about the images. On one level, the weekly series succeeded in introducing the television viewer to homes and lives in America different from those presented on such shows as *Father Knows Best* in the 1950s or *The Brady Bunch* in the late 1960s. America now acknowledged its Black population. Yet many of the new Black sitcoms had been weak and pallid, their basic situations and family relationships having been defined by people—white writers, directors, producers—from an entirely different cultural experience and perspective. Seldom presenting a sensitive, intimate portrait of Black life, the shows had also been littered with stereotypes and clichéd images. Serious weekly dramatic African American programs were still missing from the airwaves. Thus with all the advances for African Americans in television in the 1970s, one still had the nagging feeling that the more things changed, the more they hadn't changed enough.

COMMERCIAL BREAK

COMMERCIAL BREAK

Madonna and Pepsi partnered in 1989 to debut her song "Like a Prayer" as the soundtrack to a soft drink commercial. In "Desperately Selling Soda" (1994), **Leslie Savan** explores the deal that was struck, the advertisement that resulted, and how the concept of an artist "selling out" lost its force.

Desperately Selling Soda

Leslie Savan

There's never been a media buy like it. Madonna, the commercialized girl who's played hard to get for commercials, debuted the title cut from her still-unreleased album *Like a Prayer* on—whoa, *as*—a Pepsi commercial last Thursday. The ad was seen the same night in forty countries by 300 million or so people. A teaser spot running the week before and featuring an aborigine traipsing through the Australian outback (actually the California outback) to catch the commercial conveyed the pancultural ambitions of both soda pop and pop star: "No matter where you are in the world," the teaser instructed, "on March 2 get to a TV and see Pepsi present *Madonna*."

"We believe this is the single largest one-day media buy in the history of advertising," says Pepsi spokesman Ken Ross, figuring the two minutes of prime time planetary fame cost more than $5 million. And this wasn't just a Eurotrash media buy. Fans in Turkey, Indonesia, and even "war-torn countries like El Salvador" were also able to put aside their low-intensity conflicts to get down. (Despite Pepsi's earlier made-in-Moscow ad, called *Glasnost*, the Russians refused to air the spot.)

Even Michael Jackson didn't hit the cathode universe with such a bang. His Pepsi spots globetrotted only after they had run in the USA; and his songs were huge hits *before* he used them to sell something he reportedly won't drink. Just a few months ago George Michael, a sort of Madonna with facial hair, almost beat her to it: snatches of sound from *his* unreleased album popped up in a confused matador/superstar spot for Diet Coke. For her efforts—another Pepsi ad later this year and a

Pepsi-sponsored tour—Madonna will make "short of $10 million," says an industry source, some of which will go to covering tour costs.

The faint pang of disgust raised by Neil Young's video parody of Jackson, Whitney Houston, Eric Clapton, and other corp-rock sell-outs last year seems to have passed like a kidney stone. The sheer size and glamour of this ad, coupled with the built-in consensus that arty/vulgar Madonna was made for this kind of thing, has left questions of "artistic integrity" to Massachusetts liberals.

But the ad itself, if viewed as video, is so canny it cooks. It opens with something all us narcissists can relate to: watching home movies of our own childhood. There's Little Madonna at her eighth birthday party (actually filmed circa 1988) being viewed by the big, real Madonna, looking peacefully lovely (in part because for once she's the spectator, albeit of herself). The entire spot is as recursive as a Rod Serling plot, which lends it the sentimental fantasy of most music videos. Now Little Madonna, cine-magically transported out of vid-world and into full-color life, watches the famous Madonna on the black-and-white screen. The star goes back to the mid-'60s, singing and dancing on urban, interracial streets, where the kids don't moonwalk perfectly. There's Madonna back at her Catholic girls' school, a black-clad sylph with a crucifix in her cleavage towering over the linen-collared uniforms. Everyone marches in timid lockstep until they glimpse an old poster of the bleached superstar—and suddenly the screen is full of flying frocks as they dance with the lapsed brunette in their midst.

The lyrics have power ("Life is a mystery/Everyone must stand alone/I hear you call my name and it feels like home/When you call my name, it's like a little prayer"), and the music's hooky, but it doesn't really swing until Madonna lets the gospel spirit of the Andre Crouch singers take over. (This is definitely the commercial version; the actual video, which ran on MTV the following day, is a much more daring mix of black soul and Catholic funk. Madonna is kissed by the reliquary of a black saint, gives herself the stigmata, and jitterbugs in front of a row of burning crosses. Madonna is the kind of Catholic girl who forgets to wear a hat in church—or a dress over her slip. RAI TV in Rome, under pressure from Catholic groups, has banned the video.)*

---

* And shortly after I wrote this, Pepsi pulled the ad in the United States—and *only* in the United States—because of uproar over the video.

At the end, Little Madonna, back in the black-and-white home movie, looks eerily from across time into the eyes of the real Madonna. As the child toasts her with a bottle of Pepsi, Madonna responds in kind with a can: "Go ahead. Make a wish." The tagline comes on— "Pepsi. A Generation Ahead"—and the loop is made: if Madonna Louise Veronica Ciccone could wish herself into stardom through the magic of video, a little cola consumer in Thailand or Paraguay can be like a star through the magic of advertising.

The ad is like a wet spot where all this season's hot TV topics have condensed: finding yourself by finding your "inner child"; depending on yourself (and not on men like Sean); the nostalgia of baby boomers for their 8-mm wonder years; Catholicism as the fashionable ethnicity to come *from*, because it's new traditionalist yet earthy; interracial mixing as a symbol of mature hipness (not unrelated to the way TV white guys establish soul by playing basketball with black guys). In a *Rolling Stone* interview, Madonna said that when she was little, all her girlfriends were black, and that she *feels* black.

All those very American themes would seem to make the ad too parochial to have the big, vague vavavavoom required for global marketing. What's a Tasaday in the Philippines to make of St. Mary schoolgirls in a chorus line? Actually, global marketing—crafting a commercial so that advertisers can use the same or nearly the same campaigns around the planet with little or no adjustments for language—was the big drive a few years ago. But it never really clicked—except with teenagers.

Marketeers believe that modern communications have spawned a "global teen," kids who have more in common with kids halfway across the earth than they do with other generations in the next room. Their percussive hormones drive them to Levi's and Swatch, Benetton and BIC perfume. Two new "global TV" shows—*Buzz* on MTV, which previewed Tuesday, and Fox network's *Revolution*, premiering in mid-May—are both rock-and-roll "lifestyle magazine" programs that flash at a superfast pace. And they're both thirsting for Pepsi or Coke as sponsors.

Music is the universal language and all that, but more importantly, cola is the universal solvent. Fit for any lifestyle, its image mutable, cola is truly *fluid*. Aesthetically, at least on American TV, where hard liquor ads are banned, soda spots are the kickiest, and they've become the alcoholic content of advertising. Cola is the teen caffeine, accounting for 70 percent of all soft drink sales. Pepsi, marketed in 150 countries, is still trying to catch up to Coke worldwide (the real thing outsells Pepsi two-and-a-half to one internationally). But their two corporate cultures share world hegemony, and to these titans, it's no longer enough to be just an *American* artist. Madonna has sold 75 million records worldwide—according to some, she's the most famous woman in the world. Naturally, Pepsi wants to use her to ensure its universal solvency.

As Madonna told *Rolling Stone*, "I like the challenge of merging art and commerce. As far as I'm concerned, making a video is also a commercial. The Pepsi spot is a great and different way to expose the record. Record companies just don't have the money to finance that kind of publicity. As it is, the music will be playing in the background, and the can of Pepsi is positioned very subliminally. The camera pans by it so it's not a hard sell commercial."

It's the *subtlety* of the sell that corporate-sponsored rock stars are increasingly judged by, not the fact that they're selling at all. For years, Madonna refused to do an ad—except in Japan (for Mitsubishi), like other big stars (David Byrne, Woody Allen, Paul Newman) who feel advertising would be crass here but is okay there, where they don't have relatives. One factor in Madonna's decision to do the Pepsi ad was the guarantee of exposure. "I wouldn't say [the long list of countries] was a prerequisite," says an industry source, "but there was discussion with Madonna's management and Warner Bros. about the number of people reached, or GRPs [gross rating points]. There was discussion of media weight."

The sense that the inevitable destination of all celebrity journeys is a Pepsi commercial validates the Big Shill of celebrity. Only the networks forged by the multinational soda pop vendors are vast enough to provide a stage for celeb/aristos like Madonna; only they heft enough media weight. We were always supposed to love Madonna *because* she luxuriates in media hype, writing jingles for teenage abandon. A Pepsi promo video has *Billboard* exec Sam Holdsworth kind of saying it all: "She's a commercial character. She's changed her persona three or four times in her career already, from the vamp ingenue to the punk to the techno girl to the who knows what, and I think Pepsi's done the same."

But in the next breath, he inadvertently spells out what's wrong with the sense that corp-rock is inevitable: "The whole push in promoting artists nowadays is how do you reach people, how do you reach people that either haven't heard of them, or haven't heard a particular album, or whose image hasn't really penetrated. And that's what advertising is and that's what promotion is, and I think that's what artists are really more and more about these days. Because it's an electronic medium, music's not a personal medium, and to be an international artist you really have to fly on that higher media plane."

In a press release, Pepsi lays its plans for world domination bare: "The groundbreaking deal is expected to change the way popular tunes from major artists are released in the future. Traditionally, new songs have been made public through heavy radio airplay. In an innovative twist, the Pepsi-Madonna deal uses television to provide unparalleled international exposure for her new single."

But if that's the way to enter the pantheon, then what does that make Pepsi and Coke? They are the medium through which the word is passed. They are universal, speaking no language and all languages. And each art/ad is like a prayer unto them.

I'M NOT A DOCTOR,

BUT I PLAY ONE ON REALITY TV

I'M NOT A DOCTOR, BUT I PLAY ONE ON REALITY TV

The pieces in this section consider the complex relationship between reality and television, taking up not only reality shows but also how our lived reality shapes and is shaped by televised stories.

In his short story "The TV" (2011), **Ben Loory** explores what happens when a man discovers that it is himself he is watching on the screen.

"Television, Reality, and Cold War Citizenship" (2005), by **Alan Nadel** examines American attitudes toward objective truth, national ideals, and televised narratives during the 1950s.

Poet **Douglas Kearney**'s "In the End, They Were Born on TV" (2014) offers the story of a couple expecting twins who agree to appear on a reality show, with unexpected results.

Actor, comedian, and writer **Aziz Ansari**, in "Why Is 'Everyman' a White Guy?" (2015), asks why it is still so difficult to find television or film actors who are not white playing substantial, non-stereotypical roles.

In "Kim's Fairytale Wedding" (2014), **Kate Durbin**'s retelling of a *Keeping Up with the Kardashians* episode raises questions about how we can tell what is "real" on the screen or in life.

The TV

Ben Loory

One day the man wakes up and finds that he does not feel like going to work. He is not sick, exactly; he just doesn't feel like going to work. He calls the office and makes an excuse, then he pours himself a bowl of cereal and sits down in front of the television.

The man doesn't usually have time to watch television, so it takes him a while to find a show he's interested in, but when he eventually does find it, he sits rapt, staring, his cereal forgotten, for a very, very, very long time. The show seems to last much longer than a normal show. In fact, it seems to last all day. It is five o'clock before the main character finally leaves his job and heads home, prompting the credits to roll.

The man sets his bowl of cereal aside and stares at the floor for a while.

My God, he thinks.

He gets up, goes into the bathroom, and gets into the shower. As he washes, he thinks about the show he has just seen. He is shampooing his hair when suddenly he realizes: the show was about him. Not kind of about him, not metaphorically about him, but actually *about him*.

That's why the main character looked so familiar, he thinks, dunking his head under the water.

But how could it have taken me so long to recognize my own self? he wonders. And how did they manage to find an actor who looks so exactly like me?

The man stays home from work again the next day, claiming to have the flu. The show is on again—his show. This time he watches it with his eyes open. Yep, there he is, arriving at work. He is wearing the suit he bought last week at Macy's. There he is, waving at the security guard he always waves at in the morning. Now he's walking down the hallway toward his office, now he's moving inside, there's his desk, his chair, his inbox and his outbox, his stapler and his letter opener. It's amazing; the man can hardly believe it. On-screen, he sits down at his desk, looks at the clock, and begins to work.

The man does the same thing at work every day; it is not very exciting. But somehow watching himself do it from inside his apartment, through the TV screen, is absolutely fascinating. The man is mesmerized by all the little unconscious movements his on-screen self makes. He seems to chew on his lip a lot.

Maybe that's why my lips are always chapped, he thinks, running a finger over them. He will have to watch that in the future.

At lunchtime, the man on-screen leaves the building and goes down the block to a little sandwich shop. It is Thursday, so the old man who owns the place is in. He and the man have a conversation about the state of the world while the man eats his sandwich (roast beef, same as always) and drinks his drink (coffee, black, same as always). Then the man returns to the office and works the rest of the day. At five o'clock he finishes up and heads out the door, and once again the credits roll.

This time the man on the couch studies the credits carefully. Yep, there's his name, listed both as the main character's and as that of the actor.

So it really *is* me, the man thinks in relief. It has been bothering him to think that an actor could so perfectly play him. It made him feel foolish to be so predictable, so reproducible. This way is much better. He feels proud of his role in the whole affair.

The next day, the man goes to work. He apologizes for having been absent for the past couple of days, but no one seems to care very much. This does not surprise him, but still it seems a little sad. The man sits at his desk and does his work. It is not much fun. It has never been much fun, he reflects, but now it seems particularly burdensome. He spends most of the time trying not to chew on his lip, with little success. At lunch, he goes down to the corner store. It is Friday, so the old man who owns the place is not in, so the man sits alone at a table in the corner and remembers the conversation that his on-screen self had with the old man the day before. He smiles to himself about some of the witty and observant things the two of them said.

Something nice happens in the afternoon. The man discovers that because his on-screen self did his work so well over the past couple of days, he is now done for the week. The man can hardly believe it. He almost never finishes his full workload. Usually he has to stay late on Friday night, or even come in on Saturday or Sunday—or both— to get it all done. He sits at his desk, marveling for a long moment at the knowledge that he can go home early, and then he does. He waves goodbye to the security guard on his way out. He drives home feeling the wind in his hair and the sun on his face.

At home, the man turns on the TV and is surprised to find that his show is on. There he is, wearing the same clothes he is wearing right now, in real life—but he is *still at work*. He is sitting behind his desk, hunched over a legal pad, writing something.

But how can this be? the man thinks. All the work is finished! He squints at the TV, trying to see what exactly his other self is working on. It is hard to tell. He seems to be writing up a list of some kind.

The man notices that the man behind the desk is no longer chewing on his lip.

That night the program does not stop at five. The man in the office keeps right on working until almost nine-thirty. At home, the man has pulled a straight-backed chair up to the TV and sits staring, trying to figure out what's happening, what his other self is doing. He cannot figure it out. When the man finally finishes working on his list—or whatever it is he's working on—he slides it into his briefcase and leaves work for the day. Again. At home the man sits with his eyes glued to the front door, waiting for himself to walk in. He has lots of questions. He wants to know what this list is all about. Ten, eleven, eleven-thirty, midnight. The door does not open.

Suddenly it occurs to the man that he can just open the briefcase and take out the list and read it. After all, it is *his* briefcase. He gets up and goes into the bedroom. Now, where did he put that briefcase? He can't remember. Where does he usually put it? He can't remember that, either. In fact, he suddenly realizes, he can't remember ever owning a briefcase at all.

The next day, the man awakens confused. He sits on the edge of the bed. He feels like he is forgetting something, but can't think what it could possibly be.

The man gets to the couch early so he won't miss anything. But he is surprised to find himself already seated behind the desk when he turns on the TV. There he is, with his feet up, reading a book. The book is lying open in his lap, so the man cannot tell what it is. It is very thick, though. There are other books stacked neatly nearby on the desk. The man squints to make out the titles, wondering what they're all about. Some of them seem to be about business management, but one is about calculus, and there are others about art and history, and one narrow volume seems to be a collection of poetry. The man smiles when he sees that. What on earth is going on?

When nine o'clock rolls around, the man behind the desk closes the book he's reading (is it the *dictionary*?) and gets down to work. He works quickly and with an air of extreme concentration. At home, the man on the couch, though filled with admiration for his other, better self, feels a twinge of jealousy, and even, strangely enough, something that feels like fear.

At lunch, the man on-screen does not go to the shop on the corner. Instead, he fixes his tie and then heads down the corridor in the direction of his boss's office. The man on the couch cannot believe what he's seeing. He watches as he knocks firmly on the boss's door and then goes inside, closing the door behind him and staying inside for some time. When he emerges fifteen minutes later, he is smiling. He stops and calls back to the person inside, something in the way of an affirmation, and then heads off along the hall, a spring in his step. With the remainder of his lunch hour, he eats a sandwich he has brought to work in a brown paper bag, and drinks a bottle of water.

The man at home does not know what's happening. He has never purposely gone to speak to his boss. In fact, he can't imagine ever wanting to do such a thing. Still, he admires his on-screen self for doing it. Perhaps something good will come of it—maybe a raise. The man goes into the kitchen and grabs a bag of cookies from the cupboard. But when he returns to the living room, he finds that his on-screen self has left early for the day. His office is clean, his outbox is full, his pile of books is gone.

The man sits staring at his empty office for some time. He begins to get antsy. Where has he gone? There is no way to know. What did he say to his boss? What was on the list? And what are all the books for? The man is beginning to feel nauseous thinking about it all. He is making himself sick. He has to think about something else. Perhaps there is something else on the television.

The man changes the channel. There is a cartoon about a coyote, a commercial for an exercise machine, someone talking about the weather, and, oh wait, what's this? There's the man again. He's in his car now, driving down a street with which the man on the couch is unfamiliar. He stops outside a building, an office building, and he goes inside. He speaks to a receptionist, and is then ushered into a conference room.

In the room are a number of men, all of whom look very serious. At home, the man on the couch is frightened. But his other self looks perfectly at ease. He places his briefcase carefully on the table, unlocks it with a pair of decisive clicks, and opens it up. Inside is a stack of papers. He begins to hand them out and, as he does so, he begins to speak. He speaks about things the man on the couch does not understand. Stocks and bonds and financial matters, things like that. The man on the couch furrows his brow, trying to follow it all. He can't, but he is relieved to see that the men in the room seem to be following it quite well and, what's more, seem to be quite happy with what they're hearing.

At the end of the meeting, the men rise, smiling, and spend quite some time congratulating the man on what he has said and done. Cigars are passed around and the man takes one and sees himself smoking it with a practiced air, despite the fact that he has never smoked a cigar before in his life, and wouldn't ever want to, as they are disgusting. Still, he has to admit, it is quite enjoyable.

When the man leaves the meeting, however, the show does not follow him. It stays in the conference room with the other men, and after a while—despite the fact that these other men are beginning to seem vaguely familiar—the man on the couch starts to tire of their banter. He figures he's probably gotten back to the office by now, so he changes the channel again.

He is almost back to his original station when suddenly he recognizes himself on a show about doctors. He is in surgery, raising his hands in the air as a nurse slips a pair of latex gloves over them. He almost didn't recognize himself, thanks to the mask that covers half his face, but there's no doubt about it, it's him—after all, if a man can't recognize himself, what *can* he recognize? This is his first day as a surgeon. Apparently the man has been going to night school. The man on the couch is impressed. He didn't know you could go to night school to become a surgeon, and yet it turns out that he himself has actually been doing it this whole time! He marvels at himself as he cuts open some poor man's chest and begins to operate on his malfunctioning heart. He hopes the operation will go well, and it does. The nurses congratulate him as he sews the man back together. Later on they all go out drinking and the man makes love to one of the nurses—the more attractive one—in the bathroom of the club. It is the best sex the man has had in years.

On another station, the man finds himself foiling a gang of jewel thieves. He had infiltrated the gang thanks to some ingenious plastic surgery and a number of carefully constructed lies. He waits until the last possible moment and then he springs the trap. Everyone is arrested and found guilty and after the trial the man is singled out for bravery and is given a medal and a monument is erected to him in a park downtown. Lovers sit on a bench beside the monument and feel safe. Still, it is sad because the man's father once died in a botched robbery, and while what the man has done makes himself feel better, as though he has finally evened out the situation, he knows that nothing he can do will ever bring his father back from the dead. Still, though, perhaps his work has prevented other innocent fathers from being killed.

Meanwhile, the man is a scientist who has invented a way to bring people back from the dead. He uses it to bring back his wife, who died a few years ago, but then he learns that she didn't love him after all and that it is better not to mess with bringing people back from the dead. He is a better man for learning this, but still he can't help but feel sorry for himself, as he misses his wife and the love that he thought she had for him. On another station, the man is punching another man—himself?—in the face over and over again. The man sees the glory and the horror in this, but he doesn't feel like watching it right now. On another station the man has become the head of a warlike country and is threatening to unleash Armageddon on the world if his barbarous demands are not met. The man becomes afraid of himself and changes the channel. Now he is murdering a small boy in a field with a rusty knife and he feels absolutely terrible. Whatever happened to night school and books about poetry? He changes the channel again. There he is, trying to sell himself some kind of cleaning product. And now he is running down the street faster than an airplane thanks to the wonderful shoes he has invented, and blackmailing a political figure even though he himself is not without sin. The man is beginning to become confused. He is proud of himself and everything he has accomplished, very proud indeed—he always knew he had it in him. But at the same time he is scared of what he sees. There are things about himself that he doesn't want to know, things he does that he doesn't want to think about. He wishes there were some way he could choose what he does and does not do. But it is beyond his control. He runs rampant across the world, helping and killing and saving and selling, buying and raping and stealing and feeling and making love and running away and laughing and crying and dying and being born and dying and being born and dying and being born and dying and being born. The man cannot take it anymore, he can't take it anymore. He walks into the other room and puts a shotgun in his mouth and just then the show comes abruptly to an end. Eventually the man comes to see that he has a mind, and that his mind is like a fist, wrapped tightly around a single thought. He cannot open the fist to look at the thought, for fear that it will fly away, but he knows that it is very important and that he must hang on to it, no matter the cost. He stares at the fist and hopes that it is very strong. He feels like a man who has fallen asleep at the wheel and has awakened to find his car lurching off a cliff. He has applied the brake, he has swung the wheel to the side, he has offered up a silent prayer, but it is as yet too soon to see whether he has done these things in time. He can only wait for the next moment to come, and hope as hard as he can.

Finally the next moment comes. The man realizes that the thing in his hand is not a thought but the end of an electrical cord. He looks down and finds that the electrical cord leads to the television—now a dark, silent box lying on the floor at his feet. The man feels a rush of triumph. He has come out on top, he has won. He grins to himself as he contemplates his next move. He decides that the best thing to do is to take the TV down to the trash and get rid of it. And this is exactly what he does.

But in the stairwell on the way back from the trash, the man passes himself carrying the television down to the trash. He stops to congratulate himself on his wisdom and strength, but his other self averts his eyes, hoping not to be noticed. The man begins to take offense and is about to say something, when both of them are elbowed aside by a third version of the man who is carrying his TV back up from the trash. The man hurries after himself, yelling No, No, I don't want that anymore! but he doesn't listen. As they enter the apartment, the man on the couch looks up from the TV in irritation. Why can't everyone leave him alone? The room is packed with versions of the man, running here and there, talking to himself about this and that, making plans on the phone and staring out the window and falling in love and falling out of love and finding himself loved and unloved and hated and feared and liked and disliked and ignored and unknown and known. He is fired, promoted, rehired, and refired, has found a new place to live and is moving out, is moving in and repainting, is in the other room dying and in the kitchen being born. There is too much going on. The man walks out the door and down the hall and into the next apartment. Mommy, Mommy, scream his children, what's for breakfast? The man makes French toast and waffles and ham and eggs and pancakes and cereal and Pop-Tarts and brownies and hot dogs and hamburgers and Baked Alaska and a birthday cake in the shape of a castle and pours glasses of milk and orange juice and coffee and Tang and Kool-Aid and water and puts ice in all the glasses, trying to ignore himself as he murders each and every one of the kids over and over and over again in hundreds of different ways and gets a job in another country under an assumed name and pees all over the dining room floor and draws on the wall in crayon. He takes the kids down to the bus stop seven hundred times and he drives the bus to school—drunk, sober, hungover, on acid, pot, cocaine, uppers and downers, or nothing at all—it doesn't matter in the least, he gets in an accident every foot of the way, or he doesn't. At school, he gets in a fight on the playground and is sent to the office, or doesn't and isn't, or does and isn't, or doesn't and is. He gives himself a good lecture, maybe, winks at the secretary he has or has not been banging for the past two weeks, or four weeks, or ten weeks, or no weeks, then hurries slowly to the women's room, realizing that it is or is not his time of the month, mops none or half or all of the gym, and goes out back to have a smoke or stare at the sky or remember the time he accidentally ate a spider or became president or something else or nothing else or everything else. He flies to the next town over and perches in all the trees, then falls to the ground in several different countries and is blown away by the wind, which hammers endlessly in all the ears he has—more than he is capable of counting—for approximately 93 billion years, as good a guess as any to a time outside of time.

The man especially loves it when he is a doctor, a lawyer, a caveman, a cowboy, an old man who owns a luncheonette and talks to the people who come in to eat every day. He hates it when he is a doctor, a lawyer, a caveman, a cowboy, an old man who owns a luncheonette and talks to the people who come in to eat every day, but he loves it when he is a comedian, a beautiful young model, an astronaut, the king of England, a profiler working for the Federal Bureau of Investigation. It is very exciting. He loves to taunt the profiler by sending him long, cryptic notes written in human blood. He knows he will never catch him, and even if he does, it doesn't really matter because he is already dead and buried and being eaten by worms and will probably just get another medal and a raise anyway.

Sometimes the man cries himself to sleep at night, but usually he just changes the channel. He has not been able to find his way to the office; he doesn't know where they put it. He rings and rings, but the nurse no longer answers his calls. One night he discovers that his lips are horribly chapped. This strikes him as the worst thing that has ever happened, and he sobs uncontrollably for almost fourteen seconds. Then, once more, he opens the fist.

Television, Reality, and Cold War Citizenship

(selection)

Alan Nadel

THE INSTRUMENT OF TRUTH

Television fostered its reputation for objectivity from its status as a technological phenomenon even more than from its programming. Part of television's power, in this regard, was owed to a faith in visual representation that has dominated Western thought since the Renaissance. "Seeing is believing," we have come to believe. "Pictures never lie." "Ocular proof," Othello demanded of Iago before he would accept assertions of Desdemona's infidelity. Modern science depends on the empirical method. The solution to every mystery, Sherlock Holmes demonstrated, begins with observation. Noting the commercial value of television, a 1946 article about the use of the close-up, by H. G. Christensen, in the fledgling trade journal *Television* explains "another important thing: By *visual* demonstration *actual proof* can be submitted of many things that now must be accepted on mere statement."[1]

Christensen was not referring to news, science, nature, or education but to a sponsor's claim about the storage capacity of a refrigerator. As another example, Christensen describes a show that demonstrated that Chef Boyardee spaghetti could be prepared in twelve minutes: "During the entire broadcast, with all the changes of camera angles, the pot on the stove *was always* in the scene." The climax of the show was that the meal was served to the audience members. "There was an integrated commercial that not only didn't interfere with the rest of the show but certainly did a better selling job than ever could be done by oratorical radio."[2] The quality of the food was validated by the sight of the audience eating it.

For some people, television even represented an extension of the natural order. "A man will come home at night," stated a 1949 book, "and open the magic window of television, which will bring him information and entertainment from all over the world. . . . He will have lost the habit of using his ears for what they were never meant to do, and sight will have been restored to its natural place in his life."[3] Television was predicted to be so powerful a medium as to activate more than the natural senses of sight and sound. "So magic is the performance of the electron tube," wrote one commentator in 1942, "and so diversified is the service it already performs, that an engineer in describing its versatility reports that it can hear, see, taste, feel, smell, remember, calculate, count, measure, and talk."[4]

Television's stunning visual power was enhanced by its potential for immediacy. Television gave Americans access to a new level of truth not only because it let people see things but allegedly let them see things *immediately*, before reality could undergo alteration. Rather than perform actions, television ostensibly allowed events to be performed.

"The public," James Caddigan wrote in *Television*, "is being given the promise now of 'seeing things as they happen.' It is their most enthusiastic expectation of the immediacy of television that will present a challenge to every station to present the 'scoop' news in as speedy and complete a manner as possible." Unlike print media, which have to wait for the story to unfold, then write it up, print it, and distribute it, television would, in effect, eliminate the middlemen. The television public, Caddigan believed, would expect to witness news rather than read about it.

Clearly the public that Caddigan had in mind in 1947, when he wrote this dictum, was the general American populace, not the tiny minority that actually owned television sets. Caddigan's huge imaginary audience, moreover, would have access to a competing array of news broadcasts integrated into a constant flow of programming, for "the immediacy of television" was as much temporal as physical. Gilbert Seldes, an early pioneer in television programming and one of the medium's most articulate critics, wrote, "The fact that television can transmit actuality is of prime psychological importance. It invites us to 'the conception of things as they are'; it sets us on the way to maturity. . . . The essential thing is to determine that television will satisfy the deep human desire to look, at times, on the face of reality."[5]

A significant pillar of the argument rested on underscoring "spontaneity." As Orin Dunlap pointed out in 1942, "Telecasting of spot news is mostly a matter of luck. The biggest thrills in newscasting are likely to be surprises." And, as early as 1948, *Time* was lauding television's power of the spontaneous: "The unexpected makes some of television's brightest moments: a rainstorm breaks, and the camera shows groundkeepers covering the pitcher's box with canvas, then sweeps across the bleachers, singling out soaked fans huddling under newspapers. The key man is the camera director, who must watch on small screens the action of three or four cameras, to decide which image to send over the air at any moment."[6]

The newscasts, the same article noted, were generally disappointing, with the exception of "such foreseeable events as political rallies where the cameras, being set in place, catch unscheduled incidents."[7] In this interesting mix of the "foreseeable" and the "unexpected," wherein surprise depends on prediction, we can see in the moments of television's initial mass reception that the television viewer was in effect seen as a paragon of the surveillance state. The viewer tuned in to one event, but because that event was live, the viewer might unexpectedly find a second event hidden within the first. The brightest moments were those in which orchestrated order was disrupted, and the anonymous spectator glimpsed moments of something "unexpected." Even though the event—a ball game, a speech, a performance—came with the immediacy of a live broadcast, it was validated by the unexpected, as if its claim to be real required the proof of a second level of reality. In order to appreciate the full richness of television's potential, therefore, the viewer had to be on the alert.

That glowing reality—"some of television's *brightest* moments"—relied crucially on the camera, which must already be in place so as to "catch unscheduled events," and the camera director, who must "decide which image to send at any moment." The unexpected constituted both the bane of television programming and its validation. It gave people an extra reason to watch the limited and fuzzy perspective that it afforded; it invested the ordinary with extraordinary value and untapped potential. Caddigan noted,

> Many of the so-called special events productions give little warning of their coming, and should a television production staff wait until an incident or a story is looming over the production horizon, before moving toward preparation, the story will either be poorly produced or lost entirely. Preparation for the unexpected seems like a larger order to fill, yet, that is exactly the job that must be handled if the special event or news incident is to be produced with the "immediacy" that television promises. The television audience of the future is being educated at the present time to expect sight of an incident "as it happens."[8]

Although television heavily encouraged that expectation, in 1952 less than half of all households had television sets, and because of an FCC licensing freeze between 1948 and 1952, broadcasting was concentrated regionally. As a whole, therefore, the nation was incapable of seeing things as they happened. Beyond that, the technology of broadcasting—the size and cost of the cameras, the expense and difficulty of remote hookups, the limited picture quality—rendered "spontaneity" a relatively rare commodity. Far more regularly, television offered a mix of staged, rehearsed performances, broadcast live, and action or adventure shows on film, augmented by old movies, often cut into bits. Aside from sports, few events were presented as they happened, and the total amount of sportscasting, especially on network television, was very low.

While the capacity for the whole nation to see something "as it happened" was facilitated by the completion in 1953 of the transcontinental coaxial cable, connecting television signals from coast to coast, such moments were still infrequent. The cable facilitated viewing such national events as, for example, President Eisenhower's inauguration, but it contributed relatively little, in the regular flow of programming, to support television's promise to put all Americans in touch with everything at exactly the moment that everything happened. It is vital to keep in mind, nevertheless, how pervasively the television industry in its formative years asserted that it was providing a conduit to reality, and consequently how many of its programming strategies contributed to bolstering that assertion.

Television projected a sense of intimacy, surrounded by an aura of verisimilitude, as if to augment its less-than-fulfilled promise of immediacy. To that end, even talk shows such as *Today* manifested "togetherness" by bringing the world to the viewer, filtered through an ersatz family of hosts and assistants. One early *Today* host, Ernie Kovacs, used his wife, Edie Adams, as part of the cast; another host, Dave Garroway, included in his morning family J. Fred Muggs, a chimp who vividly merged the traits of the viewers' diapered baby boomer infants and their adored house pets.

Perhaps the most interesting ways in which television programming asserted the medium's veracity clustered around those portions of the schedule lacking the prima facie assumption of "truth" that accrued, for example, to a live sporting event. Arthur Godfrey, who in the early 1950s had three separate, highly successful television shows running simultaneously, owed much of his success to his ability to capitalize on television's investment in intimacy and reality. Although no one argued that he was an exceptionally talented performer, Godfrey was popular both with daytime and prime time audiences because his ad libs and informal conversational style conveyed the sense that he was expressing his true personality, that he was genuine. As one pair of television historians succinctly noted, "People did not tire of him because he was an interesting person to listen to. He was himself."[9]

Godfrey epitomized an attitude toward television as the magic place where things were themselves. Most early sitcoms were live, and when they were not, they used obligatory laugh tracks to suggest spontaneity. Many of those shows employed what has been called an "I-me-mine" formula in which a celebrity played him- or herself or appeared as a fictional character who had much in common with the real-life performer. The "real" personality of the performer thus created a sense of intimacy that diminished the show's fictional aspects and created a comfort zone: the viewers were taking the performers into their living rooms, and the performers seemed to be reciprocating.

One particularly successful early sitcom of this sort, *The Adventures of Ozzie and Harriet* (1952–1966), focused on the domestic setting of the real band leader Ozzie Nelson, his real wife and former lead singer, Harriet, and their two sons, all of whom played themselves. *The Burns and Allen Show* similarly had George Burns and Gracie Allen playing themselves, enacting episodes chiefly from their domestic rather than professional lives. *Make Room for Daddy*, starring Danny Thomas as himself, followed a similar formula, as did a number of less successful shows such as *Mary Kay and Johnny* (1948), a sitcom about the trials and tribulations of a real married couple of entertainers.[10]

At a very slight remove from these shows were those in which celebrity performers played characters with fictional names and, sometimes, fictional occupations, who nevertheless very closely resembled the celebrities who played them. These included *Where's Raymond?*, starring Ray Bolger; *Bonino*, starring Ezio Pinza; and perhaps the most famous sitcom of all time, *I Love Lucy*. In that series the character Lucy, played by Lucille Ball, was married to Ricky Ricardo, a Cuban band leader, played by Desi Arnaz, the Cuban band leader to whom Ball was actually married. The show, which premiered in 1950, quickly became the most popular sitcom in the country, and Lucille Ball's pregnancy, mirrored on the show by Lucy's pregnancy, became the focus of the 1952–1953 season. In the midst of the postwar baby boom, pregnancy no doubt was one of the greatest common denominators shared by the television audience, so the pregnant Lucille Ball mirrored not only her character but also her viewers. In Lucy's pregnancy, television was providing the newest member of the family at the same time that the television set was becoming the newest addition. Millions of home-bound new mothers welcomed television into their growing family with the same alacrity with which they awaited Lucy's delivery.

Indeed, this visual instrument not only functioned as a member of the household and a figure of authority; it also self-consciously positioned itself as the representative of religious and domestic norms. To that end, for example, a rabbi, a priest, and a minister were present on the set for the filming of all the Lucy episodes dealing with the pregnancy. Throughout those episodes, the word *pregnant* was never used, nor, throughout the entire run of the series, were Lucy and Ricky ever portrayed as sleeping in the same bed.

THE SURVEILLANCE STATE

The members of the clergy observing the filming of the pregnant-Lucy episodes, while guaranteeing that the episodes were in good taste, could also guard against some indecency that went undetected by the actors, writers, producers, directors, that is, by the normal mechanisms of television production. These religious leaders served as the invited agents of the ultimate surveillance state; under their watchful eyes, it would be impossible, even inadvertently, to subvert American mores, to deviate from the approved domestic norms. This need for elaborately self-conscious layers of censorship in the form of self-observation, like the odd symbiotic relationship between the planned and the unpredictable so valued by early television critics, implicitly identified television with the surveillance-state mentality that informed American life at the moment of the medium's proliferation.

As has been extensively noted, the manifestations of Cold War containment extended to all aspects of American life.[11] Loyalty oaths proliferated. College faculties were being purged.[12] The US Senate and House of Representatives were conducting continuous investigations to safeguard the nation from subversion. The FBI, the Central Intelligence Agency (CIA), and sundry private organizations were gathering files on people whose actions might reveal disloyalty. Television, as the technology that allowed one to see everything, fitted well into the cultural logic of Cold War observation and intelligence gathering.

"Television's surveillance potential," Jeanne Allen points out, "was quickly associated with aircraft intelligence gathering."[13] Army intelligence, in fact, was the model Caddigan recommended for television newsgathering. News divisions, he believed, should set up for each area a "television intelligence file" that would include notification contacts, topographic data, weather reports, and correct credentials because, "at the time of an incident, intelligence from the field will be most important to the production staff working on the script at the station."[14] This form of military-style intelligence gathering was "a never ending job as each new production will provide added information that can be used to advantage on some future show."[15]

A world under surveillance made sense to post–World War II Americans locked in the throes of the Cold War frenzy. At exactly the moment that the television curtain rose, the iron curtain was descending not only on Eastern Europe but also on world consciousness. Fears of the spread of communism outside American borders and the subversion of American ideals from within inundated the nation with an aura of suspicion. Thus, at every turn television differentiated American acts and values from un-American activities and objectives. People who did not consider religious broadcasts a form of public service, people who had not allowed their families to pray or stay together, people who embraced controversial positions or associated with those who did (or were even accused of associating with them)—these people were suspect.

The search for subversion, for deviance, after all, requires a set of norms against which to measure deviation, and nothing would supply the norms more prolifically and more rigidly than television. Enabling Americans to distinguish the true American from the imposter was therefore a task fundamentally consistent with the idea of television. As we have seen, television promoted itself as the medium of truth, not artifice. This describes to an equal degree the industry's self-image and the public image it promoted. With extreme versatility, television devoted its strong authority to the cause of the Cold War. The anticommunist message, as J. Fred MacDonald has extensively documented, took numerous forms.[16] Bishop Fulton J. Sheen may have been the most successful and the most explicitly anticommunist of the religious broadcasters, but he was far from the only one performing the public service of helping the nation align itself on the side of God in confirmed opposition to the godless communists. "The fundamental depravity explaining all Red actions was alleged to be the atheism basic to Communism."[17]

The broadcast schedule, through the mid-1950s, was replete with spy series, action-adventure series, and military and space adventure shows that shared a set of common Cold War motifs. Each episode of *Superman* reminded us that he was the superhuman, interplanetary agent of "truth, justice, and the American way." *Captain Video*'s Video Rangers swore "to support forever the cause of Freedom, Truth, and Justice throughout the universe," and children watching *Rod Brown of the Rocket Rangers* in order to join the Junior Rocket Rangers had to pledge to "always chart my course according to the Constitution of the

United States of America."[18] *Captain Midnight*, a jet pilot and the commander of a secret squadron based in a secret mountaintop location, so regularly dealt with issues of national defense and problems caused by enemy agents that J. Fred MacDonald calls it "thoroughly Cold War in its orientation."[19]

Television documentaries on the US military also dotted the programming landscape. One of the most successful, *The Big Picture*, filmed by the US Army Signal Corps, produced 828 episodes between 1951 and 1971,[20] each beginning with the announcement: "From Korea to Germany, from Alaska to Puerto Rico, all over the world the United States Army is on the alert to defend our country—you, the American people—against aggression."[21] This connection between foreign policy and "you, the American people" at home watching television is very revealing. Television was indeed the instrument that connected the everyday life, the leisure activity of the American people, to their national agenda: "Our country" meant "you the television viewer."

If watching television made one the definitive citizen, we need to consider how that practice defined citizenship. Certainly the connections to the monopolistic aspects of television broadcasting are implicit. If watching television were a multifarious, diversified, and fragmentary experience, each person's participation would be somewhat unique. Assorted Americans would receive sundry messages and be exposed to wide-ranging values and opinions. (Consider for example the fact that although most of the European countries in the Western bloc—the North Atlantic Treaty Organization [NATO] nations—had active, often successful socialist parties, a socialist's acquiring any serious television exposure in America would be impossible even today, much less during the black-and-white era.) Under a more diversified broadcast system, citizenship might have been defined by the right to watch and respond to an array of viewpoints and values, not by the message one received. Exactly the opposite was true under the heavily monopolized system of American Cold War television, in which a small number of stations conformed to very similar norms. "The aim of television," as David Marc so aptly puts it, "is to be normal. The industry is obsessed with the problem of norms."[22]

The (white) nuclear family watching *The Big Picture* was the normative unit of domestic security in the nuclear age. As such, it received relentless instructions on how to be normal at the same time that it was the measure of television's normal range of expression. From its inception, radio sought to reach the broadest audience by presenting that which was most common. Television not only inherited the informing principle of *broad*casting but also turned that principle into a national ideal.

Its monopolistic structure allowed television programming to be dominated by two networks, each competing for a simple majority of viewers. Each week in the months of January and February 1957, for example, the CBS half-hour adventure show *Robin Hood* was watched on between 48 percent and 51 percent of the sets in use, composing just under one-third of the total potential television audience. In none of those weeks, however, did *Robin Hood*'s ratings put it among the top twenty shows.[23] Under such circumstances, alienating even a relatively small segment of the audience could put a broadcaster or network at a great disadvantage. If the FCC had not created an artificial scarcity of stations, then worsened the scarcity by freezing the issuing of licenses for three years; if it had not aligned itself so strongly with patents and technology controlled by one company and ignored the need for public television, one could, in theory, imagine circumstances in the early 1950s that would have allowed most populated areas to have over a dozen stations, and for the thousands of stations throughout the country to be affiliated with one or more of a few dozen networks, producing shows that spanned a broad range of opinions, ideas, and interests. One could imagine, for example, stations and networks organized around the interests of targeted minorities, or political values, or regional and local concerns. The narrower the broadcast frequency spectrum, the lower the frequency of dissent and the smaller the spectrum of opinion. Under the commercial, legal, and technological structure of television in its formative years, the safe, the clichéd, and the uncontroversial had an enormous advantage over the experimental, the original, and the challenging.

The economic pressure to maximize the number of viewers when applied to the concept of citizenship thus encouraged a very conservative citizen, so that television could be the site of debate in the public forum only so long as the parameters of the debate did not exceed the most common of accepted notions. At the height of the Cold War in America, any position fell outside the normal spectrum if it could be associated, for example, with socialism. Although national health care was becoming the norm in post–World War II Europe and the bulk of the industrialized world, because it was branded "creeping socialism" or "socialized medicine" it could not be treated seriously in US news coverage, public affairs broadcasting, or television dramas. Homosexuality, premarital sex, and atheism were as unacceptable as plunging necklines or, for the most part, men with facial hair. An unqualified endorsement of capitalism and Judeo-Christian religious belief provided a tacit foundation for all of the positions expressed in virtually all programming.

This set of conditions mandated many programming decisions. Because delivering consumers to sponsors seemed, at least ostensibly, connected to head counting, the network or program that could deliver the largest audience was the most valuable. Unlike industries that rely chiefly on niche audiences, television, especially in the first decades, sought a degree of universality. The consequent pressure to maintain huge audiences demanded inoffensive programming.

In order to assure that programming was inoffensive, the National Association of Radio and Television Broadcasters in 1956 codified its norms with a television code. The preamble, stressing the fact that television was a common national activity, began with its informing principle: "Television is seen and heard in every type of American home."[24] Therefore, "it is the responsibility of television to bear constantly in mind that the audience is primarily a home audience, and consequently that television's relationship to the viewers is that between guest and host."[25] This metaphor treated the viewer and the show as equal in kind. The television show was not some object to be accepted, rejected, evaluated, or consumed; it was a guest, someone like the viewer, to be invited in and attended to.

At the same time that the broadcasters were guests who must display good manners, they also had to provide the viewer with the *best*: "American businesses . . . are reminded that their responsibilities are not limited to the sales of goods and the creation of a favorable attitude toward the sponsor. . . . They include, as well, responsibility for utilizing television to bring the best programs . . . into the American home."[26]

The notion that television had the capacity to deliver the best was a long-accepted axiom of the medium. During World War II, television was used in New York City to train air-raid wardens, who received their lessons from sets installed at local police stations. This program of instruction was based on the idea that "there is always a best lecturer for any subject and through television he can actually instruct all the parties instantly and uniformly. Standardization of training is thus introduced into the defense plans."[27]

The technology of television, as its use in police stations in the interest of national defense illustrated, allowed Americans to receive the best as a universal standard. "In this war program," Dunlap explains, "light has been shed on the ability of television to put into practical use the unlimited possibilities envisaged for it after the war."[28] After the war, through television, the best would become the standard; the standard would become uniform and available for universal access. The broadcasters' code merely codified that prediction by elaborately detailing the characteristics of the best programming. It included using television as a "means of augmenting the educational and cultural influences of schools, institutions of learning, the home, the church, museums," with the understanding that education "via television may be taken as to mean that process by which the individual is brought toward informed adjustment to his society."[29] Televisual education, in other words, is a form of regulation that validates social norms and brings the individual in line with them.

Here are some examples of appropriate adjustments found in the code's twenty-nine-item list of acceptable program material: "Reverence is to mark any mention of the name of God, His attributes and powers"; "illicit sex relations are not to be treated as commendable"; "law enforcement shall be upheld, and the officers of the law are to be portrayed with respect and dignity"; "camera angles shall avoid such views of performers as to emphasize anatomical details indecently."[30] As part of television's obligation to provide the best programming, the code unequivocally stated, "It is the responsibility of a television broadcaster to make available to the community as part of a well-balanced program schedule adequate opportunity for religious presentations."[31]

This code clearly delimited television's options within a rigid Cold War agenda that supplemented the medium's role as a virtual arm of government propaganda. The power of propaganda, of course, is directly correlated with its invisibility, that is, its ability to disappear beneath the veil of "truth." During the height of the Cold War, American "truth" comprised a narrowly construed and pervasively deployed consensus. The strategy of "containment," as originally articulated by George Kennan, charged all American citizens with the task of checking the spread of communism through a combination of vigilance and self-scrutiny that would produce a uniformly attractive image of American life.[32] Because the Cold War was being fought for hearts and minds, on a chiefly symbolic battleground, the ability to deliver and solidify images proved as effective in some ways as any form of hardware, just as the principle of "deterrence" depended on the symbolic rather than the material value of planes, missiles, and nuclear warheads.

Since containment rendered the American family a form of symbolic capital, the best programming taught Americans how, implicitly in the national interest, to be normal. If television was a guest, it was a very knowledgeable and instructive guest visiting a compliant and amenable host, one who was receptive to a national agenda and in touch with national norms and mores. Dedicated to normalizing and affirming the values and lifestyles of its audience, the television broadcasting system aimed, one could argue, at becoming a seamless extension of the television set, the piece of living room furniture that made those projections part of the flow of everyday life. "Television," *House Beautiful* announced in 1951, "has become a member of the family."[33] As such, of course, it could not be controversial, for the home, after all, was the repository of postwar values, and the nuclear family, by consolidating the values for which the Cold War was being fought, implicitly validated the nuclear arms race.

A stunning example of television's avoidance of controversy could be seen in the treatment of the actress Jeanne Muir, a regular in the early hit sitcom *The Aldrich Family*. Muir was charged with participation in left-wing activities. Although she denied the charges, General Foods, the show's sponsor, indicated that it made no difference whether or not she were guilty; the mere fact that she had been accused could hurt sales. "This reasoning became a model for other blacklisting cases. . . . The very fact that someone had been charged made them guilty of being too controversial."[34] In the obsessively normal world of black-and-white television, a person innocent of any substantive charge could nevertheless be guilty of being controversial. This latter category—being controversial—which comprised the blacklist's largest group by far was, as Thomas Doherty points out, "infinitely elastic in application and maddeningly circular in reasoning."[35] If television was the site of exemplary citizenship—the apotheosis of democracy—it was a new kind of democracy, one forging consensus by precluding controversy. And since television was *the* American activity, anything not suitable for broadcast, by implication, was un-American.

With the outbreak of the Korean War, suspicion became an even more overt obligation. "At home the question of Communist influence in America was no longer restricted to the theoretical level—the nation was at war. With American boys being felled by Red bullets, no sponsor wanted to be charged with satisfying the Communists by putting one of their fellow-travelers on national television. Publications such as *Red Channels* became the unofficial Madison Avenue bibles on performers with alleged Communist connections."[36] *Red Channels*, published in June 1950, was devoted to identifying "subversives." The American Communist Party newspaper, *The Daily Worker*, "as vetted by *Red Channels* was not the only source of names," Doherty explained. "Page after page of lists and publications, notations culled from rumor, supplemented by innuendo, and littered with transcription errors, might also render a personality controversial."[37]

Despite the need to rely on dubious information, networks and ad agencies vetted prospective hires in all aspects of production. A company executive in charge of personnel security reviewed the names with "consultants" working for organizations such as AWARE, Incorporated, an anticommunist arm of the broadcast industry founded by Vincent Hartnett, the chief author of *Red Channels*. Producer David Susskind testified to having submitted for approval about *five thousand* names.[38] People who were not approved were virtually unemployable unless they were cleared by AWARE. For such clearance, Hartnett received substantial fees and/or exacted favors as proof of loyalty. Since producers were instructed never to reveal the reason they had failed to hire someone, it often took people time to discover that they were being blacklisted—and, unless they overtly succumbed to a financial or ethical shakedown, even longer to find out they had been removed from the list.

Such was the case of Philip Loeb, the costar of *The Goldbergs*, a hit comedy in the late 1940s. In 1950 he was named by *Red Channels* because of his progressive political activities in the 1930s and the show's sponsor attempted to buy out his contract. He refused and continued to appear on the show until the end of the season, when CBS canceled it despite its high ratings. When NBC picked it up, the new network required, despite the protestations of the show's producer and star, Gertrude Berg, that Loeb be replaced. From 1952 on, the FBI kept Loeb under surveillance while he struggled to find sparse work. In August 1955, the bureau decided that Loeb should be removed from its list of suspects. One month later, with no knowledge of his cleared status, Loeb committed suicide.

One sign of a possible subversive was an interest in civil rights. Security investigators often regarded a black employee's participation in civil rights activities as incriminating evidence.[39] Hazel Scott, a black singer and performer, in 1950 briefly had a program on the DuMont network until she was listed by *Red Channels*. Although she testified before the House Un-American Activities Committee (HUAC) at her own request, categorically denying any interest in the Communist Party, she was unable to save her show. Even if Scott had, for some unlikely reason, triumphed over the blacklist, there's a strong chance she would not have survived the end of the FCC license freeze in 1952, for that moment marked the point at which television would enter the South at a large scale. Once the South made up a significant portion of the market, any network found that alienating viewers in that region was a risk it could not take. It was fear of Southern backlash, not the complaints of the National Association for the Advancement of Colored People (NAACP), that led to *Amos 'n' Andy*'s cancellation. The South simply was not ready to accept a black television show. That attitude made black shows controversial, and controversy was anathema to television. In 1954, for example, a woman in CBS's personnel department asserted that the network did not practice discrimination in hiring but that in certain positions, such as receptionist or "script girls who sit in on shows with the client," it "might not be advisable to use Negroes."[40] Blacks were clearly too controversial for visible roles. Even more shocking evidence came from NBC's failed attempt at *The Nat King Cole Show* in 1956. The content of the show was not controversial, nor was the star. It was basic high-quality music entertainment, which started out as a fifteen-minute show and was later expanded to half an hour. It was tried out in a number of time slots. Because it was clear that the show's success would be a breakthrough for blacks in television, it got a great deal of support from major stars—black and white—who offered to appear on the show for scale (a few hundred dollars) instead of the five-figure salaries that they normally received for television appearances. Thus, Cole's guests included Sammy Davis Jr., Mel Torme, Ella Fitzgerald, and Peggy Lee. Nevertheless, no matter how NBC packaged the deal, the show was unable to attract a major sponsor. With its ratings slowing, even a plan allowing local affiliates to elect the show and sell the time locally met with inadequate success. "The collapse of *The Nat King Cole Show* served only to reaffirm what many be felt to be true: television was no place for Afro-American talents to seek success."[41]

Series featuring blacks or even individual dramas about blacks were too controversial for television. In an exemplary case, Rod Serling's attempt to dramatize the story of Emmett Till (a Northern black teenager brutally killed for looking at a white woman while visiting family in the South) underwent so many changes that in the final version the victim was no longer black and the locale was not Southern.[42] According to a 1957 *Television Age* article, "in the matter of segregation, it would be difficult to present a dramatization dealing with some aspects of this problem on a sponsored program, particularly at a time when the subject is considered highly inflammatory. . . . It would be impossible to maintain any balance of dramatization highlighting one side of such a currently explosive issue as segregation in a sponsored *entertainment* program."[43]

The network was thus applying the same principle to the episode's content that it applied to hiring: it didn't want to be controversial. This principle not only drove black faces from the air but also curbed the anthology shows of the sort that Serling worked for in that period, such as *Playhouse 90* or *Kraft Theater*, which provided weekly hour-long or ninety-minute dramas. Although these shows might engage slightly more controversial themes, they too became normalized by the realities of commercial television, which saw the triumph of the Hollywood-influenced, West Coast sensibility over the Broadway-influenced East Coast approach. The Hollywood sensibility valued entertainment above serious engagement with social or moral issues, a system that resulted in even less divergence from the already narrow, normative Cold War agenda. The motivation was as much commercial as political. Fred Wizbar, director of the Hollywood-based filmed drama series *Fireside Theater*, explained, "We sell little pieces of soap, so our approach must be the broadest possible. . . . We never take a depressing story."[44]

PUBLIC SPACE, NATIONAL IDENTITY, WHITE CONSUMER

If television was constructing an ideal citizen, that citizen not only believed in truth, justice, and the American way but also understood that his or her defining role was as a consumer. Henry Clay Gipson made the same assumption about television as an educational tool:

> As the world grows older, people are bound to have more leisure. These people must find something to do with their non-reproductive time. . . . Almost everyone will have a hobby and want to learn something. Through television we can give people the proper knowhow. We can acquaint them with the skill required to use many varied products. *And what could be finer advertising than to actually show the use of a product?* (italics in the original)[45]

In some ways, television's role in the production of consumers was an implicit possibility from the outset: In his 1927 exhibition in a department store, Philo Farnsworth gave the first public demonstration of television by transmitting to a small screen for sixty seconds the image of a dollar sign.[46] In a manner of speaking, we could say that television began with a commercial and the shows were filled in later. Much evidence would support this premise, but "television," as James Monaco pointed out, "did not cause consumer capitalism, it just made it easier to construct a society built on waste and economic exploitation."[47]

If the televisual citizen was the consumer, then everything he or she saw was the object of consumption. Like Farnsworth's first televised dollar sign, the message, the commercial, and the implicit meaning coalesced under a single visual image so that every television show constituted a form of product placement, a point not lost, for example, on Mary Gannon, commenting on a 1945 television show presented by *Mademoiselle* magazine: "Beyond the opening and closing announcement which said simply CBS presents this program as a public service prepared in collaboration with the staff of *Mademoiselle*, no further mention was made that the merchandize came from the pages of the magazine—it was just inferred." The sequences were used as "natural incidents in a closely related theme."[48]

Since people were more likely to consume when they were happy, television favored happy endings. Viewers also had to consume the appropriate products. Nina Leibman cites, for example, this 1959 memo from the J. Walter Thompson advertising agency to the Screen Gems advertising liaison, regarding an episode of *Father Knows Best* sponsored by the agency's client Scott Paper:

> Unfortunately, I notice there is a very grievous error on Page 2, namely the business where Margaret wipes the paint off the refrigerator. The author has boldly written, "She gets a *cloth* and wipes off the paint." Were Mr. Elliotte a new and untried author I would not have been so shocked. Surely this young man has been most derelict in failing to watch the Scott commercials. Else, he would not possibly have failed to realize that no material performs the disagreeable task of absorbing paint so well as a Scott Paper Towel.
>
> From past experience I am sure that when this scene is shot Margaret will instinctively use a Scott Paper Towel. Correct? If so, you may consider this letter to constitute client approval.[49]

Notably, this memo situated the sponsor as the protector of reality rather than the promoter of contrivance, indicating that the writer was being unrealistic. In reality "no material performs the disagreeable task of absorbing paint so well as a Scott Paper Towel," a fact established by Scott commercials. Ignoring the commercials, the writer was not being true to life, thus differentiating himself from the character, Margaret, who in reality would never succumb to the writer's unnatural instructions. Margaret, the ad man was sure, remaining true to her instinct, would use a Scott Paper towel. The script from this viewpoint did not provide an artificial display for consumer products but rather reflected accurately the truth contained in the Scott commercials.

Television, as this memo illustrated, uniquely merged the economic realities of its production with the reality it professed to deliver, establishing itself in the postwar American scene as a two-way circuit. It professed to bring the real world to the viewers and to bring the viewers to the reality of consumerism. Scott Paper, like almost all Cold War television sponsors, was doing more than commodifying reality; it was keeping that reality shiny white by adhering to the principle articulated by network executives to writer-producer Robert Alan Arthur when he tried to limit the number of commercials: "The Crest story is really very important. The strange thing about television is that the Crest story is really more important, and the drama is something that goes between the commercials and will be sacrificed at any given time for that purpose."[50] Crest toothpaste and Scott Paper towels were doing more than selling white teeth and refrigerators with shiny white surfaces. They were promoting the notion of a stable, transparently normal nation, unambiguous and without controversy or dissent. Lacking partisan emotions, political positions, or minority opinions, much less minority complexions, the Americans featured by television mirrored the products they were supposed to consume: white bread, vanilla. In this sense, whiteness means the absence of emotional, political, or philosophical pigmentation. Cold War television—in regard to anything but communism—was white in the sense that white is the most neutral of colors, deployed by a medium that had honed the craft of equating neutrality with normality.

AMERICAN DESTINY

By the mid-1950s, television was fulfilling its destiny as the apparatus that would allow Americans to fulfill theirs. In 1942, when less than one in a thousand Americans had ever seen a television program, one author predicted that "television is destined to bring into the home total means for participation in the sights and sounds of the entire world. When it projects the instantaneous present rather than the past it will be more realistic than the motion picture. The sense of being present as a living witness of distant events as they transpire is one utterly unique."[51]

The emphasis on "participation" rather than simply on seeing is very significant. Television not only delivered the messages of reality but also brought those messages home in such a way as to make the viewer a participant. To put it another way, watching television became a form of participation—but participation in *what*? The simple answer was "everything." Television would allow the viewer to participate in the nation and the world.

Perhaps the most powerful expression of this perception came in 1952 from Pat Weaver, at the time a vice president at the Young and Rubicam advertising agency, who would shortly become the head of NBC programming:

> Having the all-family, all-home circulation through a planned radio-television schedule, we can create a new stature in our citizens. The miracles of attending every event of importance, meeting every personality of importance in your world, getting to observe members of every group, racial, national, sectional, cultural, religious; recognizing every city, every country, every river and mountain on sight; having full contact with the explanations of every mystery of physics, mechanics and the sciences; sitting at the feet of the most brilliant teachers, and being exposed to the whole range of diversity of mankind's past, present, and the aspirations for mankind's future—these and many other miracles are not assessed yet. But I believe that we vastly underestimate what will happen.[52]

Like others a decade earlier, Weaver connected the immediacy of television with a notion of citizenship. Televisual citizenship, technically superior to more ignorant, more pedestrian, more limited, and secondhand citizenship, represented the ideal to which each American could aspire.

This ideal of course narrowed the range of debate over political or social issues, whether that debate took the form of news or drama. Television could function, therefore, as the site of "democracy" to the extent that "democracy"—representing what the most people had in common—was defined in opposition to "idiosyncrasy." Broadcasting nationalized the common person in every way that his or her values were common rather than unique, clichéd rather than original, status quo rather than progressive. Necessarily entrenched in the past not the future, broadcasting proliferated narratives of a conservative utopia, sine qua non: what "ought to have been"—America in the past-perfect conditional tense—as the model for "what ought to be." Instead of delivering entertainment to audiences, it constructed "reality" as a form of entertainment, allowed free consumption of that entertainment, and then delivered the consumers to the organizations that sponsored the delivery. When Lucille Ball and Lucy Ricardo gave birth within twenty-four hours of one another, on the eve of Dwight Eisenhower's nationally broadcast presidential inauguration, the show in fact delivered "Little Ricky" to America at the same moment that it delivered America to televisual reality, an odd hyper-reality that substituted immediacy for veracity, normality for individuality, idolatry for religion.

Notes

1. H. G. Christensen, "Long Shots and Close-Ups," *Television: The Magazine of Video Fact* 3, no. 2 (February 1946), p. 29.
2. Ibid.
3. Maurice Gorham, *Television: Medium of the Future* (London: Percival Marshall, 1949), p. 130.
4. Orin E. Dunlap Jr., *The Future of Television* (New York: Harper and Bros., 1942), p. 165.
5. Gilbert Seldes, "The Future of Television," *Atlantic* 3 (1949), p. 36.
6. *Time*, May 24, 1948, p. 72.
7. Ibid., p. 73.
8. James Caddigan, "Station Operations: Setting Up a Special Events Department," *Television: The Magazine of Video Fact* 2, no. 10 (December 1945), p. 12.
9. Harry Castleman and Walter Podrazik, *Watching TV: Four Decades of American Television* (New York: McGraw-Hill, 1982), p. 19.

10. Ibid., p. 33.
11. See Alan Nadel, *Containment Culture: American Narratives, Postmodernism, and the Atomic Age* (Durham, NC: Duke University Press, 1995); Tom Engelhardt, *The End of Victory Culture: Cold War America and the Disillusioning of a Generation* (New York: Basic Books, 1995); Elaine Tyler May, *Homeward Bound: American Families in the Cold War Era* (New York: Basic Books, 1988); Lary May, ed., *Recasting America: Culture and Politics in the Age of Cold War* (Chicago: University of Chicago Press, 1989); Ellen Schrecker, *Many Are the Crimes: McCarthyism in America* (Boston: Little, Brown, 1998); Stephen J. Whitfield, *The Culture of the Cold War* (Baltimore: Johns Hopkins University Press, 1991).
12. See Ellen Schrecker, *No Ivory Tower: McCarthyism and the Universities* (New York: Oxford University Press, 1986).
13. Jeanne Allen, "The Social Matrix of Television: Invention in the United States," in E. Ann Kaplan, ed., *Regarding Television: Critical Approaches— An Anthology* (Los Angeles: American Film Institute, 1983), p. 112.
14. Caddigan, "Station Operations," p. 13.
15. Ibid.
16. J. Fred MacDonald, *Television and the Red Menace: The Video Road to Vietnam* (New York: Praeger, 1985).
17. Ibid., p. 126.
18. Ibid., p. 124.
19. Ibid., p. 122.
20. Only in the mid-1950s were these shows on network television.
21. MacDonald, *Television and the Red Menace*, p. 117.
22. David Marc, *Demographic Vistas: Television in American Culture* (Philadelphia: University of Pennsylvania Press, 1984), p. 5.
23. J. Fred MacDonald, *Blacks and White TV: Afro-Americans in Television since 1948* (Chicago: Nelson-Hall, 1983), p. 59.
24. "The Television Code of the National Association of Radio and Television Broadcasters," in William Y. Elliott, ed., *Television's Impact on American Culture* (East Lansing: Michigan State University Press, 1956), p. 328.
25. Ibid.
26. Ibid., p. 329.
27. Dunlap, *The Future of Television*, p. 15.
28. Ibid., p. 16.
29. "The Television Code," p. 329.
30. Ibid., pp. 330–31.
31. Ibid., p. 334.
32. George Kennan, "The Sources of Soviet Conduct," *Foreign Affairs* 25 (1947), pp. 566–82.
33. Quoted in Lynn Spigel, "Television in the Family Circle: The Popular Reception of a New Medium," in Patricia Mellencamp, ed., *Logics of*

Television: Essays in Cultural Criticism (Bloomington: Indiana University Press, 1990), p. 81.

34. Castleman and Podrazik, *Watching TV*, p. 53.
35. Thomas Doherty, *Cold War, Cool Medium: Television, McCarthyism, and American Culture* (New York: Columbia University Press, 2003), p. 31.
36. Castleman and Podrazik, *Watching TV*, p. 53.
37. Doherty, *Cold War, Cool Medium*, p. 25.
38. Ellen Schrecker, *The Age of McCarthyism: A Brief History with Documents* (Boston: Bedford Books, 1994), p. 224.
39. Ibid., p. 154.
40. Quoted in Erik Barnouw, *A Tube of Plenty: The Evolution of American Television*, 2d rev. ed. (New York: Oxford University Press, 1990), p. 207.
41. MacDonald, *Blacks and White TV*, p. 64.
42. See William Boddy, *Fifties Television: The Industry and Its Critics* (Urbana: University of Illinois Press, 1990), p. 201; Erik Barnouw, *The Television Writer* (New York: Hill and Wang, 1962), p. 28.
43. Harold A. Carlborg, "Billion Dollar Whipping Boy," *Television Age*, November 4, 1957, p. 90.
44. Castleman and Podrazik, *Watching TV*, p. 78.
45. Henry Clay Gipson, "Educational Films and Television," *Television: The Magazine of Video Fact* 2, no. 4 (May 1945), pp. 13–14.
46. David Marc, "Beginning to Begin Again," in Horace Newcomb, ed., *Television: The Critical View*, 4th ed. (New York: Oxford University Press, 1987), pp. 323–60.
47. James Monaco, "The TV Plexus," in Carl Lowe, ed., *Television and American Culture* (New York: H. W. Wilson, 1981), p. 24.
48. Mary Gannon, "*Mademoiselle* Tries Out Television," *Television: The Magazine of Video Fact* 2, no. 8 (October 1945), p. 11.
49. Nina Leibman, *Living Room Lectures: The Fifties Family in Film and Television* (Austin: University of Texas Press, 1995), p. 111.
50. Boddy, *Fifties Television*, p. 196.
51. Lee De Forest, *Television Today and Tomorrow* (New York: Dial Press, 1942), pp. 349–50.
52. Quoted in MacDonald, *One Nation under Television*, p. 54. It is worth noting the ways in which Weaver anticipated claims about the World Wide Web.

In the End, They Were Born on TV

Douglas Kearney

i. good reality TV

a couple wanted to be -to-be and TV wants the couple-to-be
to be on TV. the people from TV believe we'd be good TV
because we had wanted to be to-be and failed and now might.

to be good at TV make-like TV isn't. make-like living in our
    living room
and the TV crew isn't there and the boom isn't there
saving the woman from TV's voice that won't be there
saying *tell us about the miscarriage.* in the teeming evening
and some dog barking at all we cannot hear.

ii. would you be willing to be on TV?

people in their house on TV are ghosts haunting a house haunting
    houses.
pregnant women in their houses on TV are haunted houses haunting a
    house haunting houses.
our living room a set set for us ghosts to tell ghost stories on us.

would you be to-be on TV?
to be the we we weren't to be and the we we're-to-be to be on TV.
the pregnant woman agrees to being a haunted house
haunting flickering houses. yes ok yeah yes.

iii. forms

in the waiting room for the doctor to TV the pregnant woman's insides
out on a little TV on TV. filling a form on TV is to flesh into words
on a sheet that fills up with you. yes yes and turn to the receptionist
only to turn back to a ghost waiting to be officially haunted yes.

a magazine riffles itself on TV; loud pages, a startled parrot
calls your name then alighting on magazines
and waddle the hall you -to-be and the TV crew that isn't going to
    be there
on TV and the doctor and you are looking at her little TV on TV
    the doctor
says *see? there they are.* ghosts sound themselves out to flicker on the
    little TV.
there they go to the pregnant woman scared to be such good TV.

iv. cut

to one-more-time-from-the-top yourself
is to ta-daaaaa breathing. the curtain drops, plush guillotine.
would you talk about the miscarriage one more time? ta-daaaaa

v. all the little people out there

after she was a haunted house before we haunted us for TV then
the pregnant woman watched TV. vomit on her teeth like sequins.

our TV stayed pregnant with the people from TV's TV show
pregnant with haunted houses wailing then smiling up into our
    living room.

it helps she said of the people from TV's TV show so *yes* then to TV
    to help,
she said, the haunted houses in the living rooms we said *yes* to help
thousands of wailing houses.

vi. only with some effort

the best ghosts trust they're not dead. no
no the best ghosts don't know how not to be alive.
like being good at TV.

inside the pregnant woman, the -to-be of the family-who-failed-
but-now-might-be-to-be were good TV.
but the we-who-failed butterfingered and stuttered,
held our hands like we just got them.

we've been trying so long we said *we can't believe it this is finally
    happening.*

vii. scheduled c-section: reality TV

and they're born made of meats on TV!
the doctor voilàs them from the woman's red guts
into the little punch bowls.

the new mother says *I want to see them my babies!*

the doctor shoves the new mother's guts back, express lane grocer.

the demure camera good TVs up two meat babies into wailing ghosts.

off, the new mother's blood like spilled nail polish.

viii. ghost story

did you know about dogs and ghosts? one barking at one's nothing?

ix. the miscarriage: exposition for reality TV

it helps to be on TV. we want to be good on TV. ok yes.
to help we want to be good TV. yeah yes.
please tell me about the miscarriage.

the woman from TV wants good TV and *something specific that gets
    you right*
in the tear to the eye to milk the pregnant woman's breasts
    heavy with—.

good, we talk about the dead one on TV.

it was horrible, the blood was everywhere that morning a dog barks.
one-more-time-from-the-top. *it was horrible, the blood was
    everywherrrrr*
doggone dog goes on. on to take three and *it was horri*BOOM
in the boom goes the barking and bad TV! bad TV! we want to help
being good TV *please tell me about the miscarriage*
one more time *it was*

x. after the c-section was more like

the doctor shoving the new mother's guts in, jilted lover packing a
    duffel.

xi. talking about the miscarriage: behind the scenes

please tell me about the miscarriage
please tell me about the miscarriage
please tell me about the miscarriage
please tell me about the miscarriage
the fifth take and *it was horrible*, that's all.
they call them takes, again we're robbed.

xii.

did it help watching a house fill with haunting every room
or help haunting the house? watch! here we are:
an expanding family of ghosts. we aren't here but yes ok yeah yes.
did it help? and even now know yes they were born on TV
but before *it was horrible* wasn't it must have been. please tell me
about the miscarriage for I don't know how not to be telling
and the dog growls still and still and still

Why Is "Everyman" a White Guy?

Aziz Ansari

Fisher Stevens was cooking dinner when I got him on the phone. I had wanted to talk to him for years because, as I recount in my new Netflix series *Master of None*, this actor played a strange role in my relationship to television and film.

The first time I saw an Indian character in an American movie was *Short Circuit 2*, a 1988 film in which a humanized robot named Johnny 5 goes to New York and bonds with an Indian scientist named Benjamin Jarhvi.

Seeing an Indian character in a lead role had a powerful effect on me, but it was only as I got older that I realized what an anomaly it was. I rarely saw any Indians on TV or film, except for brief appearances as a cabdriver or a convenience store worker literally servicing white characters who were off to more interesting adventures. This made *Short Circuit 2* special. An Indian lead character? With a Caucasian love interest? In the 1980s? What's going on here? A bold foray into diversity far ahead of its time?

Not exactly.

One day in college, I decided to go on the television and film website IMDB to see what happened to the Indian actor from *Short Circuit 2*. Turns out, the Indian guy was a white guy.

The character was played by Mr. Stevens, a Caucasian actor in brownface. Rather than cast an Indian actor, the filmmakers had Mr. Stevens sit every morning in a makeup chair and get painted an "Indian color" before going on set and doing his "Indian voice."

As a child, I thought the villain of the film was Oscar Baldwin, the banker who tricks Johnny 5 into helping him commit a jewel heist. As an adult, I thought the bad guy was actually Mr. Stevens, who mocked my ethnicity.

And now, here I was, a real Indian man, talking to the actor who played a fake one almost thirty years ago.

After a long conversation, I can confirm Mr. Stevens is not a villain, but was, when he took the role, a well-intentioned if slightly misguided young actor who needed a job during a more culturally insensitive time.

At first, he was remarkably casual, cooking dinner as we talked, seemingly happy to recall his days with Johnny 5.

"Originally, the role of Benjamin was a white grad student, and then the director and co-writer of *Short Circuit* changed the character to Indian," he told me. They then went to Mr. Stevens and asked, "Can you play Indian?"

It was 1987, so we were all a little less savvy about the things we were doing that were actually hurtful to large groups of people, and the answer, for a twenty-one-year-old struggling actor, was yes.

What surprised me was how seriously Mr. Stevens dedicated himself to "becoming Indian." He went full Method, studying with a dialect coach, reading R. K. Narayan's *The Guide* and Hesse's *Siddhartha*. "I started taking yoga and immersed myself, because I really wanted to be as real as possible," he said. He even lived in India for a month before shooting *Short Circuit 2*.

Mr. Stevens's efforts to make the character real, and not a full-on ethnic cartoon, are admirable, despite the underlying insult of his being cast. Toward the end of the conversation, it seemed to fully hit him how insensitive his casting may have been, and he said several times that he believed the role should have been played by an Indian and that he would never take it today.

These days, Indian people—real Indian people—pop up way more in film and television, but fake Indians are still around more than you think. I loved *The Social Network*, but I have a hard time understanding why the Indian American Harvard student Divya Narendra was played by Max Minghella, a half-Chinese, half-Italian British actor. More recently, *The Martian* was based on a novel with an Indian character named Venkat Kapoor, who in the film became Vincent, a character portrayed by Chiwetel Ejiofor, a British actor of Nigerian origin. (The Indian actor Irrfan Khan was reportedly in talks to take the role, but couldn't because of a scheduling conflict.)

My efforts to get responses from people who made these decisions were unsuccessful. But I don't want to judge them before knowing the full story, especially because I know that both films made at least some attempts to pursue Indian actors. I auditioned for *The Social Network*, and I was horrible. I tried to improvise and make the role funny. I was a young actor who didn't understand what he was doing. I was also asked to audition for a part in *The Martian* (not Kapoor), but I skimmed the script and—no offense—it seemed like a boring movie about a white guy stuck on Mars for two hours who gets fired up about plants, so it didn't seem worth taking a break from my own projects. (I've heard the film is fantastic.) So, I know the filmmakers made an effort to cast Indian actors, but how hard did they try?

I had to cast an Asian actor for *Master of None*, and it was *hard*. When you cast a white person, you can get anything you want: "You need a white guy with red hair and one arm? Here's six of 'em!" But for an Asian character, there were startlingly fewer options, and with each of them, something was off. Some had the right look but didn't have comedy chops. Others were too young or old. We even debated changing the character to an Asian woman, but a week before shooting began, Kelvin Yu, an actor from Los Angeles, sent in an audition over YouTube and got the part.

So I get it: sometimes you're in a jam. Every time I've played a part that required stunts, they've been done by a white stuntman who has had to brown up. In those cases, the ethics didn't seem quite as dubious. Training an Indian to do the stunts wasn't practical, and a stuntman is not mocking Indian people; he's tricking people into thinking it's me, a real Indian. (If there is a heartbroken Indian stuntman reading this now: dude, I'm so sorry, and you really need to get a better stunt agent.)

But I still wonder if we are trying hard enough.

Even though I've sold out Madison Square Garden as a standup comedian and have appeared in several films and a TV series, when my phone rings, the roles I'm offered are often defined by ethnicity and often require accents.

Sure, things are moving in the right direction with *Empire* and *Fresh Off the Boat*. But, as far as I know, black people and Asian people were around before the last TV season. And whatever progress toward diversity we are making, the percentage of minorities playing lead roles is still painfully low. (The numbers for women are depressing as well.) In 2013, according to a recent report produced by the Ralph J. Bunche Center for African American Studies at UCLA, only 16.7 percent of lead film roles went to minorities. Broadcast TV was worse, with only 6.5 percent of lead roles going to nonwhites in the 2012–13 season. In cable, minorities did better, getting 19.3 percent of the roles.

For me, as a modern American consumer, these numbers come as zero surprise. Here's a game to play: when you look at posters for movies or TV shows, see if it makes sense to switch the title to "What's Gonna Happen to This White Guy?" (*Forrest Gump, The Martian, Black Mass*) or if there's a woman in the poster, too, "Are These White People Gonna Have Sex with Each Other?" (*Casablanca, When Harry Met Sally, The Notebook*). Even at a time when minorities account for almost 40 percent of the American population, when Hollywood wants an "everyman," what it really wants is a straight white guy. But a straight white guy is not every man. The "everyman" is everybody.

When we were looking for an Asian actor for *Master of None*, my fellow creator, Alan Yang, asked me: "How many times have you seen an Asian guy kiss someone in TV or film?" After a long hard think, we came up with two (Steven Yeun on *The Walking Dead* and Daniel Dae Kim on *Lost*). It made me realize how important it was not to give up on our search.

But I wouldn't be in the position to do any of this, and neither would Alan, unless some straight white guy, in this case Mike Schur, had given us jobs on *Parks and Recreation*. Without that opportunity, we wouldn't have developed the experience necessary to tell our stories. So if you're a straight white guy, do the industry a solid and give minorities a second look.

And to anyone worried that it may be "weird" to cast someone who looks a certain way to play a certain part because it's not what people are used to, I say: Arnold Schwarzenegger.

It's true. Arnold Schwarzenegger is an unsung pioneer for minority actors. Look at *The Terminator*. There had to be someone who heard his name tossed around for the role and thought: "Wait, why would the robot have an Austrian accent? No one's gonna buy that! We gotta get a robot that has an American accent! Just get a white guy from the States. Audiences will be confused." Nope. They weren't. Because, you know what? No one really cares.

Kim's Fairytale Wedding
(selection)

Kate Durbin

For Kanye West

We begin with the tinkling of chimes. Our first vision is of the white 1950s font of the Beverly Hills arch, cushioned with palm fronds, propped against a sparkling orange sky.

Then the fancy scrawl of the Montage Beverly Hills Hotel sign, followed by the European font of Scarpetta, a classy Italian restaurant.

The room is noisy. Family and friends of Kim and the Not-Husband hug each other in designer clothing. Sisters of Kim stand in line for flashes of light. All five wear minidresses and pumps. In the center is Kim, donning tight, white Alexander McQueen and a white short-sleeved jacket with constructed shoulders.

Brother Rob stands off to the side in a sweatshirt, hair rumpled, spooning soup into his mouth. A man in a suit stands next to him, chewing gum and moving his mouth as if he is talking. Brother Rob ignores the man.

White letters crystallize in air:
REHEARSAL
DINNER

There is a white tent. Inside the white tent is a long white table. The table is empty and flanked by white empty chairs.

In front of the table is Kim, framed by golden lights and ornate brown pillars that resemble cathedral architecture.

She says, "Even though we are arguing, we still have this huge dinner, with all our friends and family, and I'm hoping we can just forget about the tension and the drama, and let's just enjoy ourselves."

Her hair curls darkly down her shoulders. Her eyes are thickly lined, adorned with faux lashes. Her brows are arched, her lips nude. As she talks, her voice is soft, baby-ish. She looks right at us.

The Not-Husband stands on the outdoor patio of Scarpetta. Children in small suits and dresses scramble around the patio tables, touching them with tiny hands. The Not-Husband looks down at his cell phone. He stumbles forward in our direction. He looks up at us, eyebrows raised.

We are back inside the rehearsal dinner, where a blonde woman in a jungle print blouse says to the Not-Husband, "I like your suit."

"Where we sitting at?" the Not-Husband asks Kim. He looks down at his suit. "Thank you," he says to Jungle Print Woman, as if he had forgotten he was wearing a suit. "Hand stitched," he says, still looking down. "Do you like my mustache?" He loosely holds a plate of food.

The Not-Husband is taller than everyone else in the room, and his entire body is made of static.

Kim stands next to him, biting her lower lip.

"I-I-I-I," stutters a skinny man, also wearing a black suit. He is with Jungle Print Woman. "I wouldn't say that," Stuttering Man says.

"Are you saving it for the wedding?" asks Jungle Print Woman, clutching Stuttering Man's arm with French manicured nails. She laughs.

"Please talk him out of it," says Kim in a whiny voice.

The Not-Husband picks up a piece of sliced beef from his plate and wiggles it. His big thumb dips into a pile of sour cream and shredded cheese.

"On the morning of the wedding, shave it," says Stuttering Man. "Trust me."

"She'll shave it or I'll shave it?" asks the Not-Husband, staring down at his beef, pulling it.

Stuttering Man, Jungle Print Woman, and Kim stare up at him, smiling.

"Both," says Stuttering Man.

"Like, this is all I feel like I have left, is my mustache," says the Not-Husband, tugging his beef.

Jungle Print Woman laughs.

"It's the only way to send a message to Kim," the Not-Husband says, wiggling the beef. It refuses to come off the plate.

Kim, still smiling, turns. Stuttering Man and Jungle Print Woman back up, arms crossed. They look around the room.

"Where we—where we sitting at?" the Not-Husband asks. He picks up the entire piece of beef and puts it in his mouth. It falls through his static body and onto the floor. He sucks his thumb loudly. Jungle Print Woman puts her hands on Stuttering Man's shoulders and massages. She looks at Kim and smiles.

"Over there," says Kim, crossing her arms. The Not-Husband leaves in a burst of crackles.

"Nice chatting with you. How is the wedding?" Jungle Print Woman asks Kim, pointing at her own white teeth in a wide grin.

"It's—" begins Kim, grinning. White diamond earrings glitter against her dark hair.

"All normal!" says Jungle Print Woman. Her lips are bee stung and glossy.

"We hate each other. We hate each other," says Kim, still grinning. "Is that awful?"

"It's all normal. No, it's fine. No—when you walked in—" Jungle Print Woman moves her left hand so her gold wedding band shimmers. Her right hand clutches Stuttering Man's skinny bicep.

"Did you two hate each other?" interrupts Kim.

"We didn't speak really for the last two weeks before the wedding," says Stuttering Man.

Jungle Print Woman looks at him quickly, then back at Kim. "Yeah," she says.

"It's—you know—" says Stuttering Man, shaking his head.

"Really?" says Kim, flatly.

"It's totally normal," says Jungle Print Woman.

"Because I hate him," says Kim.

Jungle Print Woman laughs and says "Kim!" in a squeaky voice.

"Every last thing annoys me," says Kim, smiling, lifting her hands like a statue in worship or surrender.

The Not-Husband lumbers across the room. His body fills it to crackling.

"There he is!" yells a bald man in a suit, next to a row of suits. They stand by a round table full of food. In the center of the table is a vase stuffed with white and red roses. "Hey, what state are we in?" asks Bald Man.

"I'm ready to get out of here. When is this thing over?" says the Not-Husband, touching a chair back.

"That's his friends' table," says Kim to Jungle Print Woman and Stuttering Man. "Oh, so he's gonna sit at his friends' table and not with me. That's fun."

"Oh," says Jungle Print Woman, as Kim walks away.

The Not-Husband, sandwiched between two suits, lets out a wolf whistle. He gestures "come here" with two fingers. "Hold on," he says.

Kim, plate heaped with rice and meat, is walking across the room. She looks at the Not-Husband and keeps walking to her family's table. A man with a bowtie pulls out her seat and she settles, tucked between Sister Kourtney's Baby in a car carrier and Sister Kendall, fifteen and smoky eyed, in a YSL electric blue bandage dress.

Kim's family's table is back-to-back with the Not-Husband's friends' table. Kim and the Not-Husband's backs align. Static sizzles between their bodies.

"Hey NH, you bleeping your friends off over there?" Brother Rob asks over the two tables.

The room is loud with voices, the clang of knives and forks on plates.

"No, they're just talking about how nice you look tonight," the Not-Husband says. The girl next to him stares at nothing.

Brother Rob laughs in his red sweatshirt. His head looks small.

"Ahaha," says Husband of Sister Kourtney, Brother-in-Law Scott, in slicked back hair and brown Gucci suit. He chews meat.

Kim spoons rice between pillow lips. Sister Kendall watches.

"Helloooo," says a microphone voice.

Mom stands at the front of the room, a synthetic fire crackling inside a tall glass pillar behind her. Silver serving domes glitter in the light.

Mom has on a formfitting YSL dress with white stars and lace. Her hair is in a jagged black bob. Silver earrings fall from her ears. Her lips are cream and fat, like Kim's, her eyes smokier than all her daughters'.

As Mom begins to talk, the Not-Husband rotates his chair and sidles his big body up to Kim. The Not-Husband puts his arm around Kim's petite shoulders. Her cleavage squishes together prettily. She looks up at him, raises manicured eyebrows.

"First of all, I just want to thank everybody for being here, um, tonight," says Mom. "If you asked me where . . ." she trails off, scratching her head.

A baby shrieks.

"Don't cry," says Kim. Everyone laughs.

"Where I would want to be right now at this very moment in time it's right here," continues Mom in a trembling voice, hand to sky. A swollen diamond sits on her finger.

Mom looks at Kim and the Not-Husband. Kim looks annoyed. The Not-Husband chews meat.

"I love you guys very much and NH, I know that we've given you a really hard time over the last couple of months," Mom says, clutching the microphone. A man leaps behind her. There is a flash of light.

The Not-Husband picks up Kim's arm and twirls it. She tugs it and he drops it abruptly. Across the room a woman laughs.

"You've really proven yourself to be an amazing guy, and Kim we're really happy for you," Mom says. There is a spattering of applause.

The Not-Husband strikes his huge hands together. Kim, tiny in his arms, jolts back and forth. She sticks out her tongue.

"Whoo!" someone shouts.

Stepdad is suddenly at the front of the room. His nose is chiseled, his cheekbones sharp. The skin on his face sags. He has on a black sports jacket, unbuttoned, chest shaved and wrinkled.

"After months and months of preparation, the wedding is finally here!" he says. The room explodes in applause. Stepdad's arm is around Mom. She smiles up at him. "Sister Khloe and Son-in-Law Lamar, you were geniuses to do this in ten days," says Stepdad.

"Nine," says Mom.

"Nine days," says Stepdad.

Across the room, near a bamboo plant, Son-in-Law Lamar, a tall, bald basketball player, hugs Sister Khloe with one arm. He holds an empty wine glass in his other hand. Sister Khloe places her French manicured hand, rock on ring finger, on his belly. She smiles. Brother-in-Law Lamar kisses her shiny brown hair. Lights flash around them.

The room laughs.

"But you know Kimberly you've always had a very special part in my heart," says Stepdad.

The Not-Husband takes a gulp of water. There's a lime in his glass. He swallows the lime and it hits the floor.

"It won't be easy on Saturday to, uh, give you away," says Stepdad. Kim smiles.

"NH you have no idea what you're getting into, but you're learning," says Stepdad, raising his hand in blessing or warning. He has a gold band on his ring finger.

Stepdad smiles. Mom smiles. They look at the Not-Husband. The Not-Husband takes a gulp of water, chomps his ice. A man's body hovers behind him.

"I just wanna have the honor of wishing you guys the best of luck," finishes Stepdad.

The room cheers.

Sister Kourtney and Brother-in-Law Scott look at Kim and the Not-Husband from across the table. Sister Kourtney's hair is in a French twist, and she has on a ruffled Salvatore Ferragamo black dress. Her cheeks are glittery bronzed. Brother-in-Law Scott has a fat gold Rolex on his tanned arm. It shimmers as he claps.

"We have A Guy here. He used to be a Laker," says Mom. The room erupts. "Now, you're a Net," says Mom, laughing over at A Guy at a table. A Guy's arm is slung on the back of his chair. A woman in a cranberry Balenciaga dress sits next to A Guy and rubs his back. A Guy looks around the room, licks his lips.

A Guy comes to the front of the room, pulling another woman behind him. She has long black hair and a tight grey Carolina Herrera wrap dress that shows her tanned legs and round booty. A Guy has on a grey Tom Ford suit. His ears stick out.

"All for real. Uncensored," says the Not-Husband.

Wrap Dress Woman smiles next to A Guy at the front of the room, adjusting her shiny hair with French manicured hands. Her breasts are pushed up high and tight.

"Bein' a Laker you're kinda used to seein' celebrities and stars at the games all the time," A Guy says. "But you know, with the Nets it's really not that often."

Brother-in-Law Lamar, now sitting on a couch somewhere in the room, laughs. His long arm is draped over the couch back. A diamond-encrusted wedding band sits on his ring finger.

Kim and the Not-Husband laugh. She leans back into him.

"So when Kim came to the game, sittin' courtside with Wrap Dress Woman, that was kind of a big deal, so . . ." continues A Guy.

The Not-Husband looks down at Kim and grins. Kim laughs without looking up at him, nose crinkling cutely.

Brother Rob and Brother-in-Law Scott laugh soundlessly at something Brother-in-Law Scott is doing under the table. Sister Kylie cracks her knuckles.

"So I get a text message, from Wrap Dress Woman, um, 'Who's number forty-three?'" says A Guy. He juts his thumb at Wrap Dress Woman. She stands, hands at waist, breasts and ass jutting. "They didn't know his name, didn't know nothin' about him," says A Guy.

Kim laughs hard. She looks at Wrap Dress Woman, who also laughs. A few other people laugh. Kim shakes her hair. She leans back into the Not-Husband. He looks away, moving static lips.

"So we ended up going out as a group, had a nice dinner, all hung out. NH and I went home, and he was just telling me that he liked her, and that everything was going good. I get a text message from Wrap Dress Woman: 'This is Kim's number, give it to NH.' I was like dude, you didn't even get her number?" A Guy says.

The room laughs.

Kim looks up at the Not-Husband. He licks his lips and looks down at her. His tie is black silk with polka dots. Electricity is centralized inside the dots in the form of blue twinkles.

"You know, that was the start of it," says A Guy.

Gentle piano music begins.

The Not-Husband laughs soundlessly, jerks his head.

We are back inside the white tent alone with Kim.

As she speaks, gentle piano music continues. Two notes are being struck over and over.

"You know, hearing NH's friend's speech at the rehearsal dinner, about when we met, really kind of brings me back down to reality. This wedding is about love, it's a love that NH and I have, there's no need for any of this drama, and let's just enjoy every moment."

As she speaks, we alternate visions. We watch her cuddling up to the Not-Husband at the rehearsal dinner, his electric lips pressed into her puckering, moist ones, causing the ends of her hair to lightly spark blue.

We also watch her speaking to us, surrounded by brown pillars, eyes lined darkly to match her black silk shirt.

Back inside the rehearsal dinner, A Guy continues his speech. Lights flash around him.

"I kind of noticed little changes, you know," says A Guy. "NH went from wearin' like PF Flyers to start wearin' YSLs." The room erupts with claps and laughs. "He starts comin' to the game with a Louis Vuitton tie case." A Guy touches his heart. There is a thick gold Rolex on his arm and a thick gold band on his finger. "You know, it went from like, you know, 'We're just kinda talkin',' to like, he's textin' on the plane like, 'That's my baby, that's my baby.' I'm like, dang, really, it changed like that so fast?"

The Not-Husband enfolds Kim in static. She licks her glossy lips, turns, and smiles. They kiss. She fiddles with her ring.

Another Guy behind them watches.

"I wish you guys nothin' but the best. I thank you for upgradin' my boy," says A Guy. "Thank you guys."

Piano music begins. We clap. Kim mouths, "Thank you."

Our next vision is of the 110 parkway, heading to downtown Los Angeles. We witness the epic thrust of downtown skyscrapers against an orange sky. High desert mounds with scrub brush line the road.

Gongs, violins, and operatic singing increase the intensity of the moment.

Next, a white church-like steeple against a blue sky, a monument with birds crawling on it, a tree with leaves whipping.

A baroque-replica lamppost, clouds across a blue sky generating faster than regular clouds.

Shared Inquiry and Great Ideas in Popular Culture

Great Books Foundation editors chose the readings in *Tube Talk: Big Ideas in Television* because these selections raise multiple questions and will prompt lively discussion. Suggested discussion questions for each selection are available online at www.greatbooks.org/bigideas.

Some of the suggested questions ask about something very specific in a selection, such as the meaning of a statement or the motivation of an individual. Others ask about more general issues related to the selections; these questions are broader and invite discussion of personal insights and opinions. Addressing both kinds of questions during a discussion, without tipping the balance heavily toward one or the other, will make for a more satisfying experience that not only engages with each author's distinctive voice, but also allows participants in the group to contribute their insights in their own individual way.

A Shared Inquiry™ discussion begins when the leader of the discussion group poses an interpretive question to participants about the meaning of a reading selection. The question is substantial enough that no single answer can resolve it. Instead, several answers—even answers that are in conflict—may be valid.

Participants are free to offer answers and opinions to the group, to request clarification of points, and to raise objections to the remarks of other participants. They also discuss specific passages in the selection that bear on the interpretive question and compare their differing ideas about what these passages mean. The leader, meanwhile, asks additional questions, clarifying and expanding the interpretive question and helping group members to arrive at more cogent answers. All participants don't have to agree with all the answers—each person can decide which answer seems most convincing. This process is called Shared Inquiry.

In Shared Inquiry discussion, three kinds of questions can be raised about a reading selection: factual questions, interpretive questions, and evaluative questions. Interpretation is central to a Shared Inquiry discussion, but factual questions can bring to light evidence in support of interpretations and can clear up misunderstandings. On the other hand, evaluative questions invite partici-pants to compare the experiences and opinions of an author with their own and can introduce a personal dimension into the discussion.

The following guidelines will help keep the conversation focused on the text and ensure all participants a voice:

1. **Read the selection carefully before participating in the discussion.** This ensures that all participants are equally prepared to talk about the ideas in the reading.

2. **Discuss the ideas in the selection, and try to understand them fully.** Reflecting as individuals and as a group on what the author says makes the exploration of both the selection and related issues that will come up in the discussion more rewarding.

3. **Support interpretations of what the author says with evidence from the reading, along with insights from personal experience.** This provides focus for the group on the selection that everyone has read and builds a strong foundation for discussing related issues.

4. **Listen to other participants and respond to them directly.** Shared Inquiry is about the give-and-take of ideas, the willingness to listen to others and talk with them respectfully. Directing your comments and questions to other group members, not always to the leader, will make the discussion livelier and more dynamic.

5. **Expect the leader to mainly ask questions.** Effective leaders help participants develop their own ideas, with everyone gaining a new understanding in the process. When participants hang back and wait for the leader to suggest answers, discussion tends to falter.

Index

Acknowledgments

All possible care has been taken to trace ownership and secure permission for each selection in this anthology. The Great Books Foundation wishes to thank the following authors, publishers, and representatives for permission to reproduce copyrighted material:

The Great Divide: Norman Lear, Archie Bunker, and the Rise of the Bad Fan, by Emily Nussbaum. Copyright © 2017 by Condé Nast. First published in the *New Yorker* in 2014. Reproduced by permission of Condé Nast.

Us and Them, from DRESS YOUR FAMILY IN CORDUROY AND DENIM, by David Sedaris. Copyright © 2004 by David Sedaris. Reproduced by permission of Little, Brown and Company.

Seven Words You Can Never Say on Television, from LAST WORDS, by George Carlin. Copyright © 2009 by George's Stuff. Reproduced by permission of Free Press, a Division of Simon & Schuster, Inc.

The Amiable Madness of Green Acres, by Noel Murray, from the A.V. Club. Copyright © 2016 by Onion, Inc. Reproduced by permission of the A.V. Club.

Brad Carrigan, American, from IN PERSUASION NATION: STORIES, by George Saunders. Copyright © 2006 by George Saunders. Reproduced by permission of Riverhead, an imprint of Penguin Publishing Group, a division of Penguin Random House LLC, and International Creative Management.

Selection from "Empires of the New World," in THE FUTURE OF TELEVISION: YOUR GUIDE TO CREATING TV IN THE NEW WORLD, by Pamela Douglas. Copyright © 2015 by Pamela Douglas. Reproduced by permission of Michael Wiese Productions.

Selection from "'Time to Go': Dreaming of a Televised Future," in ANYTIME PLAYDATE: INSIDE THE PRESCHOOL ENTERTAINMENT BOOM, OR, HOW TELEVISION BECAME MY BABY'S BEST FRIEND, by Dade Hayes. Copyright © 2008 by Dade Hayes. Reproduced by permission of Atria, a division of Simon & Schuster, and the author.

Hasta Siempre, by Jean Burnet, from *Bodega Magazine*. Copyright © 2016 by Jean Burnet. Reproduced by permission of the author.

From "Lessons from Television," by Susan Stewart, from *Columbarium*. Copyright © 2003 by the University of Chicago. Reproduced by permission of the University of Chicago Press.

Pursuit of the Public Interest in the Vast Wasteland, by Walter J. Podrazik. Copyright © 2017 by Walter J. Podrazik. Reproduced by permission of the author.

What I Learned from Kristi Yamaguchi, by Nicole Chung, from the *New York Times*. Copyright © 2016 by the *New York Times*. Reproduced by permission of the *New York Times*.

Acknowledgments

Selection from "Control," in THE ART OF IMMERSION: HOW THE DIGITAL GENERATION IS REMAKING HOLLYWOOD, MADISON AVENUE, AND THE WAY WE TELL STORIES, by Frank Rose. Copyright © 2011 by Frank Rose. Reproduced by permission of W. W. Norton & Company, Inc.

Selection from "The Age of Show Business," in AMUSING OURSELVES TO DEATH: PUBLIC DISCOURSE IN THE AGE OF SHOW BUSINESS, by Neil Postman. Copyright © 1985 by Neil Postman. Reproduced by permission of Viking Books, an imprint of Penguin Publishing Group, a division of Penguin Random House LLC, and Penguin Books Ltd. (UK).

Judge in Simpson Trial Allows TV Camera in Courtroom, by David Margolick, from the *New York Times*. Copyright © 1994 by the *New York Times*. Reproduced by permission of the *New York Times*.

To Remember History You Have to Repeat It, by Tony Hoagland. Copyright © 2005 by Tony Hoagland. Reproduced by permission of Hollyridge Press.

The Moon Hours, by E. B. White and others, from the *New Yorker*. Copyright © 2017 by Condé Nast. First published in the *New Yorker* in 1969. Reproduced by permission of Condé Nast.

Getting Dirty, from BOXED IN, by Mark Crispin Miller. Copyright © 1988 by Mark Crispin Miller. Reproduced by permission of Northwestern University Press.

Selection from "The First Presidential Debate," from PRESIDENTIAL DEBATES: FIFTY YEARS OF HIGH-RISK TV, by Alan Schroeder. Copyright © 2008 by Columbia University Press. Reproduced by permission of Columbia University Press.

The Revolution Will Not Be Televised, by Gil Scott-Heron, from PIECES OF A MAN, released in 1971. Copyright © 1978 by Bienstock Publishing Company. Reproduced by permission of Bienstock Publishing Company.

The Missing Remote, by Diane Lockward. Copyright © 2003 by Diane Lockward. Reproduced by permission of the author.

Dolls and Feelings: Jill Soloway's Post-Patriarchal Television, by Ariel Levy. Copyright © 2015 by Ariel Levy. First published in the *New Yorker*. Reproduced by permission of the author.

Pop History on an Epic Scale: Roots, from "The 1980s: Superstars," in PRIME TIME BLUES: AFRICAN AMERICANS ON NETWORK TELEVISION, by Donald Bogle. Copyright © 2001 by Donald Bogle. Reproduced by permission of Farrar, Straus and Giroux.

Desperately Selling Soda, from chapter 6, "The Sponsored Life," in THE SPONSORED LIFE: ADS, TV, AND THE AMERICAN CULTURE, by Leslie Savan. Copyright © 1994 by Leslie Savan. Reproduced by permission of Temple University Press.

The TV, by Ben Loory, from STORIES FOR NIGHTTIME AND SOME FOR THE DAY. Copyright © 2011 by Ben Loory. First published in the *New Yorker*. Reproduced by permission of Funke Literary.

Selection from "Television, Reality, and Cold War Citizenship," in TELEVISION IN BLACK-AND-WHITE AMERICA: RACE AND NATIONAL IDENTITY, by Alan Nadel. Copyright © 2005 by the University Press of Kansas. Reproduced by permission of the University Press of Kansas.

In the End, They Were Born on TV, from PATTER, by Douglas Kearney. Copyright © 2014 by Douglas Kearney. Reproduced by permission of Red Hen Press.

Why is "Everyman" a White Guy?, by Aziz Ansari, from the *New York Times*. Copyright © 2015 by the *New York Times*. Reproduced by permission of the *New York Times*.

Selection from "Kim's Fairytale Wedding," by Kate Durbin, in E! ENTERTAINMENT. Copyright © 2014 Kate Durbin. Reproduced by permission of Wonder.